Learn Bridge
The 2/1 Way

Mary Jane Orock
Jacqueline Montgomery

PREFACE

♠　♥　♦　♣

Welcome to the fascinating, complex, and addictive game of bridge. As a bridge teacher, I frequently receive calls from bridge players asking me to help them learn the "new bridge". Many of these individuals have played for years, love the game, and are quite accomplished players, yet the game they play lacks the bidding techniques which have become popular over the past 40 years. A quick review of the available literature shows an abundance of texts for beginners which teach a system called Standard American which is what my callers play and most beginners are taught. The "new bridge" is an improvement over Standard American called "two-over-one game-force" or simply 2/1. This system was developed by expert, competitive players to increase the precision of bids and accuracy of contracts. The system quickly gained in popularity as shown by the estimate in the 2011 edition of *The Official ACBL Encyclopedia of Bridge* that 95% of experts use the 2/1 bidding system. This system is here to stay as evidenced by the number of texts and workbooks available to those wishing to upgrade to this bidding system. Many players entrenched in the old system find the transition very difficult and to my knowledge there is no text which brings this modern system to the beginning player.

This book will introduce you, the new player, to the most popular bridge bidding system (2/1) used in the United States today. There will be no difficult transition because you will be introduced to the wonderful, exciting world of bridge using this system from the very beginning. This challenging yet powerful introduction will prepare you to enter the world of bridge as played by the experts. You will quickly be ready to join the throng of players around the world who are engaged in the game of bridge for enjoyment and friendly competition whether at home, at a local club or on the internet.

We realize our book is chock-full of information which you will not fully incorporate into your game on first reading. It is meant to be a constant reference as you continue to learn and play this consuming game. Years of enjoyment lie ahead.

Welcome aboard.

Mary Jane Orock   and   Jacqueline Montgomery
Christmas Day, 2013

ACKNOWLEDGMENT

A special thanks to Tom Nute who provided editing assistance and displayed endless patience throughout the numerous revisions of our book.

Tom also is responsible for expertly converting our MS Word document into the required format for publication. His tireless efforts in working with us is a major factor in getting our 2/1 text into your hands.

TABLE OF CONTENTS

CHAPTER 1

CHAPTER 2

CHAPTER 3

CHAPTER 4

CHAPTER 8

CHAPTER 9

CHAPTER 10

CHAPTER 1
WHAT'S THIS GAME ALL ABOUT?

In this chapter you will learn:

- Who the players are: Partners, declarer, dummy, defenders
- About the cards: Suits and their rank; honor cards and spot cards
- About the bidding process: The auction, book, and contract
- How the play begins: The opening leader, taking tricks, placement of the cards
- A bit about scoring: Game points, trick value, vulnerability, bonus points, slam bonus

THE PLAYERS AND THE CARDS

Bridge is a partnership game for four which uses a standard deck of 52 cards. The people facing each other play as partners with one pair designated North/South and the other East/West. The object of bridge, like most games, is to outscore your opponents. The process includes bidding, card play, defensive techniques and scoring. The intricacies of bidding and card play are what make the game so fascinating for so many and what make the game such a mental challenge.

A **hand** of bridge (called a **deal**) begins when one player called the **dealer** distributes the cards one at a time in clockwise fashion to the four players. Each player receives13 cards (called his **hand**) and most players sort the cards into suits. The **rank** of the suits in descending order is spades, hearts, diamonds, and clubs. Rank is important in the bidding process and scoring. An important designation of the suits in bridge is **major** and **minor**. The major suits are spades (S) and hearts (H) which rank higher than the minors, diamonds (D) and clubs (C). The cards in descending order in each suit are A, K, Q, J, 10, 9, 8, 7, 6, 5, 4, 3, and 2. The A, K, Q, J, and 10 are **honor cards** or honors and the rest are **spot cards** or spots. Major suits are preferred over minors (more about this later) and honor cards are better than spots because of their trick-taking ability.

MAJOR SUITS (M) = Spades ♠ & Hearts ♥
MINOR SUITS (m) = Diamonds ♦ & Clubs ♣

BY THE WAY
In bridge publications, newspapers, books and teachers' lessons, spot cards are represented by a lower case x. A nice holding in the ♥ suit would look like this: AKJxxx

THE BIDDING PROCESS

The first step in the bidding process is hand evaluation which is covered in Chapter 2. After evaluating his hand, each player has the opportunity to **bid** in clockwise order beginning with the dealer. A player may bid or pass (no bid). A **bid** is a declaration or commitment to take a certain number of tricks. There are 13 tricks in each deal. A **trick** consists of four cards one contributed by each player. A bid consists of a number, one through seven, and a suit designation or a designation of **notrump.** Notrump (NT) means no suit will be "wild" or trump so that the highest card in each suit played will prevail and take the trick. Notrump outranks all the suits in the bidding hierarchy.

All **contracts** (the final bid) require you to take a **book** of six tricks plus the number specified in your bid. If a player bids 1H he is making a commitment to take seven tricks. Subsequent bids must adhere to suit rankings. Bidding 1S or 1NT is acceptable because both outrank hearts. However, if the next bidder wants to bid clubs or diamonds he must bid at least 2C or 2D over 1H because hearts is a higher-ranking suit. If a player chooses not to make a bid,

NT
SPADES
HEARTS
DIAMONDS
CLUBS

he passes at his turn. If all four players pass with none having bid, the hand is not played and is scored as passed out and the game proceeds to the next hand. If any player bids the auction continues until there are three consecutive passes which ends the auction. The player who first mentioned the last suit bid is the **declarer** for the hand. The partner of the declarer becomes the **dummy.**

> ### BY THE WAY
> The dummy's hand, which is tabled, is also called the "dummy". During play, the dummy is just that. The sole role of the dummy is to play the card declarer designates.

THE OPENING LEAD AND PLAY BEGINS

The partnership making the final bid has won the auction. They have contracted to take the number of tricks bid (plus the six for book) in the suit named in their final bid. The other pair becomes **defenders.** The defender to the left of the declarer chooses a card to play which is called the **opening lead.** The dummy then places his hand face up on the table in front of him, in four columns sorted into suits, with the trump suit placed first (declarer's left, dummy's right).

POINT OF EMPHASIS	TAKE NOTE
The **opening lead** is often critical to the success or failure of the contract. The suit selected as well as the card selected must be chosen carefully – more on this later.	The **opening lead** should be placed face down on the table before exposing its face. This prevents **a lead out of turn penalty** in case your partner was in fact the opening leader not you.

Once the opening lead has been made, play continues in a clockwise direction around the table with each player contributing a card to the trick. Declarer chooses the cards from both the dummy and his own hand. Each player must play a card in the suit led if he has one. If not, he can **discard** from another suit or play a trump card which will win the trick unless someone plays a higher trump. If all follow suit, the highest card wins the trick and that player is now on lead for the next trick. As tricks are won, place your card in a vertical position face down in front of you. If you lose the trick, place your card horizontally in front of you. This pattern allows you to quickly see how many tricks have been won or lost by either side.

Play continues until all 13 cards have been played. If the declarer has won the number of tricks specified he has made his contract. Any tricks over the number he contracted for are **overtricks** and the trick value is added to his score. Any less are **undertricks** which results in a score for the defenders.

VULNERABILITY AND SCORING

Most people play games to win or at least prefer winning to losing. A goal in bridge is to bid and make games based on the scoring system. A **game** is equal to 100 points where each trick above book (the first six tricks) scores 20 points in clubs and diamonds (minors), 30 points in hearts and spades (majors) and in notrump 40 points for the first trick and 30 points for the rest. To make a game, therefore, you must bid and make 5C or 5D (11 tricks), 4H or 4S (10 tricks), or 3NT (9 tricks). You can see that one makes a game scoring fewer tricks with both notrump and the majors than the minors. Remember there is no trick value given to the first 6 tricks (book). Therefore, to make game your bid must be high enough to equal 100 points. The table below summarizes the trick requirements to make game.

3NT (9 tricks)	40 x 1 trick + 30 x 2 tricks	100 points (game)
4H/4S (10 tricks)	30 x 4 tricks	120 points (game)
5C/5D (11 tricks)	20 x 5 tricks	100 points (game)

Winning bridge strategy includes use of the important concept of **vulnerability** related to the scoring system. On each hand a partnership is either vulnerable (V) or non-vulnerable (NV). You earn 300 bonus points for bidding and making a non-vulnerable game. When your side is vulnerable the bonus increases to 500. Any bid less than game, e. g. 4D, 2NT, 3H, results in a **partscore**. If you bid and make a partscore, you receive the trick value of your bid plus 50 bonus points.

There are big bids called **slams** where you earn additional bonus points for bidding and making contracts of six and seven ... 12 or all 13 tricks. A **small slam** is a bid of six and a bid of all seven is a **grand slam**. A NV small slam is worth 500 bonus points and V it is worth 750 points. A grand slam rewards you with 1000 points NV and 1500 points when your side is vulnerable. In both slams, you also receive the trick value and game bonus points. Pretty fun, huh?

PLAY TIP: COUNTING TRUMP

Playing in a suit contract, it is generally a good idea to play as many rounds of trump as necessary to collect all the trump cards held by the opponents. So, count how many trump cards are held by the declarer and dummy, then subtract that number from 13. This result represents the number held by the defense. Now all you need to do is watch and count the trump cards as they are played by the defenders. When the outstanding ones are all in, it is not necessary to play any more trumps.

DEFENSIVE TIP: OPENING LEADS – SEQUENCES

A good **opening lead** is the top of two or three honor cards in **sequence**. Defending notrump contracts you will need a sequence of three while a 2-card sequence is adequate in a suit contract.

Defending a notrump contract you have elected to lead a suit with one of the honor sequences shown below. Lead the underlined card:

$$\underline{A}KQ95 \qquad \underline{K}QJ4 \qquad \underline{Q}JT96 \qquad \underline{J}T953$$

Note: The card led tells your partner that you do not have the adjacent higher card. It also tells partner that you have the two cards below the card which was led.

Defending a suit contract, you would make the same lead with the holdings shown. However, you would also lead the underlined card without the third card in the sequence. Other types of sequences (**broken and interior**) are also good leads and will be discussed in future chapters.

➤ The NS pair, as partners, plays against the EW pair

➤ Declarer, with the dummy, plays offense; the other pair plays defense

➤ The rank of suits is important in bidding and scoring. Suit rank in descending order is spades (S), hearts (H), diamonds (D), and clubs (C). Notrump (NT) outranks all suits.

➤ Hearts and spades are called the majors and clubs and diamonds are called the minors; always try to play major suit or notrump games rather than minor suit games

➤ The A, K, Q, J and 10 are honor cards; the others are spot cards

➤ The bidding proceeds clockwise around the table beginning with the dealer

➤ Bids must adhere to the suit ranking hierarchy, e.g., 2H over 1S

➤ A card from each player equals a trick. There are 13 tricks in each deal

➤ Book = 6 tricks; to make its contract the declaring side must make book plus the number of tricks bid

➤ Game = 100 points: 3NT, 4S, 4H, 5C or 5D = game

➤ Non-vulnerable game (NV) = 300 bonus points; vulnerable (V) game = 500 bonus points

➤ Small slam bonus NV = 500 points and V = 750 points; grand slam bonus NV = 1000 points and V = 1500 points

➤ Count the outstanding trumps and play as many rounds of trump as necessary to collect them

➤ A good opening lead is top of a sequence of honor cards

1. Who am I? What's my bridge name?
   a. I get to play the hand
   b. I played the first card once the bidding was over
   c. My partner and I have the same name
   d. I must be quiet during the play of the hand

2. What is the number associated with these terms?
   a. Book
   b. Cards in a bridge hand
   c. A trick
   d. Game points

3. What suits are called major suits?

4. How many tricks must a declarer take to make these contracts?
   a. 4S
   b. 5D
   c. 2NT
   d. 7H
   e. 3C

5. What would be the trick value of the each of the contracts listed above?

6. Categorize the above contracts as a partscore, a game, or a slam

QUIZ ANSWERS

1. My name is:
   a. Declarer
   b. Opening leader
   c. Defenders
   d. Dummy   Note: The major players are the 3Ds!

2. The numbers game
    a. 6
    b. 13
    c. 4
    d. 100
    Note: No higher math in this game!

3. The **Majors** are hearts and spades

4. Tricks needed
    a. 10 (6 for book + 4 for the bid)
    b. 11 (6 for book + 5 for the bid)
    c. 8 (6 for book + 2 for the bid)
    d. 13 (6 for book + 7 for the bid)
    e. 9 (6 for book + 3 for the bid)
    Note: You won't see many 7H!

5. Trick values
    a. 4 x 30 = 120
    b. 5 x 20 = 100
    c. 1 x 40 + 1 x 30 = 70   Notrump is, as usual, different!
    d. 7 x 30 = 210
    e. 3 x 20 = 60

6. Partscore, game, or slam
    Partscores = c and e
    Games   = a and b
    Slam   = d
    Note: We love games but eschew games in the minors.

HAND		North
VULNERABLE:	None	♠ 4 3 2
DECLARER:	South	♥ A 6 2
CONTRACT:	4H	♦ A 9 3
OPENING LEAD:	K♠	♣ A 9 6 5

	West	East
	♠ K Q J 5	♠ T 9 7
	♥ 9	♥ 7 5 3
	♦ K J 6 2	♦ Q T 5 4
	♣ J 8 4 2	♣ Q T 7

South
♠ A 8 6
♥ K Q J T 8 4
♦ 8 7
♣ K 3

South will play four hearts requiring her to take 10 tricks.

The PLAY: South (the declarer) is in game with a wild card suit (hearts). She will look to see how many tricks she could lose:

    0 heart losers with the ace in dummy

    2 spades losers after the ace is played

    1 diamond loser (the ace in dummy covers one of her losing diamonds)

    0 club losers with the ace in dummy

    3 total losing tricks!

The contract is safe. With nine trump cards in the N-S hands declarer will just win the ace of spades and collect the four outstanding trump cards held by the opponents. Be careful to count the outstanding trump cards as they are played. Since one opponent has three trumps you will need to play trump three times to collect all the outstanding trump cards.

CHAPTER 2
LET'S GET STARTED

In this chapter you will learn:

- More about the bidding process
- How to evaluate your hand
- The requirements for opening the bidding
- About hand patterns
- What to open with different hand patterns

MORE ABOUT THE BIDDING PROCESS

Your bidding goal on each hand is to arrive at the best contract for your partnership. If and when the contract belongs to the opponents your goal is to try to defeat their contract. Points are scored when a contract is made or defeated. It is equally important, therefore, to know when not to bid and when to stop bidding lest you get too high and the opponents score the points.

Bidding is a conversation between partners which attempts to accurately describe their hands. This conversation allows the pair to reach the correct contract in both **strain** (which suit or notrump) and **level** (partscore, game or slam). The bidding conversation is limited to the numbers one through seven (level) accompanied by spades, hearts, diamonds, clubs or notrump (strain), and pass.

An opening bid, for example, you state as "one heart (1H)". During the course of an auction, your opponents may be bidding also to compete for the contract. Listen to their conversation, their bids, as well as your own. You will gather useful information which will help you play the hand or, if you are defending, to defeat their contract.

POINT OF EMPHASIS	TAKE NOTE
The bidding vocabulary is limited to only 15 words!! NUMBERS: 1-7 SUITS: S, H, D, C, & NT OUR LEAST FAVORITE: PASS + See the TAKE NOTE.	Two other words, double and redouble, are part of the bidding language but will not be used when only one partnership is bidding. Competitive bidding will be discussed later.

BRIDGE ETIQUETTE

It is unacceptable to convey information about your hand using extraneous words, facial expressions of pleasure or displeasure, gestures, sighs or groans, despite how you may feel about your hand or the bidding.

BY THE WAY

Bidding boxes are containers for each player that hold bid cards, 1C through 7NT. The player selects the card which reflects the bid he wishes to make and places it on the table in front of him. Boxes were first introduced for tournament play to eliminate voice inflections, volume change, and the like which might (advertently or inadvertently) convey unauthorized information. Now they are used almost universally in duplicate bridge games and even quite often in social bridge settings.

This method of bidding eliminates noise and also helps all players remember the auction as it is displayed on the table until the bidding is over.

The dealer occupies the first seat and has the first opportunity to bid. If he passes, any player at his turn may open the bidding. The requirements for opening the bidding vary slightly depending on your position at the table (1st, 2nd, 3rd, 4th seat).

For now, we will be discussing opening the bidding at the 1-level. Higher level openings will be discussed in later chapters. Two features of your hand are important in evaluating whether your hand meets the requirements for an opening bid: Its strength based on the number of high cards or honor cards you have and how your cards are divided among the suits. In bridge lingo, the latter is called **distribution**, or **hand pattern**, which is a very important concept.

HAND PATTERNS

Hand patterns influence which suit or strain you will choose for your opening bid as well as subsequent bids, called **rebids**. Any hand that has the 13 cards distributed among the suits in any 4-3-3-3, or 4-4-3-2, or 5-3-3-2 pattern is considered **balanced**. Note that these balanced hand patterns contain no **voids** (zero cards in a suit), no **singletons** (one card in a suit), and no more than one **doubleton** (two cards in a suit). Balanced hands are more boring unless you have lots of **high card points (HCP)**. All other hands are either **semi-balanced** (two doubletons) or unbalanced.

Unbalanced hands can be 1-suited with five, six, seven, or more cards in one suit or 2-suited with two suits of at least five and four cards in length, or 3-suited. Three-suited hands are those with at least four cards in three suits: 4-4-4-1 or 5-4-4-0. The former is one of the most difficult hand patterns to bid. Really unbalanced hands can be some of the most fun bridge hands to bid and play.

EVALUATING YOUR HAND AND OPENING THE BIDDING

In order to bid a game the partnership must have sufficient assets to take the required number of tricks. Each player evaluates her hand and during the bidding attempts to describe the strength of her hand. The combined partnership points required for games are different for the majors, the minors, and for notrump because the number of tricks required is different. It follows then that more points are required for slams. Specific points needed for games and slams are:

NT games require	25 points
Major suit games require	26 points
Minor suit games require	29 points
Small slams require	33 points
Grand slams require	37 points

So where do we get these points? In evaluating your hand, first assess the strength of your hand using a **point count system**. For each of the honor cards you hold, use these equivalents:

Ace (A)   = 4 points
King (K)   = 3 points
Queen (Q)   = 2 points
Jack (J)   = 1 point

Even though a 10 is an honor card it receives no point count but nevertheless is a valuable trick-taking card. These points are called **high card points (HCP)**. Total the points for all honor cards held to get the HCP strength of your hand. Because of the four suits, there is a total of 40 HCP distributed among the four players' hands.

Distribution, the second feature, is assessed by giving length points (LP) to any card over four in any and all suits. Thus, a suit of:

5 cards = 1 LP
6 cards = 2 LP
7 cards = 3 LP
8 cards = 4 LP

Now, add LP to your HCP to arrive at your total points (TP) which is the starting evaluation of your hand. These two factors (HCP and LP), in combination TP, determine if you can open the bidding.

HCP + LP = TP

Obviously, the more honor cards you have the stronger your hand is and the longer the suit the better, especially when your honor cards are concentrated in your long suit(s). High cards in combination are far more valuable in their trick-taking ability than if they are scattered among your suits.

COMPARE THE TWO HANDS BELOW:

♠ A K J 7   ♥ K Q T 7   ♦ 9 8   ♣ 7 5 4

♠ A J 7   ♥ K 7 6 3   ♦ Q T 5   ♣ K 7 4

With two strong major suits, the first hand looks like a great opening hand while the second hand is what some people call an ugly 13. I like all 13 TP hands so I'd open either but I sure like the first one much more.

Open the bidding in any seat with 13 TP. In first or second seat, you will at times have a hand that looks like you should open but it does not contain 13 TP. Many hands with 12 HCP are in this category. In this case, you may also open if your hand meets the "**rule of 20**". To apply the "rule of 20", add your HCP and the number of cards in your two longest suits. If the total equals 20 it is a suitable opening bid.

EXAMPLES OF OPENING BIDS

♠ A K 6 2   ♥ Q J 9   ♦ K 9 8   ♣ 7 5 4
You have 13 HCP so you should open

♠ 9 7   ♥ A Q J 9 6   ♦ K 9 8   ♣ Q 8 6
You have 12 HCP + 1 LP for 13 TP so you should open

♠ K Q 9 8   ♥ A J 9 5   ♦ Q 9 5   ♣ 8 6
You have 12 HCP + 2 four-card suits (H & S) for 8 which = 20 so you should open

---

BY THE WAY

An additional hand evaluation method is to look at "quick tricks (QT)". High honor cards, especially those in combination, provide your QT. Many players like to have two QT when they open the bidding. Here are the QT holdings:

- A K of the same suit   = 2 QT
- A Q of the same suit   = 1 ½ QT
- A or K Q in the same suit   = 1 QT
- K with another card in the same suit   = ½ QT

  Note that all the examples above also have 2 QT

If you are in the third seat and there still has not been an opening bid you may consider opening a little lighter than in first or second seat. The guidelines to open in first and second seats still apply so open if you have 13 TP or if your hand meets the "rule of 20". In third seat you may also open with less, about 11 HCP but with contingencies. Note that when your partner passed, she denied having an opening hand. If your partner bids at her next turn, you must be prepared to pass any bid she makes which will confirm that your opening bid was less than robust. Your relatively light opening bid should be made, therefore, with tolerance for any suit she might bid. Your opening bid should also suggest a suitable suit for partner to lead if you become defenders. You might open this hand in third seat and pass any bid made by your partner:

♠ K 7 6   ♥ Q 7 5   ♦ K Q 8 7   ♣ J 9 6

If you are the opening bidder in fourth seat, there is another guideline to use, the "rule of 15". Still go ahead and open your 13 TP hands, but also open hands long in the spade suit using the **"rule of 15"**. The "rule of 15" is the total of your HCPs plus the number of cards you have in the spade suit. Note that all the other players have passed before your turn to bid. If you pass, the hand will not be played. The opponents may have a nice hand which was not good enough to open but good enough to outbid you for a partscore if you open. If you hold the spade suit, however, and open the bidding, it may prevent the other side from bidding because you hold the master suit. To bid they may get too high in a lower-ranking suit giving you the chance of defeating their contract. That would be points for your side – a good deal! Here is a hand that might be opened in fourth seat:

♠ K Q T 7   ♥ 9 7 5   ♦ A Q 8   ♣ J 9 6

POINTS OF EMPHASIS

1st and 2nd seat openers require 13 TP or "rule of 20" values.
A 3rd seat opener may be as light as 11 TP.
A 4th seat opener will be either 13 TP or "rule of 15" using spades.

WHAT TO OPEN

All hands with 13-21 TP should be opened with a bid of one of a suit or a notrump bid. Remember some 12 HCP or "rule of 20" hands should also be opened.

Balanced hands generally are more suitable to be opened and played in a notrump contract. Unbalanced hands are best played in a suit contract if a fit (at least eight cards in the combined partnership holding) can be found. You should open 1NT with all balanced hands with 15-17 HCP. If your balanced hand has 20-21 HCP, you should open 2NT. All other hands in the 19-21 HCP range will be opened with one of a suit including balanced hands in the 12-14 and 18-19 HCP ranges. The balanced feature of these hands will be shown on your rebid (see TAKE NOTE below). Much more on notrump bidding will be discussed in Chapter 7.

POINTS OF EMPHASIS	TAKE NOTE
Open all hands with 13 HCP. Balanced hands are played in notrump. Unbalanced hands generally are played in a suit contract.	One of a suit followed by a 1NT rebid = 12-14 balanced points. One of a suit followed by a jump to 2NT on your rebid = 18-19 balanced points.

With an unbalanced hand and 12-21 TPs, open the bidding with one of a suit.

- Open your longest suit if it is 5 cards or longer
- With no 5-card suit, open your longer minor suit
- If your minors are equal in length and at least 4 cards long open 1D; if they are only 3 cards long, open 1C
- You must have at least 5 cards in a major suit to open 1H or 1S
- If you have 2 suits of equal length that are 5 cards or longer, open the higher-ranking suit

POINTS OF EMPHASIS
A **MAJOR SUIT** opening will never be less than 5 cards long! A **MINOR SUIT** opening will never be less than 3 cards long!

EXAMPLE HANDS

♠ K Q 8 4　♥ Q 8 6　♦ A Q　♣ K 7 5 3
16 HCP + 0 LP　= 16 TP　Open 1NT

♠ A 9　♥ K 8 6　♦ J 7 3 2　♣ A J 7 5
13 HCP + 0 LP　= 13 TP　Open 1D

♠ K Q 7 4 3　♥ J 8　♦ A Q 7 5 2　♣ 9
12 HCP + 2 LP　= 14 TP　Open 1S

♠ J 10 8 4 3　♥ A K 8 6 2　♦ 8　♣ A K
15 HCP + 2 LP　= 17 TP　Open 1S

♠ A Q 8 6 4　♥ K Q　♦ A 7 3　♣ A J 7
20 HCP + 1 LP　= 21 TP　Open 2NT

♠ A J 8 4　♥ K J 8 2　♦ A 2　♣ 9 8 5
13 HCP + 0 LP　= 13 TP　Open 1C

♠ K Q 9 7 4　♥ A Q　♦ 2　♣ A K 9 8 5
18 HCP + 2 LP　= 20 TP　Open 1S

♠ K J 8 4　♥ A Q 8 2　♦ A 9 2　♣ 8 5
14 HCP + 0 LP　= 14 TP　Open 1D

♠ Q 8 4　♥ K 9 8 2　♦ A 9 2　♣ Q 9 8 5
11 HCP + 0 LP　= 11 TP　Pass

♠ Q J 8 4　♥ K J 8　♦ A 9 2　♣ J 8 5
12 HCP + 0 LP　= 12 TP　Pass
12 points but no "rule of 20"

PLAY TIP: PLANNING THE PLAY

Once the dummy's cards are tabled you must decide how you will play the hand to take at least the number of tricks you committed to in the contract. Because play to the first trick can be crucial to the contract's success, **do not** play to the first trick until you have established your plan and have it well in mind.

Playing a notrump contract you start by counting your winners. If you bid 3NT, you will need to take nine tricks. If you can count nine immediate winners - good for you - go ahead and take them. Usually that is not the case and you will need to establish one or more winners. One way is by knocking out higher honors to establish your lower-ranking cards as trick takers. Another way to get more tricks is to establish winners in a long suit. More about notrump play later.

In a suit contract, plan your play by counting losers. There are quick losers and slow losers. Quick losers are those the opponents can take when they have the lead. Slow losers, less deadly, are those the opponents can't take right away because you have the top card(s) in that suit. However, once the top card(s) are played the remaining card(s) are losers.

In a 4H contract you can lose only three tricks. We want to count losers from the perspective of declarer's hand but you will always look at the dummy to cover some of your losers. With that in mind, try counting quick and slow losers in the hand below which you are playing in a 4H contract.

```
Dummy's hand
♠ A Q 4 3
♥ K 8 4
♦ K 2
♣ 8 7 4 3

Declarer's hand
♠ K 2
♥ A Q J 10 6 3
♦ 8 3
♣ A 5 2
```

In Spades   0 losers - dummy has the much needed ace

In Hearts   0 losers - dummy has your missing king

In Diamonds 2 losers - the potential for 2 quick losers because dummy's help is iffy

In Clubs   2 slow losers - your ace wins but there is nothing in dummy to cover your other two cards

You can see that if you lose all 4, 2 quick losers and both slow losers, you can't make your 4H contract. Your plan should now involve looking at a way to eliminate one of the losers. If you look closely at the dummy you will see that you have an extra winner in the spade suit. Since the defenders can't take any clubs right away because you own the ace, you can see that once trumps are drawn you will be able to **discard a club loser on dummy's extra spade winner** which will enable you to make the contract. That's a really good plan. You will see in a later chapter that you also have a chance for an extra trick if your left hand opponent (LHO) holds the ace of diamonds but don't count on that!

Other ways to handle losers are by ruffing them in the short trump hand (usually the dummy) and by finessing. These techniques will be discussed in other play tips.

Another element of successful play planning is the timing or sequence of your play. You may need to delay collecting trumps in order to ruff a loser from your hand in dummy. If you have a quick loser in the trump suit, again you may need to delay collecting trumps to allow you to discard (pitch) a loser before the opponents get the lead and cash their tricks. Entry considerations are a third crucial aspect of your play plan but for now assume you can move easily from one hand to the other.

DEFENSIVE TIP: LEADING FROM A K x x

In a suit contract, leading from a suit where you hold the A K along with some additional cards is a very good lead. You may have a **side suit** (any suit but trump) that looks like one of these:

A K 6   A K 9 6 5   A K J   A K J 7   A 8 6 5

When you hold the A K with one or more cards, most players today lead the ace on the opening lead. So on all the holdings (except the final one) shown above, I would lead the ace. On the last example, I don't have the king protecting my ace so I'm going to stay away from leading this suit. It is generally a losing tactic to lead an ace when you do not also hold the king; so it is best to find some other lead.

Notice that on the first two holdings, you have only the ace and king while on the third and fourth holding, you also have the jack. Examples 3 and 4 are very powerful holdings called "**broken sequences.**" Broken sequences have two in a row, a gap, and then the next high card. Here are some other examples of broken sequences. With broken sequences lead the top of the touching cards.

K Q T   K Q T 8   Q J 9 6 4   J T 8 5

When an ace is led, the leader's partner has a very important responsibility. She must tell her partner whether the lead was a good one or not using a process called **SIGNALING**. She uses her spot cards to show her **attitude** about the opening lead. If she likes the lead she plays a high spot card. If she doesn't like the lead, she plays her smallest card. HI = smiles! LOW = frowns!

What must she have to signal that her partner has found a very good lead? If she has the queen (an equal honor) that is a good thing so she would tell her partner to continue the suit by playing a HIGH spot card. Also if the leader's partner has only two cards in the suit led, she wants her partner to continue leading the suit so that she can ruff the third round of the suit. That is also a good thing so signal with a HIGH spot card.

With neither of the holdings defined above, the partner of the opening leader should play her lowest card to say "I have no help in the suit led". Now the leader should consider switching to some other suit. This message is not a command to switch it simply shows no interest in the suit led.

BY THE WAY

Attitude signals also apply to discards. A HIGH card means I like this suit, please lead it while a LOW card means I have nothing good in this suit, don't lead it.

➢ The bidding allows the partnership to arrive at the correct contract in both **strain** (what suit or NT) and **level** (partscore, game, or slam)

➢ Points required to bid games and slams
- 3NT = 25
- 4H or 4S = 26
- 5C or 5D = 29
- Small slam = 33
- Grand slam = 37

➢ The bidding vocabulary is limited to the numbers 1 thru 7, the strain, pass, double, and redouble: Just 15 words!!

➢ The dealer in the 1st seat gets to speak first and may pass or bid. The first person to bid is the **opening bidder**. The bidding then continues clockwise around the table through 2nd, 3rd, and 4th seat until there are three consecutive passes.

➢ Counting your hand:
- Add all your high card points (HCP)
  A = 4   K = 3   Q = 2   J = 1
- Then add your length points (LP)
  1 point for any card over 4 in any and all suits
- HCP + LP = TP (total points)

➢ Open the bidding in any seat with 13 TP

➢ With less than 13 TP:
- Open the bidding in 1st, 2nd, or 3rd seat if your hand meets the "rule of 20" (HCP + the number of cards in your two longest suits = 20)
- Open "light" (~ 11 HCP) in 3rd seat if you can tolerate any suit your partner may bid

- Open in 4ᵗʰ seat if your hand meets the "rule of 15" (HCP + the number of spades you hold = 15)

➤ Hand patterns are balanced, semi-balanced, and unbalanced

➤ Balanced hands contain no voids, no singletons, and no more than one doubleton. Balanced hands generally play best in NT:
- Open 1NT with 15-17 HCP and a balanced hand
- Open 2NT with 20-21 HCP and a balanced hand
- With a balanced hand and 12-14 or 18-19 points, open one of a suit planning to rebid NT

➤ Unbalanced hands may be 1-suited (5 cards or longer in one suit), 2-suited (such as two 5-card suits), or 3-suited (such as a 4-4-4-1 hand pattern)

➤ Unbalanced hands generally play best in a suit contract if the partnership has at least an 8-card fit

➤ With an unbalanced hand and 12-21 TP or "rule of 20" hand, open 1 of a suit:
- Open your longest suit if it is at least 5 cards long
- If you hold 2 suits which are equal in length and 5 cards or longer, open the higher-ranking one
- If you have no 5-card or longer suit, open your longer minor
- If your minors are equal and 4 cards long, open 1D. If they are 3 cards long, open 1C

➤ An opening bid of 1H or 1S will always be at least 5 cards long.

➤ An opening bid of 1C or 1D will always be at least 3 cards long

➤ Plan the play of the hand before playing even one card from the dummy. In a suit contract count your quick and slow losers.

➤ Lead the A from holdings with AKx(x) in a suit contract. Partner signals attitude. A high spot card says he likes your lead while a low spot card says he doesn't.

HAND EVALUATION AND OPENING BID DECISIONS

Your hand	HCP	LP	TP	Do you open?	What do you open?
♠AQ754 ♥KJ ♦K54 ♣Q95					
♠AK754 ♥Q97 ♦K52 ♣95					
♠96754 ♥AQ754 ♦KQ4 ♣ -					
♠Q754 ♥AK65 ♦A54 ♣95					
♠Q754 ♥AK65 ♦K5 ♣T95					
♠K75 ♥QT64 ♦A54 ♣Q93					
♠AQ75 ♥KQJ ♦AK5 ♣J95					
♠KQ75 ♥KJ7 ♦KQ4 ♣952					
♠754 ♥87 ♦AK54 ♣KQ95					
♠A ♥AQ754 ♦AK54 ♣QJ5					
♠AQ75 ♥KQ5 ♦KQ2 ♣975					
♠A754 ♥K8 ♦Q6432 ♣92					
♠AK754 ♥865 ♦KJ4 ♣95					
♠J54 ♥KT8 ♦AK54 ♣T95					

A SHORT QUIZ

1. What is your lead when holding these cards in spades?
   a. KQJ86   b. QJT93   c. AKQ8

2. What hand patterns are considered balanced?

3. What does it mean to say you are void in a suit?

4. An opening bid in a major will always have at least ____ cards and an opening bid in a minor will always have at least _____ cards.

EXERCISE ANSWERS

Your hand	HCP	LP	TP	Do you open?	What do you open?
♠AQ754 ♥KJ ♦K54 ♣Q95 Open 1NT even with a 5-card major and 15-17 points	15	1	16	YES	1NT Balanced
♠AK754 ♥Q97 ♦K52 ♣95 Balanced but too little for NT	12	1	13	YES	1S 5-card suit
♠96754 ♥AQ754 ♦KQ4 ♣ - With two 5-card suits open the higher one not better one	11	2	13	YES	1S 5-card suit
♠Q754 ♥AK65 ♦A54 ♣95 With no 5-card suit open your longer minor	13	0	13	YES	1D Longer minor
♠Q754 ♥AK65 ♦K5 ♣T95 12 HCP + 8 cards in your two longest suits = 20	12	0	12	YES	1C Rule of 20
♠K75 ♥QT64 ♦A54 ♣Q93 TP< 13 and does not meet the rule of 20	11	0	11	NO	N/A
♠AQ75 ♥KQJ ♦AK5 ♣J95 Big balanced hand 20-21	20	0	20	YES	2NT Balanced
♠KQ75 ♥KJ7 ♦KQ4 ♣952 No 5-card suit; too little for 1NT; equal minors (3) = 1C	14	0	14	YES	1C 3 in each minor
♠754 ♥87 ♦AK54 ♣KQ95 No 5-card suit; too little for 1NT; equal minors (4) = 1D	12	0	12	YES	1D 4 in each minor

Hand	TP	DP	Total	Open?	Bid
♠A ♥AQ754 ♦AK54 ♣QJ5 Big hand but unbalanced so open 5-card major	20	1	21	YES	1H Unbalanced
♠AQ75 ♥KQ5 ♦KQ2 ♣975 Balanced in NT range, not every suit to have a stopper	16	0	16	YES	1NT Balanced
♠A754 ♥K8 ♦Q6432 ♣92 TP<13, no "Rule of 20"	9	1	10	NO	N/A
♠AK754 ♥865 ♦KJ4 ♣95 In 3rd seat open 1S to suggest a lead. In 4th seat open 1S; meets "Rule of 15" (11 HCP+5 Spades=16)	11	1	12	NO	But open 1S in 3rd or 4th seat!
♣J54 ♥KT8 ♦AK54 ♣T95 In 3rd seat open 1D to suggest a lead – plan to pass next	11	0	11	NO	But open 1D in 3rd seat

QUIZ ANSWERS

1. Leads   a. = K   b. = Q   c. = A
   Note: You lead top of your sequence and have nothing higher!

2. Hands with 4-3-3-3 or 4-4-3-2 or 5-3-3-2 distribution

3. A void suit means that you have no cards in that suit

4. 5, 3

In bridge, balanced and unbalanced only refers to your bridge hands.

HAND #1	
VULNERABLE:	N-S
DECLARER:	South
CONTRACT:	1NT
OPENING LEAD: J♠	

North
♠ K 6
♥ K T 4 2
♦ J 9 6
♣ 9 8 5 2

West
♠ J T 9 8
♥ 9 7 5
♦ A 8 5 4
♣ Q T

East
♠ 5 4 2
♥ A 8 6
♦ Q 7 3 2
♣ K J 6

South
♠ A Q 7 3
♥ Q J 3
♦ K T
♣ A 7 4 3

THE BIDDING			
SOUTH	WEST	NORTH	EAST
1NT	P	P	P

SOUTH
16 HCP + 0 LP = 16 TP
SOUTH OPENS 1NT

The PLAY: The declarer counts his tricks and can see that he has only four (three spades and one club) before losing the lead. He will need three more tricks and can get them in the heart suit after the ace of hearts is forced out. He must be careful to lead the high cards (QJ of hearts) from the hand which is shorter in the suit before going to the king in the dummy or the defenders can keep him from collecting all his tricks. It is also important to win the first spade in his hand to preserve a later entry to the dummy. Making our contract is always nice and here careful play insures success and may even allow the declarer to make an overtrick for a very nice score of 120.

HAND #2	
VULNERABLE:	E-W
DECLARER:	South
CONTRACT:	4S
OPENING LEAD: A♥	

North
♠ 7 6 3
♥ J 6 4
♦ K Q 9 3 2
♣ Q 8

West
♠ J 5 2
♥ A K T 7 5
♦ 7 5
♣ K 7 4

East
♠ 8
♥ Q 9 2
♦ T 8 6
♣ J T 9 6 5 3

South
♠ A K Q T 9 4
♥ 8 3
♦ A J 4
♣ A 2

THE BIDDING

SOUTH	WEST	NORTH	EAST
1S	P	2S	P
4S	P	P	P

SOUTH
18 HCP + 2 LP = 20 TP
SOUTH OPENS 1S

The LEAD: The ace of hearts (A from A K). Partner plays the nine of hearts (high card encourages) to indicate interest in continuing the suit. The king is played next and then a little heart is played to the queen which declarer ruffs.

The PLAY: The declarer can see three possible losers (two hearts and a slow club loser) so his contract appears safe. He can also anticipate pitching the club loser on the long diamond suit in the dummy but must be careful to draw the opponents' trumps before playing the diamonds. The defenders have only four trump cards between them so watch for the four cards as you are drawing trump. When they are all in, it is safe to play diamonds. If you play diamonds before drawing their trumps, the opponent with only two diamonds will ruff the third diamond. You will still have a club loser and if you ruffed the heart with your lowest spade you will have no way to get back to the dummy to discard your club loser.

CHAPTER 3
BIDDING AFTER AN OPENING BID OF 1H OR 1S

In this chapter you will learn:

- About the opener's and the responder's **minimum, invitational,** and **game-forcing** hands
- How the **responder** (the partner of the opening bidder) bids to show 3-card, 4-card and 5-card support for the major when the opening bid is 1H or 1S
- How the opener rebids after various responses which show support for the opening major suit bid
- About bids which force the opener to bid again but do not promise support

MORE ABOUT THE MAJOR SUIT OPENING

When the opening bid is one of a major suit (1H or 1S), the responder knows that partner has 12-21 points and a 5-card or longer suit. When your partnership has eight or more cards in a major suit it is most desirable to play the contract in the major-suit fit. Notrump and minor suit contracts take a back seat to the majors. The option to ruff losers in a suit contract provides flexibility over notrump contracts. Major suit games require fewer tricks than minor suit games. Therefore a major goal in the bidding is to strive to reach a major suit game!

DETERMINING THE DESCRIPTIVE VALUE OF YOUR HAND

As part of the initial hand evaluation, both the opener and the responder must place their hands into one of three descriptive categories to effectively complete the bidding process. These categories are critical for accurate bidding and are involved in almost all auctions. Try to memorize this chart as you will use it a lot!

Opener's Points	Category	Responder's Points
12-15	Minimum (M)	5-10
16-18	Invitational (I)	11-12
19-21	Game-Forcing (GF)	13+

Note that the opener and responder would generally have passed with fewer points than those defined as minimum. A minimum hand will always try to make minimum sounding bids, while a player with invitational values must try to encourage partner to bid a game. When either partner has a game-forcing hand, she must tell her partner that she can't pass before a game is reached. There will be much more on this later.

LOOKING FOR A FIT AND COUNTING DUMMY POINTS

When the opening bid is 1H or 1S and the opening bidder's partner, the **responder,** has three or more cards in partner's suit the bridge game is easy and relaxing since the first question in bridge (where will we play?) is answered: We are playing in partner's suit! The only remaining question is how high do we bid: Do we settle for a partscore, or do we bid game or even slam? Now you need to communicate your joy by describing your values to your partner. But first a few steps to fully evaluating your hand.

An **8-card fit** is sufficient but an extra trump card giving the partnership a **9-card fit** is magical, and two extra trump cards giving the partnership a **10-card fit** is superb. Responder's holding in the opener's suit determines the degree of fit and it is important that your bids communicate whether your support is three, four, or five cards long.

When you have a fit and are going to become the dummy there is an additional method of evaluating your hand. You may now add points if you are short in one of the other suits. These points are called "**dummy points** (DP)" and are:

Void (0 cards)	= 5 points
Singleton (1 card)	= 3 points
Doubleton (2 cards)	= 1 point

Add these points to your high card points to obtain the true value of your hand. Now we are ready to define what to bid and what the bid shows in terms of your contribution to the total points needed to reach game in the major suit.

Responder's hand evaluation when a fit is found:

$$HCP + DP = TP$$

RESPONDER'S INITIAL BIDS WITH 4-CARD SUPPORT FOR OPENER'S MAJOR SUIT

With 4-card support, it is possible to immediately tell partner your strength and degree of support. We will use some "codes" to assist our communication. These "code" bids are called "**conventions**" which have names but it is more important to learn what the "code bids" say about your holding in partner's suit. Using the <u>heart</u> suit as our example, here are the bids:

1H	3H	(a **preemptive** raise)	= 4-6 points
1H	3D *	(a **constructive** raise)	= 7-9 points
1H	3C *	(a **limit** raise)	= 10-11 points
1H	2NT †	(a **game-forcing** raise)	= 12 + points

POINTS OF EMPHASIS	TAKE NOTE
Note the precision of the bids. Also note that the higher you bid the less strength you are showing Always show 4-card support immediately!	The names for these conventions are: * REVERSE BERGEN RAISES † JACOBY 2NT

Remember you will always have at least four cards in partner's suit to use these conventional responses. If you have five cards in partner's suit, just treat it as 4-card support with one exception: With five cards, 4-9 points, and a singleton just bid 4H; this bid allows you to express the gambling instinct inherent in all bridge players. The partnership probably does not have the 26 points necessary to bid a major suit game but you will have a very good chance of making four with your superb fit.

Here are some examples of responder's initial bid after a 1H opening. HCP means High Card Points, DP means Dummy Points and TP means Total Points.

RESPONDER'S HANDS

♠ A 8 7   ♥ K J 8 6   ♦ 8 6 5   ♣ T 9 8
8 HCP + 0 DP   = 8 TP   4-card support - Bid 3D

♠ A 8 7   ♥ K J 8 6   ♦ K 8 6 5   ♣ 8 2
11 HCP + 1 DP   = 12 TP   4-card support - Bid 3C

♠ 7   ♥ K J 8 6 3   ♦ Q 6 5   ♣ T 9 8 7
6 HCP + 3 DP   = 9 TP   5-card support - Bid a gambling 4H

♠ A 8 7   ♥ K J 8 6   ♦ K Q 6 5   ♣ T 9
13 HCP + 1 DP   = 14 TP   4-card support - Bid 2NT

♠ 8 7 4   ♥ K 9 8 6   ♦ 8 6 5 4   ♣ Q 9
5 HCP + 1 DP   = 6 TP   4-card support - Bid 3H

BY THE WAY

There is one other important convention often used by experienced players to tell their partner that they also have an opening hand and four or five cards in support of the opening bidder's major suit. This convention is called a "SPLINTER" bid and is a big jump in a new suit to show that you hold a singleton or void in the suit bid. After a 1H opening the "splinter" bids are 3S, 4C, and 4D. After a 1S opening the "splinter" bids are 4C, 4D, and 4H. This convention is very useful in slam bidding so we will not use it at present. The bid is only used with hands having 13-16 total points (high card points + dummy points)

OPENER'S REBIDS AFTER RESPONDER'S RAISES WHICH SHOW IDEAL (4 CARDS) OR SUPERB (5 CARDS) SUPPORT

Opener bids as follows after various responses by her partner.

- If partner jumped to game you will generally pass.
- If partner jumped to three (4-6 points) - game is extremely unlikely so pass unless you have a great hand - 20 or 21 points.
- If partner's bid was 3D (7-9 points) - bid game (four of the major - 4M) with 17 or more points; otherwise bid three of the major.
- If partner's bid was 3C (10-11 points) - bid game (4M) with any hand with a singleton and all other hands with 14 or more points.
- If partner's bid was 2NT (12+ points) - bid game (4M) and think about slam with 19+ points.

You are the dealer sitting in the West position.

Your hand is: Your hand evaluation is:
- ♠ K 8 7 6   3 HCP
- ♥ A Q J 9 8   7 HCP + 1 LP
- ♦ A 9 7   4 HCP
- ♣ 7   0 HCP

Total points: 14 HCP + 1 LP = 15 TP

What is your rebid on the auction given below?

West	North	East	South
1H	P	3C	P
?			

Since partner's 3C bid is showing a **limit raise** (4 hearts and 10 or 11 points) and you have a singleton club, you should bid 4H.

Had partner bid 3D or 3H (both weaker bids), you would bid 3H after 3D and pass 3H as game is probably unlikely.

If partner had bid 2NT (showing an opening hand) you would definitely bid the heart game.

Showing only three cards in support of the major suit which partner has opened is a bit more problematic. With a strong **minimum** hand (defined as 8-10 points) you will raise the major to the 2-level. Partner will know that you have a limited hand with only three cards in support. Bidding when you have 3-card support for partner's opening major suit and a very light hand (5-7 points) or an **invitational** hand (11-12 points) or a **game-forcing** hand (13+ points) will require two bids. I like to refer to these raises as the "**TEXAS TWO-STEP**". Two-step raises will be discussed in subsequent chapters.

After a single raise showing a strong minimum hand, the opener will need at least 17+ points to bid the game directly. With less, like 15-16 points, she can invite game. To invite, the opener could bid three of the agreed suit or bid a new suit where she will need you to have some high cards. **Do not pass a new suit** bid. Partner still wants to play in the already agreed suit and is just trying to get to game. If you have high cards in the new suit, jump to game (4M) otherwise bid just three in the agreed suit.

EXAMPLES:

Opener's hand: ♠ A K J 5 4 ♥ K 8 7 ♦ A 9 ♣ 8 7 4

Responder's hand: ♠ Q 8 3 ♥ 9 5 ♦ 9 6 4 2 ♣ K Q J 3

The bidding: 1S – 2S

With 16 TP the opener has an invitational hand. With a poor holding in the club suit she bids 3C to ask the responder to bid game if she has any help in clubs. With the great club holding, the responder bids 4S.

Opener's hand: ♠ A 9 6 5 4 ♥ A 8 7 ♦ A 7 ♣ K 5 4

Responder's hand: ♠ K Q 3 ♥ 9 5 ♦ 9 8 6 2 ♣ A 7 3 2

The bidding: 1S – 2S

With 16 TP the opener has an invitational hand with high cards in all the suits and poor spades so she bids three spades to ask if the responder has some honor cards in the trump suit. With two honors in spades the responder bids 4S.

All other hands with sufficient values to respond (six or more points) require the responder to start with a new suit bid or 1NT. Both the new suit and 1NT initial bids by the responder require the opener to bid again!

POINT OF EMPHASIS	TAKE NOTE
Bids that require your partner to bid again are called "**forcing bids**". Both an initial new suit and 1NT by the responder are forcing bids.	Since 1NT is a forcing bid, the responder will never get to play 1NT after a major suit opening bid.

BY THE WAY
Bids that force partner to bid again are called "forcing bids". Those that require only one more bid are called "one-round force". Those that require both partners to continue bidding until at least game is reached are called "game-forcing bids".

When you bid a new suit you must have at least four cards in the suit. New suits bid at the 1-level may be made with as little as six points and have no top value. These bids are referred to as 6+ point hands. After a major suit opening there is only one new suit which can be bid at the 1-level, that suit being 1S after a 1H opening bid. New suits bid at the 2-level require a minimum of 13 points and are also unlimited. They are called 13+ point hands. All new suits (except spades after a 1H opening) must be bid at the 2-level since they are lower on the bidding ladder than the opening bid.

These bids at the 2-level after an opening bid at the 1-level are called two-over-one and are the backbone of the modern bidding system referred to as 2/1. There will be much more on continuing the bidding after a 2/1 response in Chapter 5. For now you must know that if you make any 2/1 bid you will be telling the opening bidder that you also have opening values and therefore the partnership must reach at least game. Partscores are no longer in the bidding equation. Slams must be considered.

THE 2/1 GAME FORCING BIDS

Opener	Responder		Opener	Responder
1H	2C		1S	2C
1H	2D		1S	2D
			1S	2H

There is one other 2/1 auction which will be discussed in a later chapter. That bid is 1D - 2C. Thus, there are a total of six 2/1 auctions. We have now arrived at the critical point in modern bidding. **All hands which**

- **Cannot make an immediate raise of the opener's major suit**
- **And cannot bid a new suit at the 1-level (no spades)**
- **And cannot bid at the 2-level (too weak < 13 points)**

will respond with a forcing 1NT bid.

This initial response of 1NT covers a wide range of hand patterns and point counts (5-12 points). For this reason, the opener must bid again to allow the responder to further describe her hand. Continuing the bidding after a forcing 1NT bid will be discussed in Chapter 4. Continuing the bidding after a game-forcing 2/1 response will be discussed in Chapter 5. It is important to know that the responder may or may not have 3-card support for the opener's major suit when a 1NT or 2/1 initial response is made. Showing 3-card support for the opener's major suit will be discussed in the relevant chapters.

CONTINUING THE BIDDING AFTER 1H - 1S WHEN THE RESPONDER HAS 3-CARD SUPPORT FOR HEARTS

After the forcing 1S bid, the opener must bid again and then the responder holding 3-card support for hearts will immediately show the support by raising to the 3-level with an invitational hand (11-12 points) and jumping to game with a game-forcing hand (13+ points). After the invitational jump to the 3-level the opener will pass or bid game depending on the strength of her hand. She will pass with a very minimum hand (12-13 points) and will bid a game in the major suit with 14+ points. With the very top of her opening bid (20 or 21 points), the opener may consider bidding a slam in the major suit. The tools for bidding slam will be advanced in later chapters.

POINTS OF EMPHASIS	TAKE NOTE
Bidding 1S and then bidding 3H on your rebid shows 11 or 12 points and 3-card heart support. Bidding 1S and then bidding 4H on your rebid shows 13+ points and 3-card heart support.	With 3-card support for the opener's major and no suit to bid at the 1-level, start with 1NT forcing with 5-7 or 11-12 points, and a 2/1 new suit bid with 13+ points. MORE ON THESE AUCTIONS LATER

EXAMPLES: THE OPENING BID IS 1H
RESPONDER'S HANDS

♠ A 7 3 2   ♥ K 8 4   ♦ Q J 7 2   ♣ 9 5
10 HCP + 1 SP = 11 TP
1H - 1S
2C - 3H

♠ A 9 6 3   ♥ K 8 4   ♦ Q J 7 2   ♣ A 5
14 HCP + 1 LP = 15 TP
1H - 1S
2C - 4H

CONTINUING THE BIDDING AFTER 1H – 1S WHEN THE RESPONDER HAS < 3-CARD SUPPORT FOR HEARTS

When the responder bids 1S after an opening bid of 1H the opener must bid again. Since no suit has yet been agreed the search as to where to play the hand will continue. It is of vital importance to the search for the opener to attempt to describe both the strength and the distribution of her hand. There are four options available to the opener. She may raise the responder's suit, rebid her suit, bid a new suit, or bid NT. The level at which she bids will define her strength.

➢ With a minimum hand (12-15 points), the **opener** will make one of the following minimum bids:

- 2S - This raise generally promises four spades
- 2H - This suit rebid guarantees six hearts
- 2C or 2D - These new suit bids show a 2nd suit that is four cards or longer
- 1NT - This bid shows a balanced hand with 12-14 points

The **responder** may pass any of these bids; none are forcing bids. If the **responder** elects to pass he will also be showing a minimum hand and accepting the final bid as a suitable place to play the hand. If he continues the bidding by rebidding a 6-card spade suit or returning to the opener's suit at the 2-level (showing preference only – not real support), the **opener** must pass as both hands are minimum and game is not possible.

With more strength but not enough for game, the **responder** can bid 2NT or any old suit (one previously bid – his own or partner's) at the 3-level. With a game-going hand, the **responder** must bid a game in a previously bid suit or NT. If still unable to determine where to play, the **responder** may bid a new suit to force the **opener** to bid yet again to try to find the best final contract.

➤ With a stronger hand (16-18 points), the **opener** will make a stronger bid if possible:

- 3S – This jump bid guarantees 4-card support for the responder's suit
- 3H – This jump rebid of your suit guarantees six hearts
- 2C or 2D – These new suit bids show a 2nd suit which is at least four cards long
- 2NT – This jump bid shows a balanced hand with 18-19 points

Notice that when the **opener** next bids 2C or 2D the **responder** will not know whether the **opener's** values are minimum or invitational. This wide range rebid by the opener (12-18 points) will often make it more difficult for the **responder** to determine how high to bid.

Since the jump bids (3S, 3H, 2NT) all show extra strength and are highly invitational, the **responder** should pass only with a very minimum hand (6-7 points). With a stronger hand (8-14), the **responder** must bid a game and should have sufficient information to select an appropriate contract. With 15 or more, the **responder** must think about the possibility of slam.

> With a game-forcing hand (19-21 points) the **opener** will bid a game or make a bid which cannot be passed and, in fact, informs the **responder** that she must continue bidding until at least some game bid is reached:

- 4S - This raise to game in partner's suit promises four spades and enough points in the combined hands to bid a game (19+ by the opener and at least six by the responder = 25 total for the partnership)
- 4H - guarantees at least six strong hearts and game values
- 3C or 3D - This jump in a new suit is called a **JUMP SHIFT** and is one of the absolute game-forcing bids. Do not pass until game is reached and do not worry about getting passed if you do not immediately bid a game. Feel free to explore for the best game as both members of the partnership now know that the bidding will continue until the best contract is reached.
- 3NT - This bid may be made with a super 19 HCP. Tens and nines do not get any point value when counting our hand but these "fillers" in combination with honor cards make playing a notrump contract much easier. So our advice, looking at three or more tens or nines, is to bid it up!!

After a game bid by the **opener**, the **responder** will pass with less than 13 points and with 13 or more points (opening values) will consider bidding a slam. If the **opener** makes a jump shift, the **responder** must continue bidding until a suitable game is reached; do not violate this ageless important bidding concept.

IMPORTANT NOTES

- Two minimum hands should not bid game
- Two game-forcing hands must bid game; maybe slam
- Two invitational hands must bid game

Hands which cause problems in the bidding process are those where one player has minimum values and the other player has invitational values; some make game, many do not.

POINTS OF EMPHASIS	TAKE NOTE
The opener's JUMP SHIFT is game-forcing.	In a suit contract showing the strength of your hand is vital to determining how high to bid.
Notrump bids show slightly different numbers than those usually associated with minimum, invitational, and game-forcing hands.	M = Minimum I = Invitational GF = Game-forcing
1NT = 15-17	Opener + Responder = Level
1 of a suit, then a rebid of:	M + M = Partscore M + I = Maybe game M + GF = At least game
1NT = 12-14	I + M = Maybe game
2NT = 18-19	I + I = Game
2NT = 20-21	I + GF = At least game GF + M = Game GF + I = At least game GF + GF = Slam

BRIDGE ETIQUETTE

Try to maintain the same tempo as you play a card to each trick. Do not play your cards with undue emphasis such as snapping or flipping them on the table. Tempo is also important in bidding. Try to make all bids at the same pace so as not to convey information about your hand to your partner.

PLAY TIP: RUFFING LOSERS

In a suit contract count your losers before even playing to the first trick. A loser is a card in a side suit (any suit other than the designated trump suit) which is not protected by a high card. For example, if you are playing 4H and you have the following four holdings in the diamond suit there are some diamond losers.

Case	Diamond Holding		
1	A	7	6
2	A	K	5	3
3	K	Q	2
4	Q	J	5

1. No high cards for the 7 & 6 so they are slow losers
2. No high cards for the 5 & 3 so they are slow losers
3. The ace may capture the king and there is no high card to cover the 2 - so there is one quick and one slow loser
4. You are missing the ace and king so at least two tricks must be lost and maybe all three are losers

When this situation exists it is a good idea to see if the dummy is short in the suit where you have some losers. If so you can ruff the losing cards. We should always plan to ruff losers in the hand with the shorter trump holding. On the examples above if the dummy has only two cards in the diamond suit you could:

1. Play the ace then lose a trick in the suit and then ruff your remaining diamond
2. Play the ace and king and then ruff one or both your losing diamonds in the dummy
3. Play the king probably losing to the ace then win the queen and finally ruff your little diamond in the dummy
4. Lead from the dummy toward your Q J 5 probably losing the trick; go back to the dummy and lead toward your remaining honor and if this trick is lost you can still hope to ruff your remaining loser in the dummy

POINTS OF EMPHASIS	TAKE NOTE
To ruff **losers** in the dummy look for a suit where the dummy has fewer cards than the declarer. Often declarer must delay drawing trump to have enough trump cards remaining in the dummy to take care of losers. This most often happens after a 3-card raise.	Players often substitute the slang term "trump" for ruff. So if you hear a player say "I will trump my two losing clubs", he is simply saying that he will do what we all like to do - ruff his losers in the dummy.

DEFENSIVE TIP: THIRD HAND PLAY

When your side is defending and partner makes the opening lead you are "third hand" to play to the trick. The general rule is third hand plays high. A slight modification of the saying makes it really effective and that is "only as high as necessary to do the job". Therefore, with equal high cards it is important that you play the lowest of touching cards. If you have the QJ of a suit, play the J, the lower of equal cards. If you play the Q you deny having the J and partner will misplace that card in declarer's hand. Since the leader doesn't have it, the dummy doesn't have it, and you said you didn't have it, and it isn't on the floor, declarer has it!

Equally important is to look at the dummy and if there is a high card in the dummy you may be able to play an even lower card than the bottom of your touching cards. Let's look at some examples noting the dummy holdings and then plan third hand play when declarer plays low from the dummy.

Partner leads the 4 of spades and declarer calls for the 3 from the dummy. What card do you play from the holdings shown?

Dummy has ♠ 9 7 <u>3</u>

Case	You Hold	You Should Play
1	♠ K Q 8 2	The Q – the lower of touching cards
2	♠ A J 8	The A – highest with no touching cards
3	♠ J T 9 3	The 9 – the lowest of touching cards
4	♠ Q J 7	The J – the lower of two touching cards

Dummy has ♠ Q 7 <u>3</u>

Case	You Hold	You Should Play
1	♠ K J 8 2	The J – the K and J are equal with the Q in the dummy
2	♠ A 9 8	The A – highest with no touching or equal cards
3	♠ J T 9 3	The 9 – the lowest of touching cards
4	♠ A K J	The J – Only as "high as necessary" because the A,K, and J are all = with the Q in the dummy

---

| | SUMMARY | |

➤ Responder is the partner of the opening bidder

➤ A major suit game (4S or 4H) contract, with at least 8 cards between the partners, is the most desirable contract in bridge

➤ A major suit game usually requires 26 combined partnership TP

➤ The responder with support for opener's suit adds points for short suits, called dummy points (DP) to his HCP to determine his TP

  • Void = 5 points

  • Singleton = 3 points

  • Doubleton = 1 point

  • Responder's hand evaluation: HCP + DP = TP

➤ With support for the major, show it immediately if possible
  (See chart on page 47)

➤ Opener's rebids after responder shows 4-card or 5-card support for the major. M = the major suit opened

  • After 4M - Almost always pass

  • After 3M - Pass with < 20 points
              - Bid 4M with 20-21 points

  • After 3D - Bid 4M with 17+
              - Bid 3M with 12-16

  • After 3C - Bid 4M with 14+ or any hand with a singleton
              - Bid 3M on all others

  • After 2NT – Always bid 4M – think about slam with 19+

➤ Opener's rebid after a raise to 2M showing 3-card support and 8-10 points

  • With a poor minimum hand (12-14) pass

- With an invitational hand (15-16)
  - ✓ Bid 3M - responder bids 4M with an honor card in our suit
  - ✓ Bid a new suit - responder bids 4M with honors in the new suit, otherwise bids 3M
- Bid 4M with 17 or more points

➤ On hands which cannot immediately support the major, responder:
- Passes with < 5 points
- With 6+ points:
  - ✓ Bids 1S with 4+ spades after a 1H opener
  - ✓ Bids a new suit at the 2-level with 13+ points
  - ✓ Bids 1NT on all other hands in the 5-12 point range

➤ The only initial responses to a major suit opening that may be passed are immediate raises; all other bids are forcing for at least one round and the opener may not pass

➤ Opener's rebids after a 1S response to a 1H opening
- With a minimum hand, make a minimum bid:
  - ✓ Raise to 2S (usually showing 4-card support)
  - ✓ Rebid 2H (promises 6)
  - ✓ Bid 2C or 2D (second suit, promises 4+)
  - ✓ Bid 1NT (balanced, 12-14 points)
- With an invitational hand:
  - ✓ Jump to 3S (guarantees 4-card support)
  - ✓ Jump to 3H (guarantees 6 hearts)
  - ✓ Bid 2C or 2D (second suit, promises 4+)
  - ✓ Bid 2NT (balanced, 18-19 points)
- With a game-forcing hand:
  - ✓ Jump to 4S (promises 4-card support)
  - ✓ Jump to 4H (promises 6 strong hearts)
  - ✓ **Jump shift** to 3C or 3D (second suit promises 4+)
  - ✓ Bid 3NT (balanced super 19 HCP)

➤ A **jump shift** always promises a game-forcing hand so both partners must bid until game is reached

- Ruff losers in the dummy
- When third to play to a trick play only "as high as necessary"; lowest of touching cards with no honors in the dummy.

SHOWING SUPPORT FOR PARTNER'S OPENING MAJOR

ALL 4-CARD OR 5-CARD RAISES ARE SHOWN IMMEDIATELY (SOME BY CODED BIDS). ONLY ONE IMMEDIATE 3-CARD RAISE IS POSSIBLE. ALL OTHERS REQUIRE A TWO-STEP SEQUENCE.

	3 Card	4 Card	5 Card
Very weak	**0-4** **PASS** **5-7 Bid 1NT forcing,** **then bid 2M**	**0-3** **PASS**	**0-3** **PASS**
Weak 4-6		**3H** **3S**	**4H/4S with a** **singleton,** **3H/3S** **otherwise**
Minimum 8-10	**2H** **2S**		
Minimum 7-9		**3D**	**3D**
Invitational (Limit) 11-12	Two steps required to show support! **With 4+ spades, bid 1S* over 1H; otherwise bid 1NT†** **See Chapter 4**		
Invitational (Limit) 10-11		**3C**	**3C**
Game-forcing 13+	Two steps required to show support! **Bid any new suit*.** **See Chapter 5**		
Game-forcing 12+		**2NT**	**2NT**

* **After opener rebids over your 1S response, jump to 3H with 11-12 and 4H with 13+. See Chapter 5 for responder's rebids after a 2/1 new suit response.**

† **After an initial response of 1NT, you will jump to show 11-12 (See Chapter 4)**

EXERCISE 1 – RESPONDING TO A MAJOR SUIT OPENING: THE AUCTION STARTS WITH 1H, WHAT IS THE RESPONDER'S INITIAL BID?

Responder's hand	HCP	DP / LP	TP	Do you make an immediate raise?	What is your bid?
♠AQ7 ♥AKJ6 ♦95 ♣Q954					
♠K754 ♥Q97 ♦K52 ♣952					
♠4 ♥Q7542 ♦Q432 ♣J74					
♠Q7542 ♥K65 ♦A5 ♣K95					
♠K754 ♥A653 ♦K52 ♣92					
♠K75 ♥QT6 ♦A542 ♣Q93					
♠75 ♥KJT3 ♦K542 ♣J95					
♠KQ75 ♥KJ7 ♦KQ4 ♣952					
♠754 ♥8763 ♦75 ♣KQ95					
♠3 ♥AQ754 ♦K543 ♣QJ5					
♠K75 ♥KQ5 ♦KQ92 ♣975					
♠AKQ654 ♥K8 ♦Q64 ♣92					
♠54 ♥A865 ♦KJ432 ♣95					
♠J54 ♥T8 ♦AK543 ♣Q95					

A SHORT QUIZ – TRUE (T) OR FALSE (F)

_____ 1. A jump shift by the opener shows 19-21 points and is game-forcing

_____ 2. Responder's 2-level new suit shows 11+ points

_____ 3. 1NT by the responder may be passed

_____ 4. With four or more cards in support of the opener's major suit and 4 or more points, the responder can always make an immediate raise

ANSWERS TO EXERCISE 1
RESPONDING TO A MAJOR SUIT OPENING: THE AUCTION STARTS WITH 1H, WHAT IS THE RESPONDER'S INITIAL BID?

Responder's hand	HCP	DP / LP	TP	Do you make an immediate raise?	What is your bid?
♠AQ7 ♥AKJ6 ♦95 ♣Q954 Opening hand with 4 trump	16	1DP	17	YES	2NT
♠K754 ♥Q97 ♦K52 ♣952 8-10 with 3 trump	8	0	8	YES	2H
♠4 ♥Q7542 ♦Q432 ♣J74 4-6 HCP + 5 trump + a singleton = game gamble	5	3DP	8	YES	4H
♠Q7542 ♥K65 ♦A5 ♣K95 Opening hand with only 3 hearts so use "Texas two-step" by bidding 1S	12	1DP	13	NO	1S
♠K754 ♥A653 ♦K52 ♣92 11 support points = 3C	10	1DP	11	YES	3C
♠K75 ♥QT6 ♦A542 ♣Q93 Invitational hand with only 3 hearts, < 4 spades, so 1NT forcing is your bid	11	0	11	NO	1NT

Hand					
♠75 ♥KJT3 ♦K542 ♣J95 A nice constructive raise – 7-9 points and 4 hearts	8	1DP	9	YES	3D
♣KQ75 ♥KJ7 ♦KQ4 ♣952 Only 3 hearts but 4 spades so start with 1S	14	0	14	NO	1S
♠754 ♥8763 ♦75 ♣KQ95 4-6 points so bid a weak (preemptive) 3H	5	1DP	6	YES	3H
♠3 ♥AQ754 ♦K543 ♣QJ5 Another opening hand with superb support so use the 2NT immediate raise	12	3DP	15	YES	2NT
♠K75 ♥KQ5 ♦KQ92 ♣975 An opening hand but only 3-card support so again use the "Texas two-step" and start by bidding a 2/1 suit	13	0	13	NO	2D
♠AKQ654 ♥K8 ♦Q64 ♣92 No heart support but a great suit of your own so start with a 1S bid	14	2LP	16	NO	1S
♠54 ♥A865 ♦KJ432 ♣95 A limit raise so it's 3C	8	2DP	10	YES	3C
♠J54 ♥T8 ♦AK543 ♣Q95 < 3 hearts < 4 spades < 13 points so start with 1NT forcing	10	1LP	11	NO	1NT

ANSWERS TO SHORT QUIZ

1. **TRUE**

2. **FALSE** The 2/1 bid of a new suit shows 13+ points since it is game-forcing

3. **FALSE** 1NT is 100% forcing; the opener must bid at least one more time.

4. An emphatic **TRUE!**

EXERCISE 2
EXERCISE 2 – THE OPENER'S REBIDS:
YOU OPEN 1H AND THE RESPONDER BIDS AS SHOWN; WHAT IS YOUR REBID?

Your hand	HCP	LP	TP	Responder's initial bid	What do you rebid?
♠K75 ♥AQ975 ♦K5 ♣952	12	1	13	2NT	
♠A ♥QT542 ♦QJ32 ♣AK4	16	1	17	2H	
♠Q75 ♥AKT65 ♦A5 ♣K95	16	1	17	2H	
♠K75 ♥A6532 ♦KQ52 ♣9	12	1	13	3C	
♠75 ♥AQT62 ♦94 ♣AJ93	11	1	12	3C	
♠A7 ♥AJT32 ♦KJ4 ♣T95	13	1	14	3D	
♠K7 ♥AQ975 ♦KT52 ♣A5	16	1	17	3H	
♠KJ54 ♥AQ973 ♦K5 ♣92	13	2DP	15	1S	
♠K754 ♥AQ976 ♦AK5 ♣9	16	3DP	19	1S	

Your hand	HCP	LP	TP	Responder's initial bid	What do you rebid?
♠K75 ♥AQ975 ♦K5 ♣952 2NT is game-forcing; bid it!	12	1	13	2NT	4H
♠A ♥QT542 ♦QJ32 ♣AK4 Invites game - asks responder to bid game with an honor in hearts	16	1	17	2H	3H
♠Q75 ♥AKT65 ♦A5 ♣K95 Partner has 8-10 SP so just bid game	16	1	17	2H	4H
♠K75 ♥A6532 ♦KQ52 ♣9 With a singleton bid game!	12	1	13	3C	4H
♠75 ♥AQT62 ♦94 ♣AJ93 "Rule of 20" hand-no game	11	1	12	3C	3H
♠A7 ♥AJT32 ♦KJ4 ♣T95 Partner has 7-9 - no game	13	1	14	3D	3H
♠K7 ♥AQ975 ♦KT52 ♣A5 Partner has 4-6 – no game	16	1	17	3H	PASS
♠KJ54 ♥AQ973 ♦K5 ♣92 Minimum hand with 4-card support for spades; bid 2S	13	2DP	15	1S	2S
♠K754 ♥AQ976 ♦AK5 ♣9 Partner has 6+ points and 4+ spades so your 19 points = game with 8 card fit; so bid it!	16	3DP	19	1S	4S

HAND #1	
VULNERABLE:	Both
DECLARER:	South
CONTRACT:	4H
OPENING LEAD: 7♦	

North
♠ K 6
♥ A J 6 4
♦ K 8 3 2
♣ K 9 3

West
♠ A T 7 5
♥ T 5
♦ J 9 7
♣ Q T 7 4

East
♠ 9 8 3 2
♥ 9 2
♦ A Q 6 5
♣ 8 6 5

South
♠ Q J 4
♥ K Q 8 7 3
♦ T 4
♣ A J 2

THE BIDDING

SOUTH	WEST	NORTH	EAST
1H	P	2NT	P
4H	P	P	P

SOUTH
13HCP + 1LP = 14TP
SOUTH OPENS 1H

The LEAD: The SEVEN OF DIAMONDS. Lead small from an honor. The declarer plays a low diamond from the dummy and the East player (third hand) should play the queen of diamonds (only as high as necessary to win the trick). He next switches to the safe lead of a low heart.

THE PLAY: Declarer wins the heart return and draws the outstanding trumps being careful to count the opponents' trumps as they are played. There are now two more fast losers (the ace of spades and another diamond) and one slow loser (the little club). Declarer should drive out the ace of spades to establish two spade winners in her hand and then use one of those winners to discard the little club. Now she can play the king and ace of clubs and trump her remaining little club in the dummy.

HAND #2	
VULNERABLE:	N-S
DECLARER:	South
CONTRACT:	4S
OPENING LEAD: 5♥	

North
♠ K 8 6 3
♥ 9 4 3
♦ K 8
♣ K J 8 5

North
10 HCP + 1 DP = 11 TP
North bids 3C

West
♠ T 5 2
♥ K T 7 5
♦ Q 7 5
♣ A 7 4

East
♠ 7
♥ A Q J 8 2
♦ J T 9 2
♣ T 6 3

THE BIDDING			
SOUTH	WEST	NORTH	EAST
1S	P	3C*	P
4S	P	P	P
* Shows 4 spades & 10-12 pts			

South
♠ A Q J 9 4
♥ 6
♦ A 6 4 3
♣ Q 9 2

SOUTH
13HCP + 1LP = 14TP
SOUTH OPENS 1S

The BIDDING: South has a minimum hand but bids the game when holding a singleton after North's Bergen bid which showed four trump cards and a limit raise (10-12 points).

The LEAD: The FIVE OF HEARTS (low from an honor). East wins the opening lead with the ace of hearts (third hand high) and returns the suit which declarer ruffs.

The PLAY: South has one heart loser, two diamond losers and one club loser. One diamond loser can be ruffed in the dummy after three rounds of trump are drawn (necessary on this hand as trumps break 3-1) and the last losing diamond can be discarded on the long club (they break 3-3). It is important to play clubs to set up the winners in that suit before ruffing the diamond loser in the dummy.

CHAPTER 4
THE 1NT FORCING RESPONSE

In this chapter you will:

- Learn more about the forcing 1NT
- Learn how the opener rebids to show her strength and shape after the forcing 1NT response
- Learn how the responder shows the invitational raise with 3-card support for the opener's major suit
- Learn how the responder rebids to describe other hand patterns and hand strengths

MORE ABOUT THE 1 NT FORCING BID

When the initial response to a 1H or 1S opening bid is 1NT, the bid is 100% forcing. The opener must bid again even if her hand is minimum and balanced and she would really like to play 1NT. This is a critical element of the 2/1 bidding system. One notrump (1NT) is forcing because the responder may have as many as 12 points making game possible or she may have 3-card support for the opener's major and no other way to show the fit. One notrump (1NT) is not forcing if the opponent on your right enters the bidding.

OPENER'S REBIDS AFTER THE FORCING 1NT

Once again the options for the opener are limited. She can rebid her suit, bid a new suit, or raise NT. Rebidding her suit promises six or more cards in the suit and shows the values of minimum or invitational strength.

- Two of the major = 13-15 points
- Three of the major= 16-18 points

BY THE WAY
When the opener holds a powerful 7-card major and ~14 high card points, she may make one of those gambling bids and try game in her major after the forcing 1NT. We would bid 4S on this hand: ♠ A K J T 9 6 5   ♥ 9 7   ♦ A Q T   ♣ 9

With only a 5-card major the opener will rebid by naming the other major suit if she holds four or more cards in the suit and the values shown below:

- 2H after a 1S opening promises 4+ hearts and 13-18 points
- 3H after a 1S opening promises 4+ hearts and 19-21 points
- 2S after a 1H opening bid promises 4 spades and 16-21 points

Note the difference in the point values for these three rebids. Since 2H is a lower-ranking suit there is no way to differentiate between a minimum and an invitational hand. With a game-forcing hand (19-21) the opener shows her values by bidding 3H, a jump shift. The rebid of 2S is quite different since it is a higher-ranking suit which would require the responder to go to the 3-level to support the opener's first bid suit. When this condition occurs the bidder is making an important bridge bid called a **REVERSE**. The reverse requires at least the strength of an invitational hand (16+ points). A reverse must never be bid with a minimum strength hand but does also cover two ranges: Invitational (16-18) and game-forcing (16-21) hands.

POINT OF EMPHASIS	TAKE NOTE
The **reverse** is a powerful bridge concept. It occurs when you bid a second suit at the 2-level which is higher ranking than your first suit. It shows more cards in your first suit than your second suit (usually 5-4) and shows a minimum of 16 points.	A dilemma occurs when you hold a 6-card major and a second suit that is 4 cards long – which do you bid on your rebid? It is probably best to rebid your 4-card suit; you may get a second chance to show your 6-card major (bid 6-4-6).

When your second suit is a minor, it is treated like the heart suit when rebidding to show your strength.

- 2C or 2D = 13-18 points
- 3C or 3D (a jump shift) = 19-21 points

With only five cards in your major suit and no second suit with four or more cards to bid, the opener will be balanced and may have the values to raise the 1NT response. Two bids are possible:

- 2NT = 17-18 points
- 3NT = 19 points

The balanced hand with 12 to 14 points which was too weak to open 1NT has no good bid. You would love to pass but 1NT is 100% forcing so you must bid something. You cannot raise notrump as that would show at least 17 points. What to do? This is one of the uncomfortable times at the bridge table but it is solved by a simple maneuver similar to the one used when you had no convenient opening bid. **Bid your 3-card minor suit!**

- With two 3-card minors, bid **2C**
- With three diamonds and only two clubs, bid **2D**

EXAMPLES:

You have opened 1M and partner bid 1NT forcing. What is your rebid?

♠ A 8 7   ♥ K J 8 6 5   ♦ A 6 5   ♣ T 9
12 HCP + 1 LP = 13 TP   Minimum hand - rebid 2D

♠ A 8 7 5 3 2   ♥ K J 6   ♦ K 5   ♣ 8 2
11 HCP + 2 LP = 13 TP   Minimum - rebid 2S

♠ 7   ♥ K Q J 8 6 3   ♦ K Q 6   ♣ A 8 7
15 HCP + 2 LP = 17 TP   Invitational Hand - jump to 3H

♠ A K   ♥ K J 8 6 3   ♦ J 9 3   ♣ K Q 9
17 HCP + 1 LP = 18 TP   Balanced - rebid 2NT

♠ A Q 8 7 4 3   ♥ K 9 8 6   ♦ 4   ♣ A 9
13 HCP + 2 LP = 15 TP   6-4 hand - rebid 2H - your 2nd suit

♠ A Q 8 7   ♥ A Q J 8 6   ♦ 4   ♣ A 9
17 HCP + 1 LP = 18 TP   Open 1H - rebid by reversing to 2S

RESPONDER RAISES THE MAJOR SUIT
AFTER THE INITIAL 1NT RESPONSE

The responder holding 3-card support for the opener's major will raise to the 2-level with 8-10 points. With 13+ points, the responder starts with a new suit; 1S with four or more after a 1H opening bid or a 2/1 suit after either 1H or 1S opening (more on the continuations after a 2/1 bid in Chapter 5). On all other hands with 3-card support for the opener's major suit the responder starts with 1S (holding 4 or more after a 1H opening) or 1NT forcing.

If the forcing 1NT is bid, the responder's first obligation on her rebid is to show the 3-card support. When the responder's hand is very weak (5-7 points), she simply signs off in 2M on her rebid. Regardless of the rebid made by the opener, the responder holding the invitational raise (11-12 points) shows this support by jumping a level in the opener's original major suit. Sometimes this jump will be to the 3-level (after opener's rebid of a lower-ranking new suit) and sometimes it will be a jump to game (after the opener rebids the major, reverses, jump shifts, or bids 2NT).

After the responder shows the invitational raise, the opener will generally be able to bid game in the major. Occasionally the opener will have a really bad hand and will pass and even more rarely, the opener may have a hand good enough to try for slam. But this raise leads to a game in the major almost always – just what you hoped would happen when the hand was opened. Remember we strive to play major suit games – we love them! This is one of the Texas two-step raises. It took two bids to inform partner of the true nature of your hand. Your bidding has shown adequate support for the opener's major suit giving the partnership that magical 8-card trump fit. You have also shown your desire to play game in her opening bid major suit.

EXAMPLE

The bidding has been:
1S – 1NT
2C – ?

What is your rebid holding?

♠ Q 8 3   ♥ K 8 6   ♦ Q 9 7 6 4   ♣ A 9
11 HCP + 1 DP = 12 TP

You have a limit raise with 3-card support, jump to 3S to show this hand – do not bid your 5-card diamond suit.

OTHER REBIDS BY THE RESPONDER
AFTER THE INITIAL 1NT RESPONSE

When the responder's hand was not suitable for an immediate raise of the opening bid major, and was of insufficient strength for 2/1 bid, and could not bid 1S after a 1H opening bid, the only bid available was 1NT forcing. This initial 1NT bid will be made with a wide variety of distributional hand patterns in two strength categories:

- Minimum hands with 5-10 points
- Invitational hands with 11-12 points

After the **opener** rebids it is essential for the **responder** to define as much as possible both the distribution and strength of her hand. The **responder** may:

- Pass the **opener's** minimum rebids

If you pass a bid of 2C or 2D, you should have 5-card support and a minimum hand. Passing opener's rebid of 2H (if a new suit) would generally show 4-card support for hearts and a minimum hand. If the opener rebids her major then she is showing a 6-card suit and the responder may pass with any holding including a void in the opener's major. When this happens the bidding is over– we are done!

- Raise one of **opener's** suits

This bid would show 5-card support for a new minor, 4-card support for a new major, and 2-card support for opener's rebid of the original major. Any of these bids would promise the invitational strength hand.

The **opener** will now consider bidding game but may pass with a very minimum hand.

- Bid a game

This most often happens after opener's rebid of 2NT showing 17 or 18 points. Since only about eight points are needed for game, the **responder** should raise to 3NT with all hands except those with seven points or less.

Bidding a game in a suit would occur only if the **responder's** hand had exceptional support for a new suit bid of 2H by the opener. On this rare occasion, the **responder's** hand has really improved after the **opener** shows four or more hearts.

- Introduce a long new suit

A new suit bid should be at least six cards long. If this bid is made without jumping it shows the minimum hand and should be passed by the **opener.** If you jump into a new suit it shows the invitational hand and invites the **opener** to bid on to some game although the **opener** may pass.

- Bid 2NT

With a balanced hand of 10-12 points, the **responder** may rebid 2NT to invite game.

- Just return to **opener's** major suit

This bid by the **responder** is a "let's get out of Dodge move" meaning I have a bad hand with poor support for your major. When unable to make any of the bids outlined above, the **responder** may simply bid two of the **opener's** major suit as a desperate attempt to end the auction. Partner, please, please pass - we are high enough. The **responder** will almost always have only two cards in the major suit opened and a weak hand with less than 10 points.

Remember, if the **opener's** rebid is a **jump shift** or a **reverse,** you must bid again. Both of these bids are **forcing.** After a **jump shift** both partners must bid to at least game so just bid what you have trying to reach a suit contract with an 8-card fit or 3NT. After a **reverse** the bidding is forcing for one round so try to make a descriptive bid. Just **do not pass!**

EXAMPLES

The opening bid has been 1H, you bid 1NT forcing and the opener rebids as noted, what is your rebid?

♠ A 8 7   ♥ K 2   ♦ J 6 5 4 2   ♣ T 9 3
Opener rebid 2D - you should pass

♠ J 8 7   ♥ K 6   ♦ K 5 4 2   ♣ 9 8 4 2
Opener rebid 2D - you will show a preference for opener's first suit by bidding 2H

♠ A 7   ♥ Q 3   ♦ K Q 9 4 3 2   ♣ 9 8 7
Opener rebid 2C - invite game by jumping in your nice 6-card diamond suit - bid 3D

♠ A Q 7   ♥ K 6   ♦ J 9 3 2   ♣ Q 9 6 4
Opener rebid 2C - invite game in notrump by bidding 2NT

♠ J 4 3   ♥ 6   ♦ 9 6 4   ♣ A J 10 5 3 2
Opener rebid 2D - with this dog of a hand just bid 3C and hope partner passes as you have shown a weak hand

♠ J 8 7   ♥ A 6   ♦ Q 8 6 5 4   ♣ 9 7 4
Opener bid 3C - since this bid is forcing to game, you could show your 5-card diamond suit by bidding 3D or perhaps better is to show the good 2-card support for hearts

POINTS OF EMPHASIS	TAKE NOTE
After initially bidding 1NT, a new suit by the responder is not forcing but does show 6+ cards. A minimum bid is weak and a jump bid is invitational.	The 1NT forcing bid quite often leads to an auction where we are playing in a 5-2 major suit fit. We really like 8-card fits but in this case it's OK.

Often some of declarer's losers can be discarded (thrown away) on extra winners in the dummy. Sometimes there are immediate winners available but often the extra winners will need to be established. You are playing a contract of 4S and the holdings listed are in the club suit: Here are two holdings with immediate club winners:

	Hand #1	Hand #2
Dummy's Hands	A K 7	A K Q 4
Declarer's Hands	Q 2	8 7

On the first hand, you will lead the queen first (called the "**high card from the short side**"). Then you will lead your 2 over to the dummy where you can **discard** (pitch) a loser on dummy's remaining high card.

On the second hand, just lead one of your small cards to the dummy and there is an extra winner to use for a **discard**.

The next set of hands shows some club suits needing to be established before you can pitch losers.

	Hand #1	Hand #2	Hand #3
Dummy's Hands	K Q J	Q J T 6	A K 7 6 2
Declarer's Hands	9 8	5 4	4 3

On the first hand you will lead your small card to the dummy and play high cards until an opponent wins the ace. If the ace is played on the first or second lead, your third card in the suit will provide a discard for a loser.

On the second hand, you can lead top clubs until the ace and king are forced out and then the 10 becomes a winner for a discard.

On the third hand a slightly different concept is present. Clearly you have two winners and only two cards in the suit in your hand so no more winners are easily seen as available. On this hand, if the dummy has lots of entries you could play the ace and the king then give up a trick. If the six outstanding cards are distributed 3-3 in the opponent's hands, you will have established two extra winners in the dummy on which you can discard losers. Playing this way you will need an **ENTRY** in the trump suit or some third suit to enjoy your established winners for discards.

Another way to handle this situation if you have no outside entry is to just give up a trick early. When you lead your first small card just **DUCK** (play small) and allow the opponent to win the first trick rather than the third trick. Now you have a second small club to lead to the dummy and enjoy all the established winners.

Sometimes to create that all-important **entry** to the dummy or your hand, you may need to **overtake** an honor card with a higher honor. Holding A Q T in the dummy and K J 9 in your hand, you can get to the dummy three times if you play the nine to the 10, then the J to the Q and finally the K to the A. Or to get to your hand you have two entries: The 10 to the J and then the Q to the K. Pretty slick!

DEFENSIVE TIP: OTHER OPENING LEADS

The goal of the defenders is to always strive to defeat the contract. Since the opening lead is often a game-changer related to the success or failure of the contract, give careful consideration to which suit and which card to lead. Listen to the bidding for possible weaknesses such as an unbid suit by the opponents. Once the suit is selected it is important that you select the correct card.

If you hold four or more cards in the suit you plan to lead and the suit is not headed by a sequence, you have what is called a **broken suit**. When leading from a broken suit we generally lead 4th best, that is, the 4th card down from the top. **In a suit contract do not lead away from an ace** - find some other lead.

In these examples lead the underlined card:

K J 7 <u>3</u>   Q T 6 <u>4</u>   J 8 4 <u>2</u>   Q 7 4 <u>2</u>   K T 9 <u>5</u>

If you hold only three cards in a suit headed by an honor, lead your smallest card. Generally the lead of a low card tells your partner you hold an honor and a higher card says you don't.

K 8 <u>4</u>   Q 9 <u>8</u>   J 9 <u>5</u>

When leading a suit where you hold a doubleton lead the top card.

$\underline{K}$ 9 $\underline{9}$ 8 $\underline{Q}$ J

If you hold three inconsequential cards in a side suit such as 7 5 2, lead the 5, next time play the 7, and finally the 2. This lead is called MUD (acronym for $\underline{M}$iddle, $\underline{U}$p, $\underline{D}$own) and signifies you have three cards (not two) and probably no better lead!

7 $\underline{5}$ 2   9 $\underline{7}$ 3   8 $\underline{6}$ 3

➤ Responder's initial bid of 1NT is 100% forcing after a major suit opening bid

➤ Opener's rebids after the forcing 1NT bid
  - 2 of the major = 6 cards and 13-15 points
  - 3 of the major = 6 cards and 16-18 points
  - Game in the major = 7 cards and ~ 14 points
  - 2NT = balanced with 17 or 18 points
  - 3NT = balanced with 19 points
  - 2H after a 1S opening = 4+ hearts and 12-18 points
  - 2S after a 1H opening = 4 spades and 16-21 points
  - 3C, 3D = 4+ cards in the suit and 19-21 points
  - 3H after a 1S opening = 4+ hearts and 19-21 points
  - 2C, 2D = 3+ cards in the suit and 12-14 points if balanced and 4+ cards and 12-18 points if unbalanced

➤ Responder continues the bidding by defining his strength and distribution
  - Jump raise the major with 3-card support and 11-12 points
  - Pass the opener's rebid if a fit is found and your hand is minimum (5-10)
  - With 11- 12 points, raise a new suit with support or bid 2NT- if balanced
  - Bid a new suit with 6 cards. Jump in the suit (if possible) with 11 or 12 points
  - When no good bid is available, return to partner's major suit with 2 cards and a bad hand

➤ Set up a long suit in the dummy to discards losers

➤ Lead 4th best from broken suits and MUD from 3 little cards in the suit you are leading

---

EXERCISE 1 – OPENER'S REBID AFTER A 1NT FORCING RESPONSE TO A MAJOR SUIT OPENING: WHAT IS THE OPENER'S REBID AFTER 1S – 1NT?

Opener's hand	HCP	LP	TP	What is your rebid?	Is it forcing?
♠AQ7532 ♥AKJ6 ♦9 ♣Q9					
♠KQ754 ♥AQ97 ♦K5 ♣95					
♠AJT94 ♥Q75 ♦Q42 ♣K7					
♠AQ742 ♥K65 ♦A5 ♣KQ5					
♠KQJ75 ♥A6 ♦AK52 ♣K2					
♠KJ532 ♥QT6 ♦A5 ♣Q93					
♠KQT75 ♥KJT53 ♦K5 ♣J					
♠KQ754 ♥K ♦K4 ♣QT952					
♠AKJ754 ♥87 ♦A5 ♣KT9					
♠JT963 ♥AQ4 ♦K543 ♣Q					
♠KQT75 ♥KQ5 ♦KQ9 ♣A7					
♠AKQ64 ♥AK82 ♦K6 ♣92					
♠KQ9854 ♥A8 ♦K432 ♣9					
♠KJ543 ♥T ♦AK543 ♣Q9					

A SHORT QUIZ

How many points does the opener show with these rebids after the responder bids 1NT forcing?

1. A jump in your suit?

2. A raise to 2NT?

3. A jump in a new suit?

4. A reverse of 2S after a 1H opening?

5. A bid of 2C or 2D?

ANSWERS TO EXERCISE 1
OPENER'S REBID AFTER A 1NT FORCING RESPONSE TO A MAJOR SUIT OPENING: WHAT IS THE OPENER'S REBID AFTER 1S – 1NT?

Opener's hand	HCP	LP	TP	What is your rebid?	Is it forcing?
♠AQ7532 ♥AKJ6 ♦9 ♣Q9 With 6-4, bid your 4-card suit on your rebid	16	2	18	2H	NO
♠KQ754 ♥AQ97 ♦K5 ♣95 Always show the heart suit	14	1	15	2H	NO
♠AJT94 ♥Q75 ♦Q42 ♣K7 Would like to pass but must bid so it's the 3-card diamond suit	12	1	13	2D	NO
♠AQ742 ♥K65 ♦A5 ♣KJ5 Raise NT with 17 or 18	17	1	18	2NT	NO
♠KQJ75 ♥A6 ♦AK52 ♣K2 Bid 3D - a game-forcing jump shift	20	1	21	3D	YES-GF

♠KJ532 ♥QT6 ♦A5 ♣Q93 Another ugly hand - forced to rebid your 3-card club suit	12	1	13	2C	NO
♠KQT75 ♥KJT53 ♦K5 ♣J It's nice to have a 2nd 5-card suit to bid	13	2	15	2H	NO
♠KQ754 ♥K ♦K4 ♣QT952 I like this club rebid better than the last one - still minimum, so just 2C	13	2	15	2C	NO
♠AKJ754 ♥87 ♦A5 ♣KT9 A nice suit and an invitational strength hand - jump in your suit	15	2	17	3S	NO
♠JT963 ♥AQ4 ♦K543 ♣Q A bad suit and a bad hand - but a 2nd suit to bid	12	1	13	2D	NO
♠KQT75 ♥KQ5 ♦KQ9 ♣A7 19 HCP is worth a raise of NT to game	19	1	20	3NT	NO
♠AKQ64 ♥AK82 ♦K6 ♣92 Another game-forcing jump shift	19	1	20	3H	YES-GF
♠KQ9854 ♥A8 ♦K432 ♣9 A fair 6-card suit and a minimum hand so it is 2S	12	2	14	2S	NO
♠KJ543 ♥T ♦AK543 ♣Q9 A pretty good hand and a fine 2nd suit but too weak to jump shift, so just 2D for now	13	2	15	2D	NO

ANSWERS TO A SHORT QUIZ

1. 16-18 TP

2. 17-18 HCP

3. 19-21 TP

4. 16-21 TP

5. 12-18 HCP

EXERCISE 2 – RESPONDER'S REBID AFTER AN AUCTION THAT STARTS 1S – 1NT AND THE OPENER REBIDS AS SHOWN: WHAT IS THE RESPONDER'S NEXT BID?

Responder's hand	HCP	LP	TP	Opener's rebid	What is your rebid?
♠K75 ♥K975 ♦K5 ♣Q752				2C	
♠K75 ♥K975 ♦K5 ♣Q532				3D	
♠K75 ♥K975 ♦K5 ♣Q532				2S	
♠K75 ♥K975 ♦K5 ♣Q532				2H	
♠75 ♥AT6 ♦9432 ♣KJ93				2D	
♠A5 ♥JT32 ♦KJ4 ♣QT95				2D	
♠A7 ♥JT32 ♦KJ4 ♣QT95				2S	
♠65 ♥AQ9732 ♦J5 ♣932				2D	
♠K7 ♥976 ♦AK765 ♣932				2D	

ANSWERS TO EXERCISE 2
RESPONDER'S REBID AFTER AN AUCTION THAT
STARTS 1S – 1NT AND THE OPENER REBIDS AS SHOWN:
WHAT IS THE RESPONDER'S NEXT BID?

Responder's hand	HCP	DP / LP	TP	Opener's rebid	What is your rebid?
♠K75 ♥K975 ♦K5 ♣Q752 Jump in spades to show the invitational 3-card raise	11	1DP	12	2C	3S
♠K75 ♥K975 ♦K5 ♣Q532 Jump in spades with the 3-card invitational raise	11	1DP	12	3D	4S
♠K75 ♥K975 ♦K5 ♣Q532 Jump in spades to show a limit raise with 3 spades	11	1DP	12	2S	4S
♠K75 ♥K975 ♦K5 ♣Q532 With a 4-4 fit in hearts, raise hearts to invite to game in hearts rather than play in the 5-3 fit in spades	11	1DP	12	2H	3H
♠75 ♥AT6 ♦9432 ♣KJ93 We don't like it but a return to the opener's 1st bid suit shows a bad hand - often with only 2-card support	8	0	8	2D	2S
♠A5 ♥JT32 ♦KJ4 ♣QT95 A better hand with only 2 spades invites in NT	11	0	11	2D	2NT
♠A7 ♥JT32 ♦KJ4 ♣QT95 Since the opener has shown 6 spades, a non-jump raise shows 2 good spades and an invitational hand	11	0	11	2S	3S

♠65 ♥AQ9732 ♦J5 ♣932 A bad hand with a long suit of your own - bid it now - partner should pass	7	2LP	9	2D	2H
♠K7 ♥976 ♦AK765 ♣932 An invitational hand with 5-card support for partner's suit is worth a raise	10	1LP	11	2D	3D

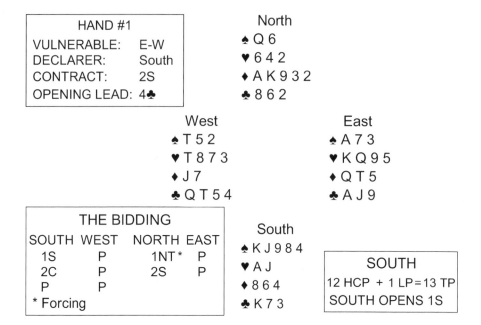

HAND #1

VULNERABLE:	E-W
DECLARER:	South
CONTRACT:	2S
OPENING LEAD: 4♣	

North
♠ Q 6
♥ 6 4 2
♦ A K 9 3 2
♣ 8 6 2

West
♠ T 5 2
♥ T 8 7 3
♦ J 7
♣ Q T 5 4

East
♠ A 7 3
♥ K Q 9 5
♦ Q T 5
♣ A J 9

THE BIDDING

SOUTH	WEST	NORTH	EAST
1S	P	1NT*	P
2C	P	2S	P
P	P		

* Forcing

South
♠ K J 9 8 4
♥ A J
♦ 8 6 4
♣ K 7 3

SOUTH
12 HCP + 1 LP = 13 TP
SOUTH OPENS 1S

The BIDDING: When North bids 1NT South must bid again even with a very minimum hand so bids his 3-card club suit. North might be tempted to bid his nice diamond suit but instead should bid 2S returning to partner's opening bid suit with a doubleton spade. This is a very common occurrence when playing the 2/1 game forcing system.

The LEAD: The FOUR OF CLUBS. Leading from a broken suit headed by an honor card is a common and acceptable lead. When leading from a broken suit, you lead a low card - fourth best or small from three.

The PLAY: After the lead of the small club won by East and a club return, your king of clubs becomes a winner but you still have two club losers, a trump loser, a diamond loser and a heart loser. That's only five losers so your contract is safe. It's time to try for an extra trick. Drive out the ace of trump after which the opponents will cash the club winner and may then just return the remaining club which you will ruff. Now since you have a diamond loser don't cash the ace and king rather play a small diamond and just duck it (play small from dummy) allowing the opponents to win a cheap trick. Now win the ace of hearts when they lead back a heart and play a diamond to your ace and king. This move will pick up all the remaining diamonds held by the opponents and your little diamond will provide a place to discard your losing heart. Wasn't that fun and the overtrick is a real bonus. Note that the defenders could have prevented you from making an overtrick by returning a heart after cashing the club winner.

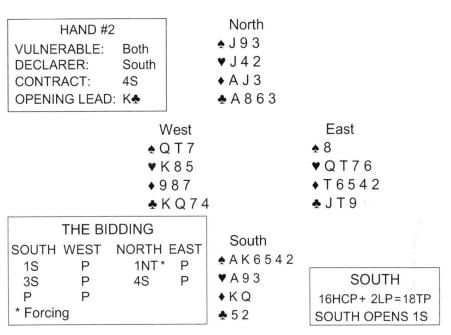

HAND #2	
VULNERABLE:	Both
DECLARER:	South
CONTRACT:	4S
OPENING LEAD: K♣	

North
♠ J 9 3
♥ J 4 2
♦ A J 3
♣ A 8 6 3

West
♠ Q T 7
♥ K 8 5
♦ 9 8 7
♣ K Q 7 4

East
♠ 8
♥ Q T 7 6
♦ T 6 5 4 2
♣ J T 9

THE BIDDING

SOUTH	WEST	NORTH	EAST
1S	P	1NT*	P
3S	P	4S	P
P	P		
* Forcing			

South
♠ A K 6 5 4 2
♥ A 9 3
♦ K Q
♣ 5 2

SOUTH
16HCP+ 2LP = 18TP
SOUTH OPENS 1S

The LEAD: The KING OF CLUBS (the top of two touching honor cards against a suit contract)

The PLAY: You can see a club loser, two heart losers, and a possible loser in spades. You elect to win the first club trick with the ace and play the ace and king of spades hoping the queen falls. When it does not you have a spade loser. You see an extra winner in the diamond suit but are out of entries to the dummy. This is the time to play the king of diamonds then the queen and overtake it with the ace. Now cash the jack of diamonds and pitch (discard) one of your losers in the heart suit or your losing club. Now the hand is made and you played the hand like a pro.

CHAPTER 5
THE TWO-OVER-ONE (2/1)
GAME-FORCING BIDS

In this chapter you will:

- Learn more about the game-forcing 2/1 bids
- Learn how the opener rebids to show her strength and shape including a bit about the infrequent jump rebids
- Learn how the responder continues the bidding after initially bidding a new suit at the 2-level
- Learn about the "Principle of Fast Arrival"

MORE ABOUT 2/1

When a major suit is opened, the responder has four choices: Pass, raise the major, bid 1NT forcing, or bid a new suit. The new suit may be 1S after an opening 1H bid or a new suit at the 2-level (2/1). A 2/1 bid shows an opening hand and is absolutely game-forcing provided the responder is not a passed hand and that your right hand opponent (RHO) does not bid. If you have passed you cannot have an opening hand so the 2-level bid shows about 10-12 points and the opener is not obligated to bid again. Bidding when the opponents compete will be discussed in a later chapter. Since solid values are needed when the responder wants to insist on game, the 2/1 bidder must have a sound opening hand. I like to define this opening hand as:

13 HCP

This restrictive definition may be relaxed when the **responder** has three cards in the **opener's** major suit and intends to raise the major on her rebid. In this case, 12 HCP are adequate for a 2/1 bid.

A 2/1 bid sends out exhilarating vibes between the partners. Why? When the responder bids a 2/1 suit both partners know that the bidding will continue until at least game is reached. This means that there is much less stress involved during the auction. A partscore is no longer an option because you have committed the partnership to a game. You can now concentrate on bidding naturally while looking for the best strain (what suit or NT). Once agreement is reached as to strain the only remaining question is: Do we stop in game or do we have enough strength for a slam?

THE 2/1 BIDS FOLLOWING A MAJOR SUIT OPENING

A bid of 2C over a major suit opening shows four or more clubs and 13 or more points. A bid of 2D over a major suit opening shows four or more diamonds and 13 or more points. With 13+ points and two 4-card minors, bid the lower-ranking suit (2C) to allow room to explore all possible strains at a low level. A bid of 2H over a 1S opening promises five or more hearts and 13 or more points. Remember, partner will never pass this 2/1 bid.

POINTS OF EMPHASIS	TAKE NOTE
Minors over a major suit opening may be only 4 cards long. **2H over 1S always promises 5 or more hearts**.	Partner has opened 1S. You have a dilemma. Your hand is: ♠Q 6 5 ♥A J 8 6 ♦K 9 7 ♣A 7 6 • No immediate spade raise! • < 4 in a minor & < 5 hearts • What to bid? An extremely rare tiny lie – bid 2C!!

In general we bid our longest suit first when we hold two suits of unequal length. In general we also like to try to find a major suit fit as soon as possible. These two ideas may clash at times when our two suits are spades and a minor after partner opens 1H. Which suit should you bid first? Consider the two hands below:

♠ A 7 4 3　　♥ K 3　　♦ K 7 6 3 2　　♣ 9 6

Your hand is not strong enough to bid 2D (a 2/1 game-force) so you should bid the 4-card spade suit to try to find a fit in spades – bid 1S. This bid is very natural and acceptable and certainly meets our objective of looking for the major suit fit.

♠ A 7 4 3　　♥ K 3　　♦ A K 6 3 2　　♣ 9 6

You have an opening hand so absolutely should bid your longer suit first – bid 2D. This bid does not preclude finding a fit in spades as you will have a chance to show your 4 spades later. By bidding 2D you have also established a game-forcing auction which is a really good thing!

MORE EXAMPLES OF 2/1 BIDS
The opening bid has been 1S.

♠ K 9 7　　♥ A J 9 7　　♦ K Q 9 6　　♣ 8 7

You have adequate support for spades (3) and 14 SP so start with a 2/1 2D bid showing your 4-card diamond suit planning to support spades next

♠ 9 7　　♥ K Q J 9 7　　♦ K Q 9 6　　♣ A 7

You have a nice 5-card heart suit and 15 HCP - start with 2H

♠ A 9　　♥ A J 9 7　　♦ K　　♣ K Q T 8 6 3

You have plenty of points (17) for a 2/1 bid and a great club suit - bid 2C

♠ K 9 7　　♥ A 9 7　　♦ K Q 9 6 2　　♣ 7 3

You have sufficient support for spades and 13 SP – start with a 2/1 bid of 2D to show your nice 5-card suit. Support spades on your rebid

On the following hands the opening bid has been 1H.

♠ A Q 7 4　　♥ A J 9　　♦ K Q 9 6 3　　♣ 8

Start by bidding your longest suit (2D) when you have an opening hand (16 HCP)

♠ Q J 8 5 2　　♥ J 9 7　　♦ K Q 9　　♣ A 7

Start with 1S (your longest suit) with this opening hand (13 HCP)

♠ 9 8   ♥ A J 7   ♦ K J 9 4   ♣ K 7 3 2

You have sufficient heart support (3 cards) and 12 HCP so start with a 2/1 bid - with two 4-card minor suits start with your lower ranking suit - bid 2C

OPENER'S REBIDS AFTER A 2/1 RESPONSE

Responder's 2/1 bid has created a game force so the opener rebids to show pattern not strength. This means that most of opener's rebids are natural and unlimited. **Jumps to show extra strength are not needed and not made!**

Once again the **opener** only has four choices. She can:

* Rebid her suit
* Raise the responder's suit
* Bid a new suit
* Bid NT

A rebid of the major suit promises six and is unlimited.

A raise of the **responder's** minor suit will usually show four cards in support but may be made with three to an honor when other bids are not reasonable. Any raise of the minor is unlimited in strength. Raising the minor suit, while descriptive of the **opener's** hand, does not mean the partnership will play game in the minor (5C or 5D). When there is no major suit fit and the only fit is in a minor, the partnership should always try to play in notrump. It is extremely rare for a hand to make a minor suit game (11 tricks) and not be able to make 3NT (9 tricks).

A raise of **responder's** 2/1 heart suit may be made with any 3-card support because the **responder** has promised five. Since a fit is known, the **opener** should now attempt to show his strength by using the **"principle of fast arrival"** when raising the **responder's** suit. A jump to game when raising the **responder's** heart suit shows a hand with 12-14 points and no interest in slam. With 15 or more points, the **opener** raises the suit to the 3-level to suggest slam is possible if the **responder** has some extra values.

Any second suit of at least four cards should be bid if the partnership has not already found a fit. This new suit may be bid with a very minimum hand. However, the strength of the opener's hand is still unlimited and could be quite strong.

Two notrump should be rebid an all balanced hands which are not suitable for a raise of the responder's suit. This rebid shows a hand that has either minimum points (12-14) or maximum points (18-19). With the very strong hand, the opener will try for slam later in the auction.

EXAMPLES
The bidding has been:
1H – 2C
What is your rebid?

♠ A J 8   ♥ K Q 9 7 2   ♦ K J 2   ♣ T 9 3
You have a balanced 14 HCP so rebid 2NT

♠ A 3   ♥ K Q 9 6 3   ♦ 5 4   ♣ A J 4 2
With great support for clubs, raise to 3C

♠ A 8 7 5   ♥ A Q 9 7 3   ♦ K 4   ♣ 9 8
Bid your second suit - 2S; this bid is technically a reverse but in a 2/1 auction it doesn't require 16+ HCP

♠ A Q 7   ♥ A K J 6 4   ♦ K 9 3   ♣ Q 4
Bid 2NT with your balanced 19 point hand; plan to bid 4NT later in the auction to show the strength of this hand

♠ A 3   ♥ A J 9 8 6 2   ♦ K J 4   ♣ A 2
Bid only 2H to show your 6-card suit; there is no need to jump at this point even though you have a very nice hand

---

Defining the "Principle of Fast Arrival"
When a major suit fit is found and you are in a game-forcing auction, a jump to game is weaker than bidding three of the major. Both partners can apply this principle to their rebids. Using this idea when the **responder** bids 2H over a 1S opening, opener can jump to 4H with a 12-14 point opener and bid 3H with 15 or more points:

1S – 2H		1S – 2H
4H	is weaker than	3H

TWO IMPORTANT JUMP REBIDS

Finally, a brief look at two types of hands where the opener may want to make a jump rebid. Remember, jumps are not used to show strength since the auction is already game-forcing.

With a hand with a solid 6-card major suit, it is acceptable to jump in your suit to inform the responder that your suit is trump and there is no need to look further for the place to play. Your jump does not show extra points just a great suit.

EXAMPLES:

HAND #1	HAND #2
♠ A K Q J T 8	♠ 9
♥ K 8	♥ A K Q J T 9 8
♦ J 8 7	♦ K J
♣ 9 8	♣ A 7 6
Open 1S	Open 1H
Rebid 3S after a 2/1 bid by the responder	Rebid 3H after a 2/1 bid by the responder

The second hand where it is acceptable to jump on your rebid is when you have four cards or more in support of the responder's suit and a singleton or void in some unbid suit. A jump in the new suit shows your fit and shortness in the new suit. Remember, there is no need to jump to show strength but rather use your jump to show shape or pattern.

EXAMPLES:

HAND #1	HAND #2
♠ A Q J 8 7	♠ A 9 7
♥ 8	♥ K Q J 9 8
♦ K J 8 6	♦ 9
♣ K 4 2	♣ A K 6 4
Open 1S	Open 1H
Rebid 3H if the responder bids 2D	Rebid 3D after responder bids 2C

These jump rebids (called splinter bids) are critical elements in advanced 2/1 bidding. They are difficult concepts which you may want to add to your bidding later. You can do fine for now without them.

RESPONDER RAISES THE MAJOR SUIT
AFTER THE INITIAL 2/1 RESPONSE

Showing three cards in support of the opener's major suit is the responder's first priority on her rebid. Again the **"principle of fast arrival"** comes into play. With minimum values (12-14 points) for your 2/1 bid, jump to game in the major suit on your rebid. With 15 or more HCP, make a minimum raise of the major suit. This minimum raise will encourage the opener to try for slam if she also holds some extra values. Slam bidding will be discussed in Chapter 9.

EXAMPLES:

Partner has opened 1H, you bid 2D (2/1) and your partner rebid 2H.

1H - 2D
2H - ?

What is your rebid?

♠ A Q 7 4   ♥ A J 9   ♦ K Q 9 6 3   ♣ 85

Your initial bid with this hand was 2D which denied 4-card support for hearts and showed your game-forcing values and your suit (diamonds). Now is the time to tell your partner that you have 3-card support for her suit and a really nice hand. Using the **"principle of fast arrival"** as your guide this hand is much too good (17 SP) for a jump to 4H. Bid 3H which is a much more encouraging bid and shows a hand with 15+ points.

♠ 9 8   ♥ A J 7   ♦ K J 9 4 3   ♣ K 7 2

With 3 cards in support of hearts your hand is just barely sufficient (12 HCP) for your 2/1 initial response of 2D. Tell your partner about your support and that you have a very minimum hand for your previous bidding by jumping to 4H. This is the final Texas two-step raise of the opener's major suit. Much like after the 1NT forcing bid it takes two bids after 2/1 to inform partner of the true nature of your hand - the adequate support giving the partnership that magical 8-card trump fit and your desire to play game in her opening bid major suit.

POINT OF EMPHASIS	TAKE NOTE
Raising partner's major on your rebid should always show 3-card support even when partner rebids the major promising a 6-card suit.	Partner's rebid of the major = 6 so if you have 2 cards in the suit there is an 8-card fit – that's great. But be patient and wait to show the support.

OTHER REBIDS BY THE RESPONDER AFTER THE INITIAL 2/1 RESPONSE

If you do not have the 3-card raise just continue making natural bids to describe your hand pattern. There is no need to jump to try to show extra values. Here are some of the rebids the **responder** may make and what they will show about pattern.

- Rebid your suit to show six
- Raise the **opener's** second suit

This bid would always promise four cards in support because the **opener** only needs four cards in the suit to bid a second suit.

- Bid a new suit of your own

This bid would promise four cards in the second suit. Quite often you will have more cards in your first suit since bidding two suits usually shows an unbalanced hand.

- Bid 2NT

This bid shows a balanced hand with 13-14 HCP or 18-19 HCP. With the big hand you will bid aggressively later in the auction to try to reach slam.

Above all else, do not pass until at least game is reached. Keep bidding what you have until a fit is found or the partnership agrees to play notrump. Strive to bid game in a major or notrump. Only bid a minor suit game as a remote final option. Slams in any strain are acceptable. Bidding options to get to slams will be shown later.

BRIDGE ETIQUETTE

Being a supportive, patient, and calm partner, even when faced with bidding "disasters" or major playing "blunders", makes the game more pleasant for all - especially when your partner made the mistake! Be a good sport - gracious in both victory and defeat. Every bridge player has made mistakes!

PLAY TIP: THE FINESSE

You can attempt to turn a potential loser into a winner by **finessing**. You finesse by playing toward a card which you hope will win the trick even when the opponents have a higher card which could capture your lower card. A successful finesse depends on a favorable position of the outstanding higher card. Your finesse will be successful about 50% of the time.

THIS IS AN EXAMPLE OF A BASIC FINESSE

Dummy's hand: A
                 Q

Your hand: 7
                 4

Dummy has A Q in a suit where you have two little cards. The ace is clearly a winner but the queen is in jeopardy because one of the opponents holds the king. If the opponent on your left (LHO) has the king it is "in the pocket". When you lead a small card from your hand, plan to play the queen if the opponent plays a small card. Do not play the ace unless the LHO puts up the king. The queen becomes a winner! However, if the king is in your right hand opponent's (RHO) hand the queen is captured by the king. This maneuver is a 50/50 proposition which is much better than 0% which you will almost always get if you simply play the ace and then the queen. So finesses are classy techniques for gaining extra tricks.

HERE ARE SOME OTHER FINESSING EXAMPLES

Hands	#1	#2	#3	#4	#5	#6
Dummy's Hand	K	Q	Q	Q	K	A
	J	4	J	J	9	J
	7	2	T	7	7	T
	6					9
Your Hand	A	A	A	A	8	8
	4	9	7	6	4	6
	2	6	4	4		4
				3		

Hand #1

First lead the ace from your hand. If both defenders follow suit and the queen doesn't drop, lead small from your hand planning to put in the jack. If your LHO plays the queen, of course you will play the king to win the trick and your jack is now good. If your finesse wins you will take three tricks in the suit and four tricks if the six outstanding cards are evenly split (3-3) between the defenders. How cool is that?

Hand #2

Lead the ace and then low from your hand toward the queen, hoping LHO has the king. If LHO plays small, put up the queen which wins the trick if the King is with your LHO but loses if it is with your RHO … a 50/50 proposition.

Hand #3

This hand is a bit different from Hand #2. Here you have a nice sequence with not only the queen but also the jack and 10 so you will try to trap the king by leading the queen rather than leading toward the queen. As in all finesse situations it is important that the lead starts from the correct hand. With these cards, begin in the dummy's hand by leading the queen. Play small from your hand unless RHO covers the queen with the king. If RHO plays the king take the trick with the ace in your hand. Now your jack and 10 are both winners and you have made all three tricks good with your successful finesse of the king.

Hand #4

Compare this hand with the previous one. Having only two cards in sequence, this time it is correct to lead from your hand toward the queen hoping LHO has the king. If so, you can win three tricks. If, instead, you lead the queen from the dummy and RHO covers with the king, you will take only two tricks with high cards - try it! Likewise if you lead the queen and it loses to the king in LHO's hand, you will still get only two high card tricks. To get three tricks if you lead the queen you will need the suit to divide 3-3 in which case your last little card will win a trick.

Hand #5

With this unsightly holding there is little hope for a winning trick. Don't give up yet as a successful finesse could net one trick. Lead small from your hand toward the king in the dummy hoping your LHO has the ace. If so, you'll get a trick with the king. If not, there's always next time.

Hand #6

On this hand you are missing both the king and queen. You will need to lead twice from your hand and hope at least one of the high cards is in your LHO's hand. Small to the nine - maybe it loses to the king - go back to your hand and lead again and put in the 10 if your LHO plays low. Of course, if LHO at any time plays the king or queen, win the trick with the ace and then simply drive out the other high honor scoring three tricks in the suit.

As you can see finesses are a bit complex; sometimes we lead toward the honor and other times we lead an honor card to try to trap a higher card. It depends on whether we have a nice sequence in the suit or not - with the sequence, lead one of the honor cards. In both situations success depends on the location of the outstanding higher honor card. Finesses are fun when they work and that's about half the time. I know you will say like lots of experienced players "my finesses never work" but I won't believe you because they really do work part of the time. Be a winner and take that 50% chance - you'll love the success!

DEFENSIVE TIP: SECOND HAND PLAY

When you are second to play to a trick you will generally play low. It does not matter whether declarer is leading from the dummy or from her hand. This is to allow your partner who will be last to play to the trick to try to capture whatever is played in the third hand. This second hand low guideline is almost always followed when a small card is led but generally changes when declarer leads an honor card and you have a higher honor card.

If declarer leads an honor you should cover the honor with a higher honor **if it promotes (or may promote) a trick** in your hand or your partner's hand. If declarer plays the queen from dummy holding Q 4 2 and you hold K 10 9, you can see that playing your king over the queen forces the declarer to play the ace to win the trick. When this happens, you can see that your 10 has been promoted and will win a trick after the jack is played.

Dummy has:
Q 4 2

You hold:
K 10 9

Declarer has:
A J 4

On an even stronger holding like K J T, you promote two winners by covering the queen with the king.

If you have no possible tricks in your hand in the suit (like K 9 7), cover the honor played with your honor if you believe partner has length in the suit and there is a high probability that you will be able to promote a trick for her. If neither of these conditions exists, just play low.

If declarer has touching honors in the dummy such as J T 6 cover the second of the touching cards, not the first. The general rule is to cover the last of touching honors.

Obvious exceptions to the second hand low guideline are when you hold the ace and declarer, playing in a suit contract, leads a singleton in that suit from the dummy. Another example is when there is a doubleton in the dummy and you hold the A K 6. Take your tricks before they get ruffed.

➢ In a noncompetitive auction any new suit bid at the 2-level by a responder who has not previously passed is game-forcing

➢ A game-forcing 2/1 bid requires 13 HCP or 12 HCP and a fit for the major suit opened

➢ Only games and slams are involved after a 2/1 response

➢ A minor suit 2/1 bid requires only 4 cards while a bid of 2H after a 1S opening always promises 5 cards in the suit

➢ With a full opening bid, the responder always bids her longest suit first

➢ Opener's rebids after a 2/1 response:
- Rebidding the major suit promises 6
- Raising the responder's minor suit usually shows 4
- Raising the responder's heart suit uses the "principle of fast arrival" where a jump to 4H is weaker than 3H
- Bidding a new suit shows an unbalanced hand and a second suit of at least 4 cards
- Bidding 2NT shows a balanced hand and 12-14 or 18-19 HCP
- Jump rebids are rarely used and show pattern not strength:
  - ✓ A jump to 3 of your major shows a self-sufficient suit which must be trump
  - ✓ A jump in a new suit shows 4-card support for the responder's suit and a singleton or void in the new suit

➢ Responder's rebids:
- The first priority is to raise the opener's major if 3-card support is held – use the "principle of fast arrival"
- Without support, bid what you have showing pattern rather than strength until a suitable contract is reached
  - ✓ Rebidding your 2/1 suit shows 6
  - ✓ Raising opener's second suit shows 4-card support

    ✓ Bidding a new suit shows an unbalanced hand with more in the first suit than the second suit

    ✓ Bidding 2NT shows 13-14 or 18-19 HCP

  • Do not pass until game is reached

➤ The finesse (leading toward a card you hope to make a winner when the opponents hold a higher card) is a 50/50 proposition

➤ When second to play to a trick generally play low. However, if an honor is led, cover the last of touching honors. Also if you have the setting trick, it is probably best to win the trick even as second hand.

EXERCISE 1 – OPENER'S REBID
AFTER A 2/1 RESPONSE TO A MAJOR SUIT OPENING

Opener's hand	HCP	TP	Your opening bid?	Partner's bid	Your rebid?
♠Q7532 ♥AKJ6 ♦97 ♣Q9				2C	
♠KQ75 ♥KQ975 ♦K5 ♣J5				2D	
♠AJT94 ♥75 ♦KQ42 ♣K7				2H	
♠AT742 ♥K6532 ♦A ♣Q5				2D	
♠KQT75 ♥A6 ♦AK52 ♣K2				2C	
♠K32 ♥QT976 ♦AQ5 ♣Q9				2C	
♠AT7 ♥KJT532 ♦K5 ♣AK				2D	
♠AQ754 ♥6 ♦KQ4 ♣QT95				2C	
♠AKQJ75 ♥8 ♦J52 ♣KT9				2D	
♠AT963 ♥AQ4 ♦K54 ♣AQ				2H	
♠KJT75 ♥KT5 ♦Q97 ♣A7				2H	
♠AKQ64 ♥K8 ♦A62 ♣K32				2H	

SHORT QUIZ – TRUE (T) OR FALSE (F)

_____ 1. Responder's 2/1 bid promises 13 HCP

_____ 2. After an initial 2/1 bid, responder's raise of the opener's major suit always promises 3-card support

_____ 3. After a 2/1 response, opener's reverse to 2S on her rebid shows 17+ points

_____ 4. A rebid of 2NT by either partner shows a balanced hand with minimum values (12-14) or 18-19 HCP

_____ 5. Responder promises 5 hearts when he bids 2H over 1S

ANSWERS TO EXERCISE 1
OPENER'S REBID AFTER A 2/1
RESPONSE TO A MAJOR SUIT OPENING

Opener's hand	HCP	TP	Your opening bid?	Partner's bid	Your rebid?
♠Q7532 ♥AKJ6 ♦97 ♣Q9 Bid your 2nd suit	12	13	1S	2C	2H
♠KQ75 ♥KQ975 ♦K5 ♣J5 Bid your 2nd suit - you do not need extras to reverse	14	15	1H	2D	2S
♠AJT94 ♥75 ♦KQ42 ♣K7 Balanced minimum = 2NT	13	14	1S	2H	2NT
♠AT742 ♥K6532 ♦A ♣Q5 Bid your 2nd 5-card suit	13	15	1S	2D	2H
♠KQT75 ♥A6 ♦AK52 ♣K2 Yes you have a great hand but look for the fit first before showing strength	19	20	1S	2C	2D

♠K32 ♥QT976 ♦AQ5 ♣Q9 Balanced minimum = 2NT	13	14	1H	2C	2NT
♠AT7 ♥KJT532 ♦K5 ♣AK Rebid your 6-card suit - no jump in your broken suit	18	20	1H	2D	2H
♠AQ754 ♥6 ♦KQ4 ♣QT95 Raise clubs is OK. Better is a jump in a new suit (hearts) to show your singleton & promise a fit in clubs; a splinter bid	13	16	1S	2C	3C or 3H
♠AKQJ75 ♥8 ♦J52 ♣KT9 Rebid your 6-card suit is OK. Better is to jump in your suit to show that it is solid and spades will be the trump	14	16	1S	2D	2S or 3S
♠AT963 ♥AQ4 ♦K54 ♣AQ With extras and a heart fit, just bid 3H	19	20	1S	2H	3H
♠KJT75 ♥KT5 ♦Q97 ♣A7 With a minimum hand and a fit, jump to game (4H)	13	14	1S	2H	4H
♠AKQ64 ♥K8 ♦A62 ♣K32 A big balanced hand - start with a rebid of 2NT	19	20	1S	2H	2NT

ANSWERS TO A SHORT QUIZ

1. Almost true - may occasionally bid 2/1 with 12 and a fit for opener's major suit

2. True

3. False - in a 2/1 auction bid your pattern and don't worry about strength; this is a reverse but in this situation it does not promise extras

4. True

5. True

EXERCISE 2 – RESPONDER'S REBID AFTER A
2/1 RESPONSE TO A MAJOR SUIT OPENING

Responder's hand	TP	Opening bid	Your initial bid?	Opener's rebid	Your rebid?
♠Q75 ♥AJ6 ♦KQ973 ♣Q9		1H		2H	
♠K7 ♥KQ9 ♦KQ65 ♣AJ53		1H		2D	
♠AJT ♥75 ♦KQJ42 ♣K73		1H		2NT	
♠T76 ♥AK ♦A752 ♣Q532		1H		2D	
♠KQ5 ♥A6 ♦AJ52 ♣T642		1H		2S	
♠AK3 ♥QT ♦AQ5 ♣QJ962		1H		2D	
♠AT7 ♥KJT53 ♦K95 ♣AK		1S		3H	
♠A4 ♥KQ76 ♦Q4 ♣KQT95		1S		2S	
♠AJ7 ♥875 ♦KQ52 ♣KJT		1S		3H	
♠A3 ♥AKQ43 ♦542 ♣T98		1S		4H	
♠KT ♥JT5 ♦KQ97 ♣AJT7		1S		2D	
♠KT6 ♥KQJ83 ♦A62 ♣72		1S		2NT	

ANSWERS TO EXERCISE 2
RESPONDER'S REBID AFTER A
2/1 RESPONSE TO A MAJOR SUIT OPENING

Responder's hand	TP	Opening bid	Your initial bid?	Opener's rebid	Your rebid?
♠Q75 ♥AJ6 ♦KQ973 ♣Q9 Start with 2D (2/1) and then bid 3H to show 3-card support and 15 SP	15	1H	2D	2H	3H
♠K7 ♥KQ9 ♦KQ65 ♣AJ53 Bid clubs (2/1) - your lower-ranking 4-card suit. Raise opener's major with 3-card support & a great hand	18	1H	2C	2D	2H
♠AJT ♥75 ♦KQJ42 ♣K73 Start with 2D (2/1) then without heart support and a balanced hand raise to 3NT	15	1H	2D	2NT	3NT
♠T76 ♥AK ♦A752 ♣Q532 Bid your lower-ranking 2/1 suit, then raise opener's 2nd suit with 4-card support	13	1H	2C	2D	3D
♠KQ5 ♥A6 ♦AJ52 ♣T642 Bid your lower-ranking 2/1 suit then bid 2NT to show a balanced 13-14 points	14	1H	2C	2S	2NT
♠AK3 ♥QT ♦AQ5 ♣QJ962 Bid your nice 5-card suit (2/1) then show your balanced hand with 2NT even with a huge 19 points	19	1H	2C	2D	2NT
♠AT7 ♥KJT53 ♦K95 ♣AK After partner raises your 2/1 heart suit to 3H showing extras surely you have a slam (19 + 15 = 34) so just bid it	19	1S	2H	3H	6H

♠A4 ♥KQ76 ♦Q4 ♣KQT95 Show your 2nd suit (which is usually only 4 cards long) on your rebid. This sequence shows an unbalanced hand with longer clubs than hearts	16	1S	2C	2S	3H
♠AJ7 ♥875 ♦KQ52 ♣KJT Bid 2D (2/1) then show your 3-card support for spades & good hand with a 3S bid	14	1S	2D	3H	3S
♠A3 ♥AKQ43 ♦542 ♣T98 Opener's rebid shows at least 3-card support for hearts (your 2/1 suit) but a minimum hand so pass	14	1S	2H	4H	P
♠KT ♥JT5 ♦KQ97 ♣AJT7 Bid 2C (your lower-ranking suit) then raise opener's second suit with 4-card support	14	1S	2C	2D	3D
♠KT6 ♥KQJ83 ♦A62 ♣72 Show your 5 hearts by bidding 2H (2/1) then jump to 4S to show 3-card spade support and a minimum hand for your bidding	14	1S	2H	2NT	4S

HAND #1	
VULNERABLE	None
DECLARER	South
CONTRACT	4S
OPENING LEAD	T♥

North
♠ K Q 6
♥ A 4
♦ 7 6 3 2
♣ A Q 8 4

NORTH
15HCP+ 1DP=16TP
NORTH BIDS 2C

West
♠ J 5
♥ T 9 8 3 2
♦ A Q T
♣ K 7 5

East
♠ 7 3 2
♥ J 7 6 5
♦ J 9 8 5
♣ 9 6

THE BIDDING			
SOUTH	WEST	NORTH	EAST
1S	P	2C	P
3C	P	3S	P
4S	P	P	P

South
♠ A T 9 8 4
♥ K Q
♦ K 4
♣ J T 3 2

SOUTH
13HCP+ 1LP=14TP
SOUTH OPENS 1S

The BIDDING: North has enough for a 2/1 game-forcing bid of 2C. South holding four cards in support of clubs bids 3C and now North shows her good hand (15+) and 3-card spade support by bidding only 3S. With a weaker hand she would bid 4S (fast arrival).

The LEAD: The TEN OF HEARTS (top of a sequence)

The PLAY: South wins the opening lead in her hand and draws trump in three rounds ending in her hand. Next South leads the jack of clubs planning to finesse for the king of clubs by letting the jack ride if West does not cover. West covers (cover an honor with an honor) hoping to promote a winner for her partner. This is not to be and South now plays all her club winners ending in the dummy. Now it's time for the diamond finesse. South leads a small diamond from the dummy planning to play the king hoping to find the ace in East's hand (a 50% chance). South plays the king when East plays low (second hand low) and West wins the ace and can now cash a second diamond. South makes five spades since one of her two finesses worked. If both had worked she would have made six and if both had failed she would have made only four. Finesses are great fun especially when they work!

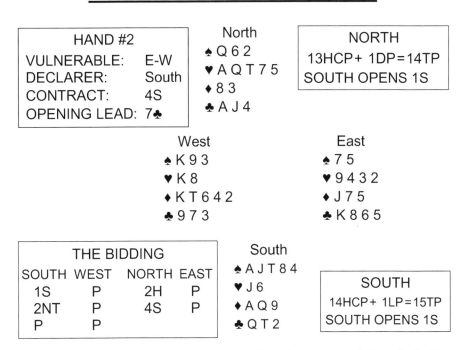

HAND #2	
VULNERABLE:	E-W
DECLARER:	South
CONTRACT:	4S
OPENING LEAD: 7♣	

North
♠ Q 6 2
♥ A Q T 7 5
♦ 8 3
♣ A J 4

NORTH
13HCP+ 1DP=14TP
SOUTH OPENS 1S

West
♠ K 9 3
♥ K 8
♦ K T 6 4 2
♣ 9 7 3

East
♠ 7 5
♥ 9 4 3 2
♦ J 7 5
♣ K 8 6 5

THE BIDDING			
SOUTH	WEST	NORTH	EAST
1S	P	2H	P
2NT	P	4S	P
P	P		

South
♠ A J T 8 4
♥ J 6
♦ A Q 9
♣ Q T 2

SOUTH
14HCP+ 1LP=15TP
SOUTH OPENS 1S

The BIDDING: North has an opening hand so can and does bid 2H - a 2/1 game-forcing bid also promising five hearts. South rebids 2NT to show her balanced hand and now North jumps to 4S which shows 3-card spade support and minimum values for her 2/1 bid.

The LEAD: The SEVEN OF CLUBS - with all other suits too dangerous to lead the seven is the middle card from three little. This lead is called MUD as you will next play the nine so middle, up and finally down, the three.

The PLAY: So many finesses! It looks like the club finesse will lose but you take it anyway and lose to the king. Back comes a diamond, another finesse which looks like it will lose, but you take the finesse for another loss. You win the diamond return and go to the dummy with the jack of clubs to take the spade finesse which also loses (a frequent lament of all bridge players that "all my finesses lose" seems to be working here). You win the club return and finish getting in the outstanding trumps. Now to make this contract you will need a successful finesse in the heart suit. So you hold your breath as you lead the jack of hearts and let it ride when West plays second hand low. The jack wins and you breathe again as you can finally see that this contract is making.

CHAPTER 6
BIDDING AFTER AN OPENING BID OF 1C OR 1D

In this chapter you will learn:

- About the responder's bidding priorities after a minor suit is opened
- How the opener rebids to describe her strength and distribution
- How the responder rebids to show minimum, invitational, and game-forcing hands

MORE ABOUT A MINOR SUIT OPENING

A minor suit opening occurs quite frequently. You will remember that a hand which cannot open 1NT (too weak/too strong, or unbalanced) or one of a major suit (no 5-card or longer major) must be opened with a minor suit bid. Remember also that we open our longer minor if unequal, one diamond if the minors are equal in length and at least four cards long, and one club when the minors are equal and three cards long. Therefore, the length of the minor opened may be as few as three but could be five cards or even longer. A 3-card club suit is much more common than a 3-card diamond suit since with 3-3 in the minors we should always open 1C. Therefore the only distribution where you would open 1D with a 3-card suit would be when you hold precisely four spades, four hearts, three diamonds and only two clubs (this only occurs about 4% of the time). Therefore partner should play you for four or more diamonds when responding to a 1D opening.

One hand pattern deserves special mention. When you hold a 5-card major and a longer (six+) minor, it is generally best to open your longer suit even though we love the majors and have sufficient length to open with a bid of one of the major. Your plan will be to next bid your major suit and given another chance, you will bid the suit again. This auction would show your 6-5 hand pattern and thereby the location of 11 of your 13 cards. You can believe that information will be extremely helpful to the responder later in the auction.

POINTS OF EMPHASIS	TAKE NOTE
The length of a minor suit is unknown and may be as few as 3 but could also be 8+.	A 1D opening with a 3-card diamond suit only occurs when the distribution of your hand is exactly:
A 3-card club suit is much more common than a 3-card diamond suit.	4=4=3=2
	This display of pattern means you have exactly 4 spades, 4 hearts, 3
Open your longer suit first - with a 6-card minor and a 5-card major, open the minor.	diamonds, and 2 clubs, as opposed to 4-4-3-2 which only shows pattern and does not define the length of specific suits.

Once a minor suit is opened the partnership has embarked on one of the most challenging bidding adventures in bridge. The minor suit length is unknown, the points cover a wide range (12-21) and you have only begun the search for the correct strain. Additionally, it is not an easy task to determine the correct level as a partscore, a game, and even a slam are all still in play. This chapter will use some of the techniques covered in previous chapters to assist in determining the strain and level of play. We will also introduce some new and exciting bidding tools which the responder will use in the ongoing effort to find the answers to the two vital questions, what level and what strain.

RESPONDER'S BIDDING PRIORITIES
AFTER A 1C OR 1D OPENING

When the responder holds at least six points, he should make some bid to keep the bidding open since the opener may have 19-21 points. Your six points and opener's 19 points mean that the combined partnership points are sufficient for game somewhere. Since the opening bidder may have a 4-card major, the responder's first obligation is to bid a major suit of at least four cards in length in an attempt to locate that magical 8-card fit. Four-card suits are bid up the line (hearts first) but if you have both majors and they are five cards in length, bid spades first. If one major is longer than the other, bid the longer one first. This new suit bid is 100% forcing so do not jump on your initial bid in an attempt to show a stronger hand. While it is somewhat controversial, we firmly believe in looking for our major suit fit and will gladly pass over a 4-card, 5-card, or even a 6-card diamond suit to get to the major. However, we also feel just as strongly about bidding your suits in natural order when you, the responder, also have an opening hand. Remember two opening hands must get to game. So if the opening bid is 1C and you have five or more diamonds and only four in your major suit and 13 or more points, your initial response should be 1D.

EXAMPLES

Partner opened 1C, what is your initial response?
You hold:

♠ K Q 9 7   ♥ 9 6 5 4   ♦ K 7 3   ♣ 9 5

Bid 1H even though your spades are much stronger. Four-card suits are bid up the line!

♠ J 9 7 6 3   ♥ K Q 5 4   ♦ A K 7   ♣ 5

Bid 1S because you have more spades than hearts

♠ A K Q J 7   ♥ A 8   ♦ K Q 3   ♣ 9 5 3

Bid 1S - this bid is forcing and keeps the bidding low while you explore for a fit. It also allows you to hear opener's rebid to help determine your total strength.

♠ K Q 9 7   ♥ 9 6   ♦ K J 7 3 2   ♣ 9 5

Bid 1S - since you have only 9 HCP, bypass your longer diamond suit to try to find a major suit fit

♠ K Q 9 7   ♥ A 5 4   ♦ K Q 7 3 2   ♣ 9

Bid 1D - with 14 HCP you are going to insist on game somewhere so start with your longest suit

When the opening bid is 1D and you hold a 5-card or longer club suit and 13+ points, bid 2C even with a 4-card major suit. This 2/1 bid creates a game force which makes the continuations easier for both partners as all bids are natural while the partnership searches for the final strain.

POINTS OF EMPHASIS	TAKE NOTE

An initial response in a new suit at the 1-level shows 6+ points and 4+ cards in your suit.
   Bid 4-card majors up the line
   After 1C, bypass a 4-card, 5-card, or 6-card diamond suit to mention a 4-card major. However, when you have an opening hand, bid a 5-card or longer diamond suit first.
	When the opening bid is 1D, it is preferable to bid the club suit if it is longer than your major and you hold the required 13 points for a 2/1 bid.
	   Some experts even prefer bidding a 4-card club suit over a 4-card major with 13+ points so as to create a game force.

If you do not hold a 4-card or longer major suit and you do not have an opening hand with a long minor (5+ cards), and your hand is somewhat balanced, the next priority is to try to play notrump. Your notrump responses show specific point count ranges making it easier for the opener to evaluate the total combined strength of the two hands. The bids and the strength shown are:

1 NT	8-10 HCP
2 NT	11-12 HCP
3 NT	13-15 HCP

These bids are quite specific and for the most part simplify the bidding. The opener knows that you are fairly balanced and that you do not have a 4-card or longer major. Your point count is pinned down to a very narrow range. Having provided all this wonderful information it is now possible to have an effective auction to the best contract for the partnership.

Finally, if you do not have four or more cards in a major suit and your hand is somewhat unbalanced with **five or more cards** in the opener's minor suit, you can raise the minor. The raises and the strength shown are listed below.

Raise to the 2-level 1C – 2C or 1D – 2D	6-10 HCP

Raise to the 3-level 1C – 3C or 1D – 3D	This is called a **limit raise** showing 11-12 HCP
Jump shift in the other minor 1C – 2D or 1D – 3C	These unusual jump bids promise an opening hand with at least 5 cards in the opening bidder's minor suit. The name for these conventional bids is **criss-cross** (another coded bid).

The opener may pass the two limited bids but must reach game after a criss-cross raise. Since playing a minor suit at the 5-level is our least desirable contract, the forcing raise of the minor suit is a signal for the opener to attempt to play notrump. If she has a really big hand she may want to try for slam in the minor rather than settle for 3NT.

OPENER'S REBIDS AFTER VARIOUS NT RESPONSES AND THE RESPONDER'S CONTINUATIONS

Let's look at the easy one first. When the **responder** bids any number of notrump she has denied a 4-card major and promised a fairly balanced hand which will include some cards (usually three or four) in your minor suit. This means the partnership need look no farther than notrump for a place to play unless the opener is interested in slam in one of the minor suits. Therefore, almost always the **opener** will pass or raise the notrump bid. **Opener's** rebids are:

- If the response was 3NT, pass or with interest in a minor suit slam bid four of the opening minor. With both minors and slam interest bid 4C. You will need a distributional hand with long minors and at least 17+ TP to show slam interest. If the **opener** rebids four of a minor, the **responder** will bid slam with a fit and 15 points. Otherwise, try 4NT or five of the minor.

- If the response was 2NT, pass with a very weak opening bid and raise 2NT to 3NT with 14+ points. If interested in a minor suit slam, bid a new suit at the 3-level to show your 5-4 distribution and your extra strength (20+ points). The **responder** will next bid 3NT or, with a fit for one of opener's minor suits, will bid six of the minor.

- If the response was 1NT, pass with a minimum and raise 1NT to 2NT with 18-19 HCP. This raise is highly invitational and, while it is a bid which may be passed, it asks the **responder** to bid 3NT when she holds a nice seven or more points. If interested in a slam in your minor suit, **jump shift** (19-21 HCP) into a second suit which is at least four cards long. This bid shows an unbalanced hand with more in your first suit than your second suit. **Responder** will raise your minor suit with a fit and the top of her 1NT response or return to 3NT to play.

EXAMPLES
The bidding has been:
1D – 2NT
What is your rebid?

♠ A 9 7　♥ Q 9 4 2　♦ A K J 3 2　♣ 8
Bid 3NT - you have a nice 5-card suit and 14 HCP. Do not worry about the club suit, your partner has some clubs since she didn't bid a major or raise diamonds.

♠ A 9 7 2　♥ Q 8 4 2　♦ A K 2　♣ 8 5
Pass - you have a very minimum hand with poor intermediate cards (10s and nines)

♠ A K 9 7　♥ Q 9 4　♦ A K J 3 2　♣ A
Bid 3S - this bid tells your partner that you have a huge hand and that you are interested in a diamond slam. Notice that you do not need to rebid your diamonds because you show an unbalanced hand with more in your first suit than your second suit when you bid a new suit at this level. So this sequence of bids shows at least five diamonds and at least four spades.

♠ A J 9 7　♥ Q 9 4　♦ A J 3 2　♣ 9 8
Pass - you have a very minimum hand so the partnership does not have the required points for a NT game

♠ A 9 7　♥ Q J　♦ A K 8 3　♣ 10 8 3 2
Bid 3NT - you have a nice 14 points so game is very likely

When the opening minor is raised the auction is once again reasonably easy. Clearly the responder's failure to bid a major suit (he doesn't have one) means that only notrump and the minor are options as to strain. There is one exception to this general observation and that is the hand where the opener has a 6-card minor and a 5-card major. On these 6-5 hands the opener's first bid is the 6-card suit and then she must bid the major twice to show this distribution. After this auction a major suit game is still possible if the responder has three cards in support of the major. On all other hands where the responder raises the minor the opener tries to play notrump unless a minor suit slam is possible. **Opener's** rebids are:

After a single raise to the 2-level, the **opener** with a minimum hand will pass. With a balanced hand and 18-19 points, bid 2NT to ask the **responder** to bid 3NT with 7-10 points. Remember that the **opener** will not have a balanced 15-17 points (she would have opened 1NT) nor 20-21 points (a 2NT opening bid).

After a limit raise to the 3-level, the **opener** will pass with a very minimum hand and bid 3NT with a nice 14 or more points. With 20-21 points and a long minor suit, the **opener** may suggest the possibility of slam by bidding 4D. The **responder** will then bid five or six of the minor depending on the degree of fit and strength of her hand.

After a jump in the other minor (the criss-cross raise) to show 13+ points and a fit in the **opener's** minor, game must be reached. The **opener** may simply bid 3NT with a minimum balanced hand with **STOPPERS** in both major suits. A stopper is an ace or a protected king, queen or jack. Something like: A 9 or K 7 or Q 9 5 or J 8 5 4. If the **opener** has a stopper in one major but not the other, she could bid the major with the stopper to suggest notrump but concern about the other major. The **responder** will cooperate by bidding 3NT when she holds a stopper in the other major; otherwise, she returns to the minor. Finally with a 5-card or longer minor and 15 or more points, the **opener** could show interest in slam in the minor by simply rebidding the minor. Don't worry as partner will not pass since he has promised to continue bidding until game is reached. If the **opener** rebids the suit (suggesting slam), the **responder** will bid 3NT if minimum with stoppers in both majors or bid four of the minor with 15+ points to say that he is also interested in slam. This raise almost always results in a minor suit slam contract.

EXAMPLES

The responder makes a limit raise in diamonds

1D – 3D

What is the opener's rebid?

♠ Q 10 9   ♥ K 9 7   ♦ A K 10 2   ♣ Q 9 8

Bid 3NT - you have 14 HCP so 3NT should be possible

♠ J 9 7 2   ♥ K J 4   ♦ A K 3 2   ♣ J 5

Pass - this one is not so good with13 bad points. 3NT just might make but the points just don't justify bidding it.

♠ A 9   ♥ K 9 4   ♦ A Q J 9 3 2   ♣ A Q

Bid 4D to suggest a diamond slam; this is a great hand

♠ J 9 7   ♥ K 9 4 2   ♦ A J 3 2   ♣ K 8

Pass - this "rule of 20" hand just doesn't make 3NT a likely successful contract

♠ K 9 7   ♥ Q   ♦ A K Q 8 3   ♣ A J 3 2

Bid 4D - this is a very nice hand with some slam potential so give partner the good news

POINTS OF EMPHASIS	TAKE NOTE

With a minor suit fit, try to play NT.
 	
   Stoppers are protected honor cards.
 	
   A jump shift in the other minor is forcing to some game
	A splinter bid is another way to show a game-forcing raise of a minor suit.
	   After a 1C opening, 3D, 3H, or 3S shows 13+ point and 5-card club support.
	   After 1D, it's 3H, 3S, or 4C.

OPENER'S REBIDS AFTER A NEW SUIT RESPONSE AND THE RESPONDER'S CONTINUATIONS

Now we will explore how to continue the bidding after the responder bids a major suit at the 1-level. This is the most difficult auction as little is known about either hand. It is very important for the opener to attempt to add some structure to the auction by making a rebid which accurately describes her strength and distribution. Remember the strength guidelines you firmly placed in your memory bank in Chapter 3.

Opener's Points	Category	Responder's Points
12-15	Minimum (M)	5-10
16-18	Invitational (I)	11-12
19-21	Game-Forcing (GF)	13+

The opener once again has the familiar four choices for her rebid:

* Raise the responder's suit
* Rebid her suit
* Bid a new suit
* Bid NT

BIDDING AFTER A RAISE OF RESPONDER'S SUIT

With 4-card support for the **responder's** major suit, the **opener** should raise to the 2-level with a minimum hand, jump raise with an invitational hand and bid game with a game-forcing hand. After any raise of the responder's suit, the strain is settled and the **responder** will simply add her points to what the **opener** has shown and pass, invite game, or bid game.

A jump raise always promises four cards in support but a simple raise to 2M may occasionally be made with only three cards. A hand with shortness in the unbid major has what is called a "**ruffing value**" and is appropriate for a simple raise. This would be a typical hand for the **opener** to raise a 1H response to 2H with only 3-card support: ♠ 5 3   ♥ K 10 6   ♦ A K 7 3   ♣ A 9 6 4

After a game raise, the **responder** generally passes but may bid slam with 13+ points. More advanced methods for slam bidding will be advanced in Chapter 9.

After a jump raise, the **responder** will pass with 6 or 7 points and bid at least game with more. Slam is possible if the **responder** has 15 or more points or a very distributional hand - more on this later.

When the **opener** has shown a minimum hand (12-15) by raising one level the **responder** will bid game when she also has an opening hand (13+) and will pass with a minimum hand. However, with an invitational hand (11-12 points), the **responder** can't be sure of game so will need to either give information about her hand or ask for more information about **opener's** hand before determining the level. A very effective way for the **responder** to continue is to bid 2NT to ask the **opener** for more information about her raise. Remember we are not trying to play notrump since we have a major-suit fit and are committed to playing in the major. This 2NT inquiry may also be useful when the **responder** has a very big hand with slam interest. The **opener** answers the inquiry by bidding:

3C = 3-card support and 12 or 13 points
3D = 3-card support and 14 or 15 points
3H = 4-card support and 12 or 13 points
3S = 4-card support and 14 or 15 points

Armed with the information provided by the **opener**, the **responder** is well-placed to bid all games which should be bid and to stay out of games when the values or support are insufficient.

Partner opened 1D and you responded 1H. Partner rebid 2H which shows support for your hearts (usually four) and 12-15 SP.

1D – 1H
2H – ?

What is your rebid?

♠ K Q 9   ♥ K 9 7 3 2   ♦ A 10 2   ♣ Q 9
Bid 4H - you have 14 HCP and at least an 8-card fit in the major

♠ J 9 7 2   ♥ K J 10 4   ♦ K 3 2   ♣ K J 5
This hand with 12 not so good points will need partner to have 14 or 15 and 4 hearts. Bid 2NT to ask partner to tell you more about her hand. Game is certainly possible in hearts or notrump.

♠ A 9   ♥ A K 10 9 4   ♦ Q J 9 3 2   ♣ A
This is a great hand with a fit in two suits – bid 6H and expect to make it

♠ J 9 7   ♥ K 9 4 2   ♦ J 3 2   ♣ K 8 5
With this minimum hand, you will pass being happy that a fit has been found at a low level

♠ K J 9 7   ♥ A Q 10 5   ♦ A Q 3   ♣ A 2
This is a very nice hand that has some slam potential so bid 2NT to find out more about your partner's hand before making a final decision

---

BIDDING AFTER THE OPENER REBIDS HER SUIT

When the **opener** does not have adequate support for responder's major suit (generally four cards), no second suit of at least four cards, and her minor suit is six cards or longer, it is appropriate to rebid the minor suit. When rebidding, the **opener** defines her strength by bidding two of the minor with 12-15 points and by jumping to three of the minor with 16-18 points.

At this point, the **responder** knows a lot about the opener's hand and bids as follows:

- With a minimum hand, pass the 2-level minor suit rebid or make a minimum rebid of your major suit if it is six cards long.

You may also bid two hearts if you hold five spades and four or five hearts. This bid is not forcing and the **opener** is asked to pass the heart bid or return to the **responder's** first bid suit. When the **opener** has jumped in her suit, as **responder** you will generally pass unless you have enough values for game (nine+). With game values any bid by you is forcing including rebidding your original suit if it is five cards or longer. If the **responder** bids any new suit, the auction is game-forcing and both partners continue with natural bids until a game is reached.

• When you hold an invitational hand and the **opener** has rebid her suit at the 2-level, you may raise the minor, jump a level in your 6-card major or rebid 2NT. Any of these bids invites game and keeps all options open. If the **opener** is at the top of her bid she will continue with any natural bid until game is reached. If the **opener's** hand is at the lower end she will pass. If the **opener** has jumped, any rebid by the **responder** is game-forcing, so make any natural bid.

• When you hold a game-forcing hand and the **opener** has made a minimum rebid of her suit, you must either bid a game if you know where you want to play or bid a new suit at the 3-level to force. If the **opener** has jumped in her suit all of responder's rebids are forcing. Make natural bids and consider slam if a fit is found and you have 15 or more points.

EXAMPLES
Partner opened 1C and rebid 2C after your 1S response

1C – 1S

2C – ?

What is your rebid?

♠ Q 10 9 4   ♥ K 9 7   ♦ A K 2   ♣ Q 9 8

Bid 3NT- you have 14 HCP and a fit with your partner so bid 3NT which will most likely make

♠ K J 9 8 7 2   ♥ K 4   ♦ A 3 2   ♣ 9 5

With 11 HCP and a fair 6-card suit you should invite game in spades by bidding 3S

♠ A J 10 9   ♥ Q 9 4   ♦ 9 3 2   ♣ A 9 5

With only 11 points and a very valuable card in your partner's suit, bid 3C to invite partner to bid a game. Hopefully he will bid 3NT.

♠ J 9 7 6   ♥ K 4 2   ♦ J 5 3 2   ♣ J 8

Pass - you barely had enough for an initial response and the partnership does have 8 cards in clubs so that contract should be just fine

♠ K 9 7 5   ♥ K J 5   ♦ K Q 8 3   ♣ 9 3

Bid 2NT to show your 12 HCP and invite game in notrump

SUMMARY

NF = NonForcing   I = Invitational   GF = Game-Forcing
m = minor   M = major

REBIDS BY ... OPENER ⌐→ RESPONDER ↓	WITH 6-10 PTS	WITH 11-12 PTS	WITH 13+ PTS
2 of the minor 1C-2C or 1D-2D 12-15 points	Pass Bid 2M with 6 (NF) Bid 2H (NF)	3m (I) 3M (I) 2NT (I)	Bid a game New suits at 3-level are GF
3 of the minor 1C-3C or 1D-3D 16-18 points	Pass All other bids are GF	All bids are GF	All bids are games or GF

BIDDING AFTER THE OPENER BIDS A NEW SUIT

With a second suit of at least four cards the **opener**, in most cases, will be able to rebid the new suit to show an unbalanced hand. Some of these bids are forcing and some may be passed. Both a rebid of 1S or 2C (a lower-ranking new suit) may be made with a minimum or invitational hand (12-18 points). A higher- ranking new suit at the 2- level is a **reverse** and requires 16 or more points. Lacking the required points for a reverse, the **opener** must not bid her second suit. She must instead find a bid which may be somewhat flawed (rebidding a 5-card minor or an unbalanced 1NT).

When the **opener** rebids 1S or 2C the **responder** may pass although the 1S bid is rarely passed. Continuing the bidding after a 1S rebid by the **opener** will be discussed in the section under notrump rebids by the **opener**.

When the **opener** rebids a lower-ranking new suit at the 2-level (2C after having opened 1D) the bid is not forcing but does cover a wide range of points. The **responder** with a minimum hand may pass or bid an old suit (one previously bid by either partner) at the 2-level. With an invitational hand, the **responder** may bid any old suit at the 3-level or 2NT. With a game-forcing hand the **responder** must bid game if the strain is known or make a bid which forces the opener to bid again and further describe her hand. The **responder's** only forcing bid after a 2-level lower suit rebid by the opener is the **fourth suit**. This bid of the fourth suit (the only suit which has not already been mentioned) is totally artificial and game-forcing. Any rebids by either partner short of game may no longer be passed.

Summary of the **responder's** rebid options following a 2C rebid by the opener

Opener's Bids		Responder's Bids		Meaning of Responder's Bids
1st Bid	1D	1st Bid	1H	4 or more hearts
2nd Bid	2C	2nd Bid	Pass, 2H or 2D	Desire to play there
			3C, 3D, 3H or 2NT	All invite game
			4H or 3NT	I've heard enough – I know where to play
			Rarely 5C or 5D	
			2S	**Fourth-suit forcing**

EXAMPLES:
The bidding has been
1D – 1H
2C – ?
What is the responder's rebid?

♠ A 7　♥ K Q 8 7　♦ Q 8 4 2　♣ 8 4 2

Jump to 3D to invite game hopefully in notrump if partner can bid it - you show good support for diamonds and the values to invite game

♠ 9 7　♥ A K Q 8 7 5　♦ K 8　♣ Q 4 2

Bid 2S which is "**fourth-suit forcing**" to establish a game-forcing auction. You plan to next rebid your hearts showing 6 and hoping to play game in hearts.

♠ A J 6　♥ Q 10 8 7　♦ Q 8 4 2　♣ Q 4 2

Bid 2NT to show your balanced invitational strength hand

♠ 7 3　♥ A J 8 7　♦ 8 4 2　♣ A Q 8 4

Bid 3C - this raise shows invitational values and 4 cards in support of clubs

♠ J 9 6　♥ Q J 7 2　♦ Q 8 4 2　♣ 8 4

With this weak hand go back to 2D to show a preference for your partner's first bid suit and a desire to play there

If the **opener** jump shifts to 2S after a 1H response or to 3C after the **responder** bids one of either major suit or 1NT, the jump shift is game-forcing. Both partners must continuing bidding until game is reached. Continue bidding naturally until a fit is found and game is bid or until someone bids 3NT.

If the **opener**, on her rebid, bids a higher-ranking suit at the 2-level, it is a **reverse** which is forcing for one round. The reverse bids after a minor suit opening are:

1C - 1H	1C – 1NT	1D – 1S
2D	2D	2H
1C – 1S	1C – 1NT	1D – 1NT
2D	2H	2H
1C – 1S	1C – 1NT	1D – 1NT
2H	2S	2S

Reverses by the opener all show 16-21 points and an unbalanced hand with more cards in the first suit than the second suit, typically 5-4. Since the **opener** may have the values for game, the reverse is absolutely forcing for one more round. The **responder's** first obligation is to rebid a 5-card major if one is held. If the **responder's** suit is only four cards long, the **responder** can raise one of the **opener's** suits at the cheapest level or rebid 2NT to show less than nine points. With 9-15 points, the **responder** must bid game in one of the **opener's** suits or 3NT. With more points, the **responder** must consider slam – more on that later.

POINTS OF EMPHASIS	TAKE NOTE
"Fourth-suit forcing" by the responder shows 13+ points and is game-forcing.	The responder may also reverse to show 13+ points and a game-forcing hand.
The jump shift by the opener shows 19-21 points and is game-forcing.	Reverses are vital to good bidding but difficult to fully understand so avoid them if another bid will suffice.
The reverse by the opener shows 16-21 points and is forcing for 1 round.	Sophisticated methods are available for bidding after a reverse but for now simple is best!

BIDDING AFTER THE OPENER REBIDS 1NT OR 2NT

If the **opener's** rebid is 2NT (either by jumping after a suit response or by raising a 1NT response) she is showing a balanced hand which was too big for 1NT and too little for 2NT. Therefore, the **responder** knows that the **opener** has 18-19 balanced points. While this bid may be passed, the **responder** must bid again with as little as seven nice points. Since the **opener** is balanced, the **responder** should just bid game in her major if it is six cards or longer. With a 5-card major, rebid it at the 3-level to see if the **opener** has three cards in support. Bidding a new 4-card suit would also promise five cards in the major. With only a 4-card major, just bid game in notrump. With 15 or more points, just bid slam in your 6-card suit or in notrump. There will be much more on slam bidding in Chapter 9.

If the **opener's** rebid is 1NT she is showing a balanced hand which was too little to open 1NT. This means that the **opener** has exactly 12-14 HCP.

If the **responder** also has a minimum hand and hears this limited 1NT rebid by the opener, he knows that game is not possible so will attempt to exit the auction at a low level. The **responder** may pass the 1NT rebid or sign off at the 2-level in a 6-card major suit. If his first bid was 1S, he may rebid 2H if he also holds four or more cards in hearts. This rebid would show more spades than hearts (5/4 or both 5-card majors). If the **responder** rebids a 6-card major suit or bids hearts after an initial bid of 1S he is showing a minimum hand. Both actions are not forcing and not even invitational. Both rebids ask the **opener** to pass or in the second case correct to 2S with less than four hearts.

When the **responder** holds an invitational or game-forcing hand and there have been any three bids at the 1-level including a 1NT rebid by the **opener**, a really neat bidding tool may be used. This conventional bid has an interesting name; it is called **XYZ**. It works this way:

THE ELEMENTS OF THE XYZ CONVENTION

- 2C is totally artificial and forces the opener to bid 2D
- 2D is totally artificial and is game-forcing
- 2NT forces the opener to bid 3C
- A jump in any previously bid suit or any lower-ranking new suit shows interest in a slam with 17+ points. More on this one later!
- Rebidding 2S after a 1H initial response is a reverse showing 13+ points and more hearts than spades (usually 5-4) and is game-forcing
- With 13-16 points and no slam interest just bid a game if you know where you want to play, otherwise bid 2D to show your game-forcing hand

When the **responder** bids 2C, the opener must next bid 2D. The **responder** may now pass and play 2D when she holds a long diamond suit or wants to return to the **opener's** original suit to play there. If the **responder** does not pass and instead bids anything else, it is showing an **invitational hand** and tells the **opener** what kind of hand she holds. All of **responder's** subsequent bids following the forced 2D rebid by the **opener** show 11-12 points. Here are possible rebids by the **responder**:

- Rebidding your major at the 2-level = a 5-card suit
- Rebidding your major at the 3-level = a 6-card suit
- Bidding 2NT = a balanced hand
- Bidding two of **opener's** second suit would show support with four cards
- Bidding a new suit would show a 5-4 hand

Easy isn't it!

When the **responder** uses the 2D rebid, a game force is established and both partners bid naturally to the best game or occasionally to a slam. The **opener's** first obligation would be to show delayed support (three cards) for the **responder's** major suit.

When the **responder** bids 2NT it forces the **opener** to bid 3C. The **responder** will then pass this bid either because she has a weak hand with a long club suit of her own or because her hand is weak and she wanted to return to the **opener's** 1st bid suit.

BY THE WAY

Bids which force partner to bid the next suit are called relay bids. The 2C and 2NT bids in the XYZ convention are examples of relay bids.

EXAMPLES

Here are five hands to see how this convention works.
The auction has been:

Auction	1C – 1H		Auction	1C – 1H
A	1NT – ?		B	1S – ?

Holding the following hands, what would the **responder's** rebid be given the two different rebids by the **opener**?

♠ A 8 5 ♥ K Q 6 4 2 ♦ 9 4 ♣ Q 8 3

A. Bid 2C - the opener will bid 2D and then you will bid 2H to show 5 and an invitational to game hand

B. Bid the same way as on the A auction

♠ A 10 5 3　♥ A Q 4 2　♦ A K 3　♣ Q 8

A. Bid 2D - this is probably a slam hand in notrump so you could just bid 6NT. The 2D bid shows a game-forcing hand and will allow you to hear more from the opener.

B. Jump to 3 spades - this bid shows 4-card spade support and interest in a spade slam.

♠ A 8　♥ J 6 4 2　♦ 9 4　♣ Q J 9 8 3

A. Bid 2NT - this bid forces the opener to bid 3C which you will then pass

B. Bid the same way as on the A auction

♠ A 8 5　♥ K Q 6 4 2　♦ A 4　♣ Q 8 3

A. Bid 2D - this bid shows a game-going hand and is looking for 3-card support for your heart suit. The opener must continue bidding until some game is reached.

B. Bid as you did on A

♠ K J 8 2　♥ Q J 8 3　♦ Q 9 3　♣ Q 8

A. Bid 2C - the opener will bid 2D and then you will bid 2NT to invite game in NT

B. Bid 2C - after the opener bids 2D as requested you will bid 2S to invite game in spades

---

SUMMARY OF RESPONDER'S REBIDS AFTER AN AUCTION WHICH STARTS WITH ANY THREE BIDS AT THE 1-LEVEL

There are nine auctions which start with a minor and may have three bids while remaining at the 1-level. Note that the opponents do not bid. Note also that an auction that starts with 1H and a response of 1S with the opener rebidding 1NT also falls in this category and will continue using XYZ.

THE OPENER REBIDS A NEW SUIT AT THE 1-LEVEL	THE OPENER REBIDS 1NT
1C – 1D 1H	1C – 1D 1NT
1C – 1D 1S	1C – 1H 1NT
1C – 1H 1S	1C – 1S 1NT
1D – 1H 1S	1D – 1H 1NT
	1D – 1S 1NT
	1H – 1S 1NT

On all 10 auctions **opener's** rebid is not forcing. However, there is a major difference in the auctions in column one and those in column two. When the **opener's** rebid is a major suit at the 1-level the strength of her hand could be anywhere from a minimum opener to as many as 18 HCP. When the rebid is 1NT it limits the **opener's** hand to exactly 12-14 HCP.

On all the auctions, if the **responder** has a minimum hand she should pass or make a minimum rebid which reflects her distribution. In column one, it is perfectly alright to raise the **opener's** major with four cards in support even with a very minimum hand. Without 4-card support for the **opener's** second suit, rebid your major if it is six cards long and bid 1NT with a balanced hand. On the auctions in column two, pass 1NT if balanced or rebid your major if you hold six. On the hands in both columns, if you want to play a minor suit either because you hold a long minor or you want to return to your partner's opening bid minor, you must ask partner to bid the suit. Bid 2C to ask partner to bid 2D and then pass if that is where you want to play. Bid 2NT to ask partner to bid 3C and then pass if that is the suit you want to play.

When the **responder** also has an opening hand but no slam interest he should just bid a game if the strain in known – usually four of the **opener's** major or 3NT. If uncertain about where to play ask the

opener for help by bidding 2D to inform the **opener** that the partnership must get to at least game but the strain is unclear.

With an invitational hand bid 2C which forces the opener to bid 2D. If you continue with any bid, including 2NT, it shows an invitational hand with 11-12 HCP and uncertainty about the strain and/or level.

POINTS OF EMPHASIS	TAKE NOTE
After any three bids at the 1-level, responder's artificial rebids are: • 2C = an invitational hand • 2D = a game-going hand • 2NT forces the opener to bid 3C	Other conventional bids are available to force the opener to bid again on these auctions, but none are as powerful or complete as **XYZ**.

BRIDGE ETIQUETTE

Good manners and common courtesies are the foundation of bridge etiquette. Once bidding has started, general conversations, especially inane chatter, should stop to allow players to focus on their hands and the game. In fact, it is unethical to use conversation as a diversionary tactic to distract opponents during the bidding and play.

PLAY TIP: MORE ON ESTABLISHING LONG SUITS FOR DISCARDS

When you are playing a suit contract and you see that you have too many losers, you will sometimes be able to establish a long suit in the dummy and then discard a loser on good cards in the dummy. Look at the two hands below: On both hands the contract is 4H and the lead is the queen of clubs.

	Dummy's hand		Dummy's hand
	♠ A 8		♠ A 8
	♥ K Q 9 6		♥ K Q 9 6
	♦ A 9 8 7 5 2		♦ A 9 8 7 5 2
#1	♣ 9	#2	♣ 9
	Declarer's hand		Declarer's hand
	♠ 9 5 2		♠ 9 5 2
	♥ A 8 4 3 2		♥ A 8 4 3 2
	♦ K 6		♦ 6 4
	♣ A 7 2		♣ A K

On the first hand declarer has two spades losers and two club losers in her hand. She could win the club lead with the ace, give up a spade and try to ruff two clubs and a spade in the dummy. Playing this way, you will have to use one of the high trump cards to ruff those losers and then maybe lose a trump to the jack. There will also be problems getting to your hand two more times to ruff all those losers. A much better plan is to try to establish dummy's long diamond suit. You can then discard some of your losers on dummy's little diamonds which are good because all the opponents' diamonds have been extracted. Notice that the dummy has six diamonds and you have two for a total of eight. When we have eight cards in a suit the opponents have only five. When there is an odd number of cards outstanding, in this case five, they tend to divide as evenly as possible between the opponents' hands, so we would expect them to be 3-2. So, on this hand, win the club, draw trump, and then play the two top diamonds and ruff a diamond. If the suit breaks as expected you will find that dummy's three remaining diamonds are good. Now, go to the dummy by ruffing a club and use the good diamonds to pitch two spades and the remaining club and make all the tricks.

When the opponents hold an even number of cards in one of our suits, they tend to divide unevenly. So, when the opponents hold six cards in a suit, we would expect them to be divided 4-2 not 3-3.

Hand #2 is very similar but the diamonds are not as strong. There are two spade losers and one diamond so the contract is safe and in fact you could give up a spade and ruff one of the spade losers making an overtrick. But you can do better. Play the club ace or king on the opening lead and then draw the outstanding trumps. Next play a small diamond from your hand and **duck** it in the dummy allowing either opponent to win the trick. Whatever suit is returned, win it and play the ace and another diamond which you will ruff. Now the diamonds are established and you can get to the dummy with a little heart to discard your spade losers on the good diamonds, making six.

POINT OF INTEREST	TAKE NOTE
If there is an odd number of cards outstanding in a suit, they tend to divide as evenly as possible while an even number of outstanding cards tend to divide unevenly.	**Ducking** to lose a trick which may not need to be lost is a valuable technique in establishing a long suit for discards.

DEFENSIVE TIP: COUNT SIGNALS

Knowledge of how many cards the partnership holds in a suit can be critical in defeating a contract. You convey information to your partner by the card you play when the declarer is leading a suit. Play a low card to show an odd number (three or five) of cards and a relatively high spot card (2nd highest from four) when you have an even number of cards (two or four).

Giving count is very important when the declarer is trying to establish a long suit in the dummy and has no outside entry to use to reach the dummy once the long suit is established. Look at the layout of the diamond suit in the example below:

Dummy

♦ K Q J 10 9

You   Partner

♦ 6 4 3   ♦ A 8 2

Declarer

♦7 5

On this example, assume that there are not other high cards or trump cards left in the dummy so there are no entries except in the suit itself. When declarer leads the seven, it is a critical defensive technique for you to play the three of diamonds thereby conveying to your partner that you hold an odd number (three) of cards in this suit. Your partner must win the trick when declarer is playing his last card in the suit to shut him off from the dummy. Partner sees three cards in his hand, adds the dummy's five and your three for a total of eleven which means declarer only has two. Now partner can make an expert play by refusing the first diamond trick and winning the second one. Dummy will have three good diamonds established but no way to get there to use them.

➢ Minor suits are opened when you have no 5-card major and do not have the points or shape for a NT opening

➢ 1C is often a 3-card suit. 1D is rarely a 3-card suit

➢ The responder's bidding priorities after a minor suit opening are:

- With 13+ points, 5 cards in the other minor, and no more than 4 cards in either major, bid the other minor

- On all other hands bid a major suit if a 4-card or longer major is held: With both majors bid the longer one first; if equal and 4-4, bid hearts first; if equal and both 5 cards or longer, bid spades first

- If no 4-card or longer major is held, bid 1NT with 6-10 points; and when balanced, bid 2NT with 11 or 12 points and 3NT with 13-15 points

- Finally, if none of the above options apply and you have 5 cards in support of the opener's minor suit, raise the minor to 2 with 6-10 points and to 3 with 11-12 points. With 13+ points and 5-card support for the opener's minor suit, jump shift in the other minor

➢ The opener rebids to show shape and strength:

- After a NT response, pass or bid game with adequate strength and balanced distribution. May also bid a second suit to show a distributional hand.

- After a raise, pass or try to reach 3NT with extras and stoppers in the major suits

- When the responder bids a new suit, the opener may:

  ✓ With 4 cards in support of the responder's suit, raise one level with a minimum, jump raise with an invitational hand and bid game with a game-forcing hand

  ✓ Rebid his suit if it is 6 cards long, jumping to show 16-18 points

✓ Bid a new suit to show an unbalanced hand. With 19-21 points, jump shift if your new suit is spades or clubs. With 16+ HCP reverse if your new suit is diamonds or hearts

✓ Bid NT if balanced: 1NT with 12-14 HCP and 2NT with 18-19 HCP

➤ The responder rebids to show shape and strength:

- If a major-suit fit is known and the strength is minimum sign off in a partscore. With game values, no slam interest and certainty about where to play, bid the major suit game

- If the opener has rebid 2C, pass or return to a previously bid suit at the 2-level with a minimum hand or the 3-level with an invitational hand. With a game-going hand and uncertainty about strain, bid "**fourth-suit forcing**" to let the opener know that game must be reached

- If the opener rebids a new suit at the 1-level or 1NT, and you are unsure of strain or level or if you want to return to a minor suit, use the **XYZ** convention where:

  ✓ 2C asks the opener to bid 2D which may be passed or if the bidding continues it shows an invitational hand

  ✓ 2D is artificial and game-forcing

  ✓ 2NT forces the opener to bid 3C which you will pass

  ✓ A jump in a previously bid suit or a lower-ranking new suit shows 17+ points and slam interest

➤ Two techniques for establishing long suits are ruffing a loser and losing an early trick in the suit by ducking

➤ Give count signals when declarer leads a side suit

A SHORT QUIZ

1. After a 1D opening, should the responder bid 1H or 2C when holding five clubs and four hearts and 10 points?

2. Same question but the responder has 15 points?

3. What should the responder bid with a balanced hand, no four card or longer major suit and 11-12 points?

4. How many points does the opener show if she raises the responder's major suit to the 3-level?

5. How many points does the opener show if she rebids 2NT after a major suit response at the 1-level?

EXERCISE #1
WHAT IS YOUR OPENING BID
ON THE FOLLOWING HANDS?

Your hand	HCP	LP	TP	Do you open?	What do you open?
♠KJ75 ♥KT75 ♦K85 ♣A2					
♠KJ7 ♥K975 ♦Q32 ♣A74					
♠5 ♥K5 ♦AQ765 ♣K9543					
♠K7 ♥A6 ♦KQJ5 ♣98653					
♠J85 ♥A ♦KJ9732 ♣AJ3					
♠7 ♥K842 ♦AKJ43 ♣T95					

ANSWERS TO A SHORT QUIZ

1. 1H - you are not strong enough to bid 2C
2. 2C - bid your longer suit with an opening hand
3. 2NT
4. 16-18 SP
5. 18-19 balanced points

ANOTHER SHORT QUIZ
TRUE (T) OR FALSE (F)

_____ 1. After the opener rebids 2C, responder's jump in her major suit is forcing

_____ 2. Opener's reverse shows 16-21 points

_____ 3. After any three bids at the 1-level, responder's 2D bid is artificial and forcing

_____ 4. Opener's rebid of 1NT shows 12-14 HCP

_____ 5. "Fourth suit forcing" is forcing for one round only.

EXERCISE 2
RESPONDER'S INITIAL BID: WHAT DOES THE
RESPONDER BID AFTER A 1C OPENING?

Responder's hand	HCP	LP	TP	Responder's initial bid	Is it forcing?
♠AK75 ♥9754 ♦K5 ♣952					
♠AKJ84 ♥QT542 ♦Q6 ♣4					
♠KJ7 ♥AKT65 ♦A5 ♣K95					
♠K75 ♥A96 ♦K52 ♣Q974					
♠K5 ♥Q6 ♦J943 ♣AJ983					
♠A ♥KJ3 ♦QJ43 ♣AQ975					

EXERCISE #3
THE OPENER'S REBID: WHAT DOES THE OPENER REBID AFTER A 1H RESPONSE TO A 1D OPENING?

Responder's handz	HCP	LP	TP	Opener's rebid?	Is it forcing?
♠KJ75 ♥K975 ♦K52 ♣A2					
♠AKJ8 ♥Q42 ♦J642 ♣K4					
♠KJ7 ♥A65 ♦AK42 ♣K95					
♠K54 ♥A ♦KQJ85 ♣AQ97					
♠K7 ♥Q6 ♦AQ8743 ♣A83					
♠A4 ♥AKJ3 ♦J943 ♣AQ9					

EXERCISE #4
RESPONDER'S REBIDS: WHAT DOES THE RESPONDER REBID AFTER A 1D OPENING, A 1H RESPONSE AND OPENER'S REBID OF 1S?

Responder's hand	HCP	LP	TP	Responer's rebid	Is it forcing?
♠A85 ♥9754 ♦K5 ♣J952					
♠AKJ8 ♥AQ542 ♦QJ6 ♣4					
♠K7 ♥AK965 ♦A52 ♣K95					
♠K75 ♥A964 ♦K52 ♣J97					
♠5 ♥Q653 ♦QJ943 ♣Q83					
♠K4 ♥AKQJ32 ♦Q7 ♣A75					

ANSWERS TO EXERCISE #1
WHAT IS YOUR OPENING BID
ON THE FOLLOWING HANDS?

Your hand	HCP	LP	TP	Do you open?	What do you open?
♠KJ75 ♥KT75 ♦K85 ♣A2 Open your longer minor	14	0	14	Yes	1D
♠KJ7 ♥K975 ♦Q32 ♣A74 With 3 cards in each minor, open 1C	13	0	13	Yes	1C
♠5 ♥K5 ♦AQ765 ♣K9543 With two 5-card suits, open the higher-ranking suit	12	2	14	Yes	1D
♠K7 ♥A6 ♦KQJ5 ♣98653 With unequal length in the minors, open the longer one	13	1	14	Yes	1C
♠J85 ♥A ♦KJ9732 ♣AJ3 Open your long suit with this unbalanced hand	14	2	16	Yes	1D
♠7 ♥K842 ♦AKJ43 ♣T95 Open this unbalanced "rule of 20" hand by bidding one of your longest suit	11	1	12	Yes	1D

ANSWERS TO EXERCISE #2
RESPONDER'S INITIAL BID: WHAT DOES THE RESPONDER BID AFTER A 1C OPENING?

Responder's hand Note: Respond with 6 or more points	HCP	LP	TP	Responder's initial bid	Is it forcing?
♠AK75 ♥9754 ♦K5 ♣952 Respond with 4-card major suits "up the line" regardless of strength	10	0	10	1H	Yes
♠AKJ84 ♥QT542 ♦Q6 ♣4 With two 5-card majors, bid the higher ranking one first.	12	2	14	1S	Yes
♠KJ7 ♥AKT65 ♦A5 ♣K95 Just bid your major suit at the 1-level - this bid is unlimited in strength and is forcing	18	1	19	1H	Yes
♠K75 ♥A96 ♦K52 ♣Q974 With no 4-card major, show your balanced 11-12 points with an invitational 2NT	12	0	12	2NT	No
♠K5 ♥Q6 ♦J943 ♣AJ983 You are unbalanced with no 4-card major so show 5-card support for clubs with a limit raise	11	1	12	3C	No
♠A ♥KJ3 ♦QJ43 ♣AQ975 A jump shift in the other minor shows an opening hand with 5-card support for the opener's minor suit. This is criss-cross	17	1	18	2D	Yes

ANSWERS TO ANOTHER SHORT QUIZ

1. False – this jump bid is invitational only
2. True
3. True
4. True
5. False – this bid is game-forcing

ANSWERS TO EXERCISE #3
THE OPENER'S REBID: WHAT DOES THE OPENER REBID AFTER A 1H RESPONSE TO A 1D OPENING?

Responder's hand	HCP	LP	TP	Opener's rebid?	Is it forcing?
♠KJ75 ♥K975 ♦K52 ♣A2 With 4-card support for responder's major suit, raise one level	14	0	14	2H	No
♠AKJ8 ♥Q42 ♦J642 ♣K4 No fit so far so show your 4-card spade suit	14	0	14	1S	No
♠KJ7 ♥A65 ♦AK42 ♣K95 With a balanced 18 points, jump in notrump	18	0	18	2NT	No
♠K54 ♥A ♦KQJ85 ♣AQ97 Jump shift into your second suit to show your 18-19 HCP points and unbalanced hand	19	1	20	3C	Yes
♠K7 ♥Q6 ♦AQ8743 ♣A83 Jump in your 6-card suit to show 16-18 TP	15	2	17	3D	No
♠A4 ♥AKJ3 ♦J943 ♣AQ9 With 4-card support for hearts and a game-going hand, just bid game	19	0	19	4H	No

Responder's hand	HCP	LP	TP	Responder's Rebid	Is it forcing?
♠A85　♥9754　♦K5　♣J952 No fit & balanced minimum = 1NT	8	0	8	1NT	No
♠AKJ8　♥AQ542　♦QJ6　♣4 With a known 8-card fit, jump in spades to suggest slam	17	3 SP	20	3S	Yes
♠K7　♥AK965　♦A52　♣K95 With no known fit, bid 2D forcing to elicit more information from the opener	17	1	18	2D	Yes
♠K75　♥A964　♦K52　♣J97 With a balanced invitational hand, bid 2C which forces 2D and then bid 2NT	11	0	11	2C	Yes
♠5　♥Q653　♦QJ943　♣Q83 Bid 2C which forces 2D which you will pass knowing you have a 9-card fit	7	1	8	2C	Yes
♠K4　♥AKQJ32　♦Q7　♣A75 Jump in your suit to show a very strong suit – 17+ points and slam interest	19	2	21	3H	Yes

HAND #1		North	NORTH
VULNERABLE:	Both	♠ K 8 7	9HCP + 1LP = 10TP
DECLARER:	South	♥ K Q T 5 4	
CONTRACT:	3NT	♦ 7 6	
OPENING LEAD: J♠		♣ J 8 4	

West	East
♠ J T 9 5	♠ Q 6 3 2
♥ 7 6 2	♥ A 9 8
♦ Q 8 3	♦ J 4 2
♣ Q 6 5	♣ 9 7 3

THE BIDDING

SOUTH	WEST	NORTH	EAST
1D	P	1H	P
3C	P	3H	P
3NT	P	P	P

South
♠ A 4
♥ J 3
♦ A K T 9 5
♣ A K T 2

SOUTH
19HCP + 1LP = 20TP
SOUTH OPENS 1D

The BIDDING: North responds to the 1D opening by bidding her 5-card heart suit. When South makes a game-forcing jump shift by rebidding 3C North must bid until game is reached. On this auction it is OK to rebid the 5-card heart suit to see if South has three hearts. No luck there so the partnership settles in 3NT.

The LEAD: The JACK OF SPADES (Top of a sequence)

The PLAY: South wins the opening lead in her hand with the ace of spades and counts her tricks. She has six top tricks and sees that she can make the contract by driving out the ace of hearts to establish four heart tricks. She leads the jack of hearts and the West player plays the deuce of hearts to show that she holds three hearts.

East, having listened to the bidding and looking at the card partner played, knows that the declarer has only two hearts so will win the second heart as declarer is playing her last card in the suit. Now the carefully preserved king of spades is the entry to the dummy to play the established hearts. After cashing the winning hearts the declarer takes her tricks making an overtrick: four hearts and two winners in each of the other three suits for 10 tricks.

HAND #2	
VULNERABLE:	None
DECLARER:	South
CONTRACT:	4S
OPENING LEAD:	Q♣

North
♠ Q J 9 5 4
♥ A Q J 8
♦ K 3
♣ 8 2

NORTH
13HCP + 1LP = 14TP

West
♠ A 2
♥ T 4 3
♦ Q 9 7 4
♣ Q J T 7

East
♠ T 8 7
♥ 5 2
♦ J T 8 6 5
♣ K 9 6

THE BIDDING

SOUTH	WEST	NORTH	EAST
1C	P	1S	P
1NT	P	2D*	P
2H	P	4H	P
P	P		

* XYZ – Artificial & Game-Forcing

South
♠ K 6 3
♥ K 9 7 6
♦ A 2
♣ A 5 4 3

SOUTH
14HCP + 0LP = 14TP
SOUTH OPENS 1C

The BIDDING: South's rebid of 1NT shows a balanced hand with 12-14 HCP. North knows that with her 14 TP the partnership has enough points for game but is unsure of the strain. To learn more about the opener's hand North bids 2D which is artificial and game-forcing. South who could not bid hearts earlier because it would have been a reverse showing more points is very happy to bid the suit now. This was all North needed to hear to bid the game in hearts.

The LEAD: The QUEEN OF CLUBS (top of a sequence)

The PLAY: South wins the club lead with the ace and draws all the opponents' trumps. Now it is time to set up the spade suit in the dummy so South leads the king of spades from her hand (high card from the short side). Since West has only two spades and South led a big honor card she should ignore the second hand low advice and capture the king. Now West can cash a club but that is the last trick for the defense. South wins the next club lead by ruffing in the dummy and discards her last club on the good spades. South will make five hearts for a very good score.

Five spades will also make but in general we prefer to play an eight card fit that is divided 4-4 rather than the 5-3 fit.

CHAPTER 7
BIDDING AFTER AN OPENING BID OF 1 NT

In this chapter you will learn:

- When to pass or raise the notrump bid
- How to look for a major-suit fit
- How to respond with a minor suit-oriented hand
- Whether the hand should be played in a notrump contract or in a suit contract

MORE ABOUT THE 1NT OPENING

When your partner opens 1NT she has described her hand within circumscribed parameters. It is balanced (no voids, no singletons, and no more than one doubleton) and has no more than 17 points and no fewer than 15 points. You usually know immediately how high the partnership should bid (partscore, game, or slam) but do not necessarily know what strain you will play. When you, the responder, have no 4-card or 5-card major suit and have no unusual length or strength in the minors, your bid will be in notrump. With a really bad hand (eight or fewer HCP) you will just pass (ugh!) and hope your partner can make the partscore contract of 1 NT. With all other hands you will be responsible for directing the auction in order to determine the best contract. In this sense you have clearly become the captain and will either set the contract or elicit more information about the opener's hand. You most often ask questions (in bridge language) and partner will answer. Sometimes you give information which is intended to assist partner in determining the correct contract. Let's see how all this works!

RESPONDING WITH A BALANCED HAND: NO 4-CARD OR 5-CARD MAJOR AND NO LONG MINOR SUIT

When you have a balanced hand and no 4-card or 5-card major your response will be a raise of the notrump opening. Remember that the combined HCP strength required for a NT game is 25. Slams require 33 HCP for a small slam and 37 HCP for a grand slam. For purposes of playing in a notrump contract, if responder has 9 HCP her hand is invitational, if she has 10-15 HCP her hand is game-forcing, and with anything in the 16+ range slam must be considered. You will raise the one notrump opening bid to the level consistent with your HCP on your first bid. With:

- 9 HCP - bid 2NT which invites partner to bid game if she is at the top of her bid (16 or 17 HCP) and to pass with the bottom (15 HCP)
- 10-15 HCP - bid 3NT because you know you just want to play game in notrump
- 16-17 HCP - bid 4NT which invites partner to bid 6NT if she is at the top of her bid (16 or 17 HCP). She is supposed to pass with only 15 HCP.
- 18-19 HCP - bid 6NT because you know you have at least the 33 HCP (15+18 = 33) needed for a small slam
- 20-21 HCP - bid 5NT **which is forcing** and invites partner to bid a grand slam (7NT) if she is at the top of her bid (16 or 17 HCP). If not, she **must bid 6NT**.
- 22+ - just bid 7NT because you have the points for the grand even when the opener has the minimum points for her 1NT opening - (22 + 15 = 37)

From your initial response your partner will know how many points you have and will pass game and slam bids when she holds minimum values. She will accept game and slam invitations when she has maximum points for her opening bid.

LET'S LOOK AT SOME EXAMPLE HANDS

♠10 9 8   ♥K Q 4   ♦J 4 3   ♣Q 7 4 2

Your hand is balanced with only 8 points so you must pass

♠ K 8 7   ♥ Q J 8   ♦ K 5 4   ♣ 8 7 4 2

You have 9 points which is enough to invite to game so bid 2NT. With 16 or 17 points partner will bid game and will pass 2NT with 15 points.

♠ K Q 8   ♥ K 6 3   ♦ Q 10 8 6 3   ♣ J 8

With 11 points you have enough for game in notrump so just bid 3NT

♠ K Q 8   ♥ A J 4   ♦ K Q 8 4   ♣ J 9 8

With this nice 16 points you have enough strength to invite to a slam in notrump. Bid 4NT to ask partner to bid 6NT if she has a maximum (16 or 17 points) for her 1NT opening.

POINTS OF EMPHASIS	TAKE NOTE
2NT invites 3NT, 4NT invites 6NT, and 5NT **forces** 6NT and invites 7NT. All these invitational responses ask partner to bid a higher level of NT if she has the top of her bid.	The 4NT response has a very special name – It is called **quantitative 4NT** and the bid is used to invite slam in NT. We will learn later that 4NT is also used to ask partner how many **keycards (the four aces and the king of the agreed trump suit)** she holds when we are looking for a slam in a suit contract.
She will accept with 16 or 17 HCP and will decline the invitation with 15 HCP.	
To raise the notrump bid, the responder will never have a 5-card major and will rarely have a 4-card major but she will often have a 5-card or 6-card minor suit.	It is vitally important to learn when 4NT is quantitative and when it is a keycard ask. Even many experienced players have difficulty with this distinction.

BIDDING TO FIND A 4-4 MAJOR-SUIT FIT: THE STAYMAN CONVENTION

As always we like to play in a major suit if we have at least an 8-card fit. After partner opens 1NT the responder doesn't freely bid 4-card major suits. Rather we use another "coded" bid (2C) to **ask** partner if her balanced hand contains a major suit which is 4-cards or 5-cards long. This "coded" bid is called the **STAYMAN** convention. Like the "coded bids" (conventions) discussed in earlier chapters this convention carries an artificial or unusual meaning in that it says nothing about clubs rather it is used to see if partner has a 4-card major which matches a 4-card major in your hand.

When you bid 2C over a 1NT opening you are not bidding a club suit but, in fact, **asking** partner if she has a 4-card major suit. To use Stayman you need at least 9 HCP and at least one 4-card major suit of your own.

After the 2C asking bid the opener bids as follows:

OPENER'S RESPONSE TO 2C	MEANING
• 2D	I have no 4-card major
• 2H	I have 4 hearts and maybe 4 spades also
• 2S	I have 4 spades and < 4 hearts

If partner responds 2D or bids the major suit that does not match your major, you will return to notrump at the level appropriate to your HCP. If the opener's response was 2H and she also holds four spades, she will know that you hold four spades and will place the contract in spades. Remember Stayman promised a 4-card major suit and if it wasn't hearts it has to be spades.

If your hand is unbalanced and you have enough points for game (10+), you could also bid a 5-card or longer minor suit rather than returning to notrump. This bid is another way to describe your hand pattern and strength.

If partner bids a major suit which matches a 4-card major which you hold you will raise the major based on your strength:

- With 9 TP: Raise the major to the 3-level. The bid invites partner to bid four of the agreed major.
- With 10-15 TP: Raise the agreed major suit to game (4M).
- With 16-17 TP: Raise the agreed major suit to the 5-level to invite partner to bid slam if she is at the top of her notrump range.
- With 18-19 TP: Bid slam (6M) in the agreed major suit.

HERE ARE SOME EXAMPLE HANDS:

♠ K Q 8 6   ♥ Q 8 7   ♦ 8 4 3   ♣ 9 7 6

Despite having a 4-card major, you must pass with only 7 points

♠ K 7 4   ♥ Q J 8 4   ♦ K 6 4 2   ♣ 8 7

This is a perfect hand for the Stayman convention. Bid 2C to ask partner if she has a 4-card heart suit. If partner bids 2D or 2S (the wrong major suit), you will bid 2NT to show 9 HCP and invite game in notrump. If partner bids 2H, you will bid 4H to show the match and your 10 TP. Did you remember to add 1 SP for the doubleton club which makes your hand worth 10 TP playing in a suit contract?

♠ K Q 8 6   ♥ K J 7 5   ♦ Q J 9   ♣ 7 6

Again a perfect hand to start with Stayman as you have both majors so bid 2C. If partner bids either major suit, raise to game. If partner's bids 2D to show no 4-card major, you will bid 3NT with your 12 HCP.

There is a situation when it is right to bid Stayman even when you have less than 9 HCP. The situation occurs when you have a void or singleton in clubs, both 4-card majors and four or five diamonds. Any response partner makes (2D, 2H, or 2S) will probably play better than 1NT which would have been the contract had you passed. This bid is referred to as **garbage Stayman**. Here's an example of when to use this Stayman variant:

♠ J 8 6 3　　♥ Q 6 4 2　　♦ 10 9 4 3　　♣ 8

Bid 2C planning to pass any response by your partner and table the dummy without apologies! You have spared your partner the agony of playing in a 1NT contract.

BY THE WAY

The Stayman convention is one of the most popular conventions used world-wide. It is so widely used that no alert is required when it is bid. An **alert** in duplicate bridge is required after a coded or conventional bid is made to inform your opponents that the bid just made has an artificial or unusual meaning.

BIDDING TO FIND A 5-3 OR A 6-2 MAJOR-SUIT FIT: THE JACOBY AND TEXAS TRANSFER BIDS

Another widely-used and useful convention ("coded" bid) in notrump bidding is the **Jacoby transfer**. It is used when you, the responder, hold a 5-card major and are looking for a 5-3 fit in your major suit. When this situation exists you want to **tell** your partner that your hand contains a 5-card major suit. He will know that he can raise your major with only three cards in support knowing that the magical 8-card fit exists. To initiate the Jacoby transfer you bid the suit (at the 2-level) directly below your 5-card major. This bid asks your partner to bid (transfer to) the next higher suit. A bid of 2D tells partner you hold at least five hearts and asks partner to transfer to 2H. A bid of 2H announces at least a 5-card spade holding and asks partner to bid 2S. Since you and your partner have agreed to incorporate this convention into your game, the opener must complete the transfer by bidding two of the requested major.

Unlike the Stayman convention which requires nine HCP, a Jacoby transfer bid should be made with any number of points, even zero. With a worthless hand and a 5-card major suit, transfer and then pass - just do it! When you have at least nine points (remember to add one for your 5-card suit) you will transfer to your suit and then return to notrump at the level consistent with your values (HCP) on your rebid. After a transfer bid, if you have sufficient values for game, you may also rebid by showing a second 4-card or 5-card minor suit rather than rebidding notrump. If your major suit is only five cards long **DO NOT** raise the major suit after partner completes the transfer - he knows you have five cards in the suit - bid notrump or a new suit.

Remember the transfers are:

2D → 2H   and   2H → 2S

THE TRANSFER FOLLOWED
BY A REBID IN NOTRUMP:

YOUR TOTAL POINTS	YOUR REBID
• 9 transfer and then	BID 2NT to invite game
• 10-15 transfer and then	BID 3NT
• 16-17 transfer and then	BID 4NT to invite slam
• 18-19 transfer and then	BID 5NT which is called "**pick a slam**" asking partner to bid 6NT or 6 of the major suit

On these sequences where you rebid notrump you are asking partner to choose between notrump and your major suit. When holding three cards in support of your major suit, partner will rebid the major suit choosing to play in the 8-card fit. With only two cards in your major she will elect to play in notrump. Let's look at some hands where your correct bid as responder is to transfer and what you should rebid.

EXAMPLES

♠ K 8 6 5 4   ♥ Q 4 2   ♦ 9 4   ♣ 8 5 2

Your initial bid should be 2H asking partner to bid 2S - you should then pass as you have only 6 TP

♠ K 8 7 6 4   ♥ K Q 2   ♦ Q 4 2   ♣ 5 2

Use the transfer bid of 2H which transfers to 2S and next jump to 3NT with your game-going hand. Partner will leave the bid in notrump with only 2 spades and bid 4S with 3 or more spades.

♠ K 7 2   ♥ K 8 7 6 4   ♦ Q 2   ♣ 7 5 2

Bid 2D which your partner will correctly announce as a transfer bid and then bid 2H. You then rebid 2NT to let partner know that in addition to your 5 hearts you have enough points to invite to game. Partner may now pass 2NT with a minimum and bid 3NT with the top of her bid when she holds only 2 hearts. With 3 or more hearts she will bid 3H or 4H depending on the strength of her hand - minimum or maximum.

♠ K Q 7 6 4   ♥ A K   ♦ Q J 4   ♣ K 10 4

Transfer to spades by bidding 2H. At your next turn, bid 5NT, telling partner to "pick a slam" which she does by bidding 6NT with 2 spades and bidding 6S with 3 or more spades.

POINTS OF EMPHASIS	TAKE NOTE
After a 1NT opening: • 2D is a transfer to 2H & • 2H is a transfer to 2S The transfer bid may be made with zero points. The opener must complete the transfer by bidding the next higher-ranking suit.	The opener may "**super accept**" the transfer by jumping to three of the requested major. To "super accept" the opener must have four or more cards in responder's major suit and 17 HCP. This rarely-occurring jump bid guarantees a superb 9-card fit!

Use the Jacoby transfer, too, when you hold a 6-card major. When partner opens 1NT you know that she has at least two cards in your major so you have the magical 8-card fit and the major suit is where you will play the contract. Transfer to your major and pass with less than six points. With 6-7 points, transfer and then invite to game by bidding three of the major. Your raise of the major informs partner you have at least six cards in the suit. If you had only five, you would have returned to notrump. Can you see how informative the partnership conversation has become?

When you have a game-forcing hand (8-13 TP) and six cards in the major, use a variation of the Jacoby transfer called a **Texas transfer** where the transfer bid starts at the 4-level. This bid shows a big hand (big as in Texas-big) with a long suit and at least game values. Instead of transferring at the 2-level, you will make the transfer request at the 4-level.

Bid 4D to transfer to hearts (4H)
Bid 4H to transfer to spades (4S)

The Texas transfer is used on hands where you just want to play game as well as on hands that are big enough to ask for keycards in an attempt to play slam (more on these really big hands in Chapter 9).

EXAMPLES:

♠ K 7 6   ♥ A Q 7 6 4 2   ♦ J 4   ♣ 8 4

With your game-going hand and 6 hearts, tell your partner just that by bidding 4D which transfers to 4H and then pass

♠ A Q 10 6 4 2   ♥ 8 4   ♦ 9 3   ♣ J 10 6

You have enough (7 HCP) to invite game with your 6 spades, so transfer at the 2-level by bidding 2H to transfer to 2S and then bid 3S at your next turn. Your bidding sequence tells partner you have 6 spades, not 5, and have enough points to invite to a game in spades.

POINT OF EMPHASIS	ANOTHER POINT OF EMPHASIS
Transfer bids allow the stronger (presumably and most often) hand to remain concealed and therefore it is more difficult to defend and usually it is advantageous for the opening lead to come into rather than through the stronger hand.	After a transfer never rebid your suit with only five. When you rebid a suit which you have transferred to you are promising at least six cards in the suit.

BY THE WAY
At duplicate bridge "coded" bids or conventional bids must be alerted or announced so that your opponents know that your bid is "phony", artificial, or unusual. A transfer bid is artificial but is so common that it is announced rather than alerted. The partner of the person making the artificial transfer request just says "transfer" immediately after the bid is made.

BIDDING WHEN THE RESPONDER HOLDS A 4-CARD MAJOR ALONG WITH FIVE OR MORE CARDS IN THE OTHER MAJOR

When you hold at least one major of exactly four cards in length along with five cards in the other major, you should start with Stayman (2C). Your rebid will depend on the strength of your hand and partner's rebid. If you hold a 4-card major and have six or more cards in the other major, just ignore the 4-card major suit and transfer to your longer major.

When you have a weak hand (0-8 TP) start with Stayman (2C) and pass if partner bids either major suit. If partner bids 2D (no 4-card major) bid your 5-card major suit at the 2-level. Partner should understand this bid to be weak with a 4-card and a 5-card major and will pass your 2-level major suit bid knowing you have a weak hand. This is a good treatment which you and your partner should adopt. If partner does not understand this bid to be weak, you will clearly get too high.

With a stronger hand (9+ TP) consider your hand as game–forcing and start with Stayman. If partner bids either major suit bid game in the major as you know you have either an 8-card or 9-card major-suit fit. If partner bids 2D, jump to the 3-level in your 5-card major suit. When you jump a level in the bidding after Stayman, you promise enough values for game and the opener must bid again. She will choose to play 3NT with only two cards in your known 5-card suit and will bid four of your major when she holds three cards in support. Example hands will illustrate these points.

EXAMPLES:

♠ K Q 8 5   ♥ Q 7 6 4 2   ♦ 9 4   ♣ 7 5

Bid 2C to see if partner has 4 cards in either major suit. If she bids either hearts or spades your call is pass which shows your weak hand. If your partner bids 2D, your bid is 2H which defines your hand as weak with 4 spades and 5 hearts - your partner should pass.

♠ K Q J 7   ♥ Q J 10 8 5   ♦ Q 7   ♣ 6 3

Again start with Stayman. If partner responds in a major, jump to game in that major to show your game-going hand. If she responds 2D (no 4-card major), jump to 3H which describes your hand as game-going with 5 cards in the suit you bid and 4 cards in the other major. Partner will now bid 4H with 3 hearts and 3NT with only 2 hearts (there is no 8-card fit).

BIDDING WHEN THE RESPONDER HOLDS FIVE CARDS IN BOTH MAJORS

When you hold at least five cards in both majors, the contract will always be in a major suit. Don't even think about playing in notrump as your partner will always have at least three cards in support of one of your major suits. Remember he will not open 1NT with doubletons in both majors. On these hands do not use Stayman or the Jacoby transfer, rather jump in one of the majors depending on the strength of your hand.

With a weak hand (0-8 TP), jump to 3H. This bid asks partner to pass or bid 3S if her spades are better than her hearts.

With a stronger hand (9+ TP) jump to 3S. This bid forces game and asks partner to pick her best major suit at the 4-level. After partner picks, you could invite slam by raising the suit to the 5-level with 16-17 TP or you could just bid slam with 18+ TP. You will learn about slam bidding in a later chapter should you be so fortunate to have a hand stronger than just a game bid. These two bids are defined as:

3H = 5/5 majors-weak

3S = 5/5 majors-strong

EXAMPLES:

♠ K 8 7 4 2   ♥ Q 9 6 5 3   ♦ 5   ♣ 6 2

After 1NT is opened, bid 3H at your first turn to tell partner you have a weak hand and 5 cards in each major. Partner will pass or correct to 3S if he likes spades better (has more) than hearts.

♠ K Q 7 4 2   ♥ Q J 7 5 3   ♦ K 7   ♣ 6

With this nice holding, jump to 3S to force partner to game in his longer or stronger major suit

RESPONDING WITH LENGTH IN THE MINORS

Since playing in a minor suit is our least desirable game contract we will generally disregard a 5-card or 6-card minor and just bid the appropriate number of notrump with game-invitational (9 TP) or game-forcing hands (10-15 TP). It is only when we have a long minor suit and either a very weak hand or a hand with slam potential that we want to mention the minor suit. All of these bids are only used when you do not also have four cards or more in a major suit.

With a 6-card minor suit and a weak hand it is generally desirable to play in the minor rather than notrump. However you will remember that both 2C (Stayman) and 2D (Jacoby transfer to 2H) are unavailable to show a weak minor suit-oriented hand. Therefore, we will use **2S to ask partner to bid 3C** (this is called a relay and says nothing about spades). After the opening bidder bids the requested 3C you will pass if clubs is your suit or correct to 3D if diamonds is your long weak minor suit. If you correct to 3D the opener must pass as you are announcing a very weak hand. Since you may have either minor suit when you bid 2S requesting partner to bid 3C, the 2S bid is called a relay rather than a transfer.

With a 6-card minor suit and slam potential (16+ TP), jump to the 3-level in your 6-card suit. Partner must bid again and will bid 3NT if she has a minimum hand (15) or if she does not have a very good fit for the minor (two or three little cards). With a nice fit or a maximum, the opening bidder should just bid slam in the minor or bid 4NT to ask for keycards (more on this in Chapter 9). The opener could also bid 6NT with 17 HCP and a fit in your minor suit. If the opener signs off in 3NT and you have 17+ TP, just bid 6NT.

EXAMPLES OF MINOR SUIT BIDDING:

♠ A 3 2   ♥ 8 6 3   ♦ K 9 8 7 3   ♣ 8 6

With only a 5-card minor and 7 points you should pass

♠ A 3 2   ♥ 8 6   ♦ K Q J 8 7 5   ♣ 8 6

With 10 HCP and 2 LP ignore the 6-card minor suit and just bid game in notump (3NT)

♠ Q 3 2   ♥ Q 8 5   ♦ K J 8 7 3   ♣ 9 6

With 9 TP bid 2NT to invite a game in notrump

♠ K 3 2   ♥ 6   ♦ K Q J 8 6 3   ♣ K Q 6

With slam invitational values (16 TP) jump to the 3-level in your long minor (3D). Partner will bid 3NT with minimum values. With support in diamonds and 16-17 points she will bid 6D. Without diamond support but maximum points for her opening bid she will go to 6NT.

♠ 10 8 6   ♥ 9 7   ♦ 8 4   ♣ Q J 8 7 4 2

This is the hand for the 2S relay; bid 2S and when partner bids 3C as requested you will pass

♠ 10 8   ♥ –   ♦ K 9 8 7 4 3   ♣ 10 8 6 4 2

Again with a weak hand bid 2S and correct 3C to 3D which will surely play much better than a 1NT contract

♠ 9 4 2   ♥ 8 7   ♦ Q 6 2   ♣ A K Q 8 7

Ignore the nice club suit and bid 3NT with your game values

POINT OF EMPHASIS	TAKE NOTE
A dictum in bridge is to "almost always" prefer a 3NT contract over a 5-level contract in a minor. Rare is the hand that will make 5D or 5C and not make 3NT. Minors are acceptable in a partscore or slam.	An extension of the two spade relay where the opener shows her minor suit preference allows for more advanced handling of the minors. For now, we will adopt the easiest way to deal with the minor suits.

Summary Of Responder's Bids After A 1NT Opening

RESPONDER BIDS	IT MEANS
• 2C	Stayman - asking the opener for a 4-card major
• 2D	Jacoby transfer to 2H
• 2H	Jacoby transfer to 2S
• 2S	A relay to 3C
• 2NT	Invitational to 3NT
• 3C	Interest in a club slam
• 3D	Interest in a diamond slam
• 3H	Weak 5-5 in the major suits
• 3S	Strong 5-5 in the majors
• 3NT	I just want to play game in NT
• 4D	Texas transfer to 4H
• 4H	Texas transfer to 4S
• 4NT	Invitational to 6NT
• 5NT	Forces 6NT & invites 7NT
• 6NT	We have the values for slam

PLAY TIP: THE HOLD-UP PLAY

The hold-up play is a technique whereby you duck, or **hold-up**, taking a trick which you could win. This technique is especially useful at a notrump contract where the opponents are trying to set up their long suit. In fact, holding-up taking a trick may allow you to make a contract that otherwise would be set. Here is an example of the hold-up play. You are playing 3NT and the leader starts with the king of spades - a suit where you have a single stopper - the ace.

Presumably the defender has led his strongest and longest suit at your contract of 3NT. Let's look at the layout of the spade suit:

Dummy
♠ 8 5

Opening leader (LHO)   Defender (RHO)
♠ K Q J 9 7   ♠ 10 3 2

♠ A 6 4
Declarer (you)

As you can see the king lead is the top card in a solid sequence. When you counted your winners you found that you had only eight and to make your contract you will have to try to establish some tricks in another suit where you are missing the ace. When you knock out the missing ace the opponents will be back on lead and may be able to cash enough tricks to set your contract. You have only one stopper in spades so you want to limit your losses in spades to, hopefully, only two. The idea is to hold on to your ace until your RHO has no more spades and, should he get the lead, he will be unable to lead a spade back to LHO's hand where the remaining spades can be cashed. To do this, you must duck two rounds of spades before winning your ace of spades on the third lead of the suit. As you can see the opening leader will have two good spades but no way to gain the lead to cash them and with no spades remaining in his partner's hand there is no way to get back to him. If you win the first or second lead of spades your contract will be defeated regardless of which opponent holds the ace you must drive out in order to make your contract.

DEFENSIVE TIP: RULE OF ELEVEN

When you are on lead against a notrump contract it is generally best to lead your longest and strongest suit. If that suit is headed by an honor sequence you will typically lead an honor card. Lacking a nice sequence in your suit it is established custom to lead the fourth best card (fourth down from the top). When your partner has led a spot card against notrump you should assume it is her fourth best in her long suit. You can apply the **"the rule of 11"** to determine how to defend. To apply the "rule of 11", subtract the number on the card she has led from 11 and the result is the number of cards higher than the card led in the other three hands (dummy, you and the declarer).

You can then determine how many, if any, cards higher than the one led are held by the declarer because you can see your cards and dummy's cards. Amazing calculation isn't it? Here's how it works:

Dummy
♥ Q 8 4

Opening leader　　　　　　　　　　You
♥ 6　　　　　　　　　　　♥ A 10 9 5

Declarer
♥ ?

When partner leads the six, subtract six from 11 and you know that there are five higher cards in the three other hands. You can see all five of the higher cards so you know that your partner's holding in the suit which he has led is ♠ K J 7 6. If declarer plays low from dummy, play your five as declarer has nothing to beat the six! You will feel so smart when you can defend like the pros! The same calculation works for declarer and he, too, can employ the "rule of 11" to his advantage (if he knows this "rule").

DEFENSIVE TIP: INTERIOR SEQUENCES

We have discussed solid sequences where you have a suit headed by three cards in a row such as K Q J 9 7. We have also looked at broken sequences where your suit has two in a row, then missing one and has the next card, a suit that looks like this A K J 7 6. One other sequence needs discussion and that is the interior sequence. An interior sequence is an honor sequence within a suit where the two lower cards are in sequence, such as K J 10 4. These kinds of sequences are also very good leads against notrump contracts.

To help partner discern what your lead means, we recommend that you use a lead convention called **coded leads** where "**jack denies, nine or 10 implies**". This means that when you lead a jack you have nothing higher in the suit led (jack denies), something like J 10 9 7. If, on the other hand, when you lead a 10 or a 9 you are promising two higher cards in the suit led or none higher, something like K J 10 8 or 10 9 8 7. Note that one of the higher cards will always be the one directly above the one led – the 10 promises the J, denies the Q, and promises either the A or K. Since the 10 is also led from sequences such as 10 9 8 4 (none higher), partner should be able to discern from his holding and dummy's which sequence the leader has.

Lead the underlined card from the following interior sequences:

♠ A Q J 8   ♠ K J 10 7   ♠ Q 10 9 4

♠ K 10 9 4   ♠ A 10 9 4   ♠ A J 10 4

➤ With a balanced hand and no 4-card or 5-card major or long weak or strong minor suit, respond to a 1NT opening as follows:

- < 8   points - pass
- 9   points - bid 2 NT to invite 3NT
- 10-15 points - bid 3 NT to play
- 16-17 points - bid 4 NT to invite 6NT
- 18-19 points - bid 6 NT to play
- 20-21 points - bid 5 NT to force 6NT and invite 7NT
- 22+   points - bid the grand (7 NT) to play

➤ With at least one 4-card major suit and 9+ HCP, bid Stayman (2C) **asking** the opener to bid a 4-card major to look for a 4-4 major-suit fit. The opener answers by:

- Bidding 2D = no 4-card major - you will now return to the appropriate level of notrump
- Bidding 2H when she holds a 4-card heart suit or 4 cards in both majors. If you fit hearts, raise - if not - return to notrump
- Bidding 2S when she holds 4 spades and < 4 hearts. If you fit, raise spades to the level of your strength - with no fit, return to notrump
- You may also use "garbage Stayman" with shortness in clubs, 4/4 in the majors and < 9 points

➤ With a 5-card or longer major suit bid the Jacoby transfer to **tell** the opener about your long suit so you can play in a 5-3 or 6-2 fit. Bid 2D to transfer to 2H and 2H to transfer to 2S

- With a 5-card suit, transfer at the 2-level, then pass or return to notrump at the level appropriate to your strength.
- Opener can "super accept" the transfer by jumping to the 3-level when she holds 4 cards and 17 HCP
- With a 6-card suit and less than game values, transfer at the 2-level, then pass or raise the major with 9 TP to invite game

- With a 6-card suit and game values (10+ TP), use the Texas transfer (4D to transfer to 4H and 4H to transfer to 4S)

➤ When Stayman fails to find a 4-4 fit in a major and after a 2-level transfer, the responder may bid a 5-card minor suit rather than returning to notrump if she holds game values

➤ With a 5-card major and a 4-card major use Stayman and
- Pass opener's major-suit bid with < 9 points
- With < 9 points bid 2 of your 5-card major if the opener bids 2D
- With 9+ points raise either major suit response to game and jump in your 5-card major suit if the opener bids 2D

➤ With at least 5-5 in the majors, bid:
- 3H with < 9TP
- 3S with 9+ TP

➤ With 6 or more cards in a minor suit and no 4-card or longer major suit:
- Just bid the appropriate number of notrump with game and game-invitational values
- With slam interest (16+ TP), jump to the 3-level in your minor suit
- With a weak hand (< 9 TP), use the 2S relay to tell the opener to bid 3C, then pass if clubs is your suit and bid 3D if your suit is diamonds

➤ The hold-up play will often help you make notrump contracts

➤ Employ the "rule of 11" when defending notrump contracts

➤ Lead "J denies, 10 or 9 implies" when you hold an interior sequence in your long suit

BRIDGE ETIQUETTE

In order to learn more about the game it's fun and usually enlightening to watch (kibitz) experienced players. It is proper to ask the player you plan to watch (whether friend or stranger) if it's OK with him. You should plan to watch only one player at a time, you should sit down, and you should not talk during the play of the hand.

A SHORT QUIZ
After a 1NT opening bid what are the numbers associated with:

1. Partnership points required for a NT game?
2. Responder points required for a NT game?
3. Points required for a 2-level transfer?
4. A 4NT response to a 1NT opening bid?
5. Points needed by the opener to "super accept" a transfer?

EXERCISE 1
WHAT IS THE RESPONDER'S INITIAL
BID AFTER A 1NT OPENING?

Responder's hand	HCP	LP	TP	Rsponder's initial bid	What does it mean?
♠A75 ♥9754 ♦K5 ♣9532					
♠AKJ84 ♥QT542 ♦Q6 ♣4					
♠KJ74 ♥AT65 ♦A5 ♣985					
♠K75 ♥A96 ♦952 ♣Q974					
♠K5 ♥Q6 ♦J93 ♣AJ9873					
♠A76 ♥KJ3 ♦QJ4 ♣AQ95					
♠K765 ♥AQJ62 ♦9 ♣J73					
♠K9865 ♥6 ♦J93 ♣9873					
♠K9 ♥KQ9642 ♦3 ♣AJ94					

♠J542 ♥Q632 ♦J9743 ♣–				
♠95 ♥Q6 ♦QJ9873 ♣732				
♠K5 ♥AQ6 ♦KJ9 ♣AJ873				
♠852 ♥KJ9652 ♦K3 ♣92				

EXERCISE 2
AFTER OPENING 1NT, WHAT DO YOU REBID
WHEN THE RESPONDER BIDS AS INDICATED?

Opener's hand	TP	Respoer's bid	Meaing?	Your rebid?
♠KQ75 ♥AJ79 ♦K87 ♣K5	16	2C		
♠AK4 ♥QT5 ♦KQ6 ♣K974	17	2C		
♠KQ7 ♥AJ9 ♦KQ75 ♣Q94	17	2NT		
♠KQ5 ♥AJ9 ♦KQ75 ♣Q76	17	2H		
♠KQ5 ♥AJ9 ♦KQ75 ♣Q76	17	4NT		
♠KQ7 ♥AJ8 ♦Q75 ♣KQ76	17	2S		
♠KQ5 ♥AJ ♦K75 ♣Q7632	16	4D		
♠KQ65 ♥A9 ♦KQJ5 ♣Q76	17	2H		
♠KQ5 ♥AJ9 ♦K975 ♣Q76	15	2NT		
♠Q53 ♥AJ9 ♦KQ97 ♣KQ6	17	5NT		

Responder's hand	Your total pts	Your initial bid	Opener's rebid	Your rebid?	The bid shows?
♠K765 ♥AQJ62 ♦9 ♣J73	12	2C	2D		
♠AKJ84 ♥QT542 ♦Q6 ♣4	14	3S	4S		
♠KJ74 ♥AT65 ♦A5 ♣985	12	2C	2H		
♠K9865 ♥6 ♦J93 ♣9873	5	2H	2S		
♠95 ♥Q6 ♦QJ9873 ♣732	7	2S	3C		
♠852 ♥KJ9652 ♦Q3 ♣J9	9	2D	2H		
♠K5 ♥AQ642 ♦KJ9 ♣973	14	2D	2H		
♠K542 ♥6 ♦K9743 ♣KQ5	12	2C	2H		
♠A964 ♥KQ2 ♦63 ♣A984	13	2C	2D		
♠K52 ♥AQ62 ♦A743 ♣K4	16	2C	2S		

ANOTHER SHORT TRUE (T) OR FALSE (F) QUIZ

_____ 1. It's OK to bid 2NT if you don't like the suit partner asked you to transfer into

_____ 2. The opener may pass if responder bids 4NT

_____ 3. If partner bids 2C (Stayman) you will bid 2H with both 4-card major suits

_____ 4. After a 2NT response, the opener always rebids 3NT

_____ 5. With six diamonds and 14 HCP the responder should bid 3D

ANSWERS TO EXERCISE 1
WHAT IS THE RESPONDER'S INITIAL
BID AFTER A 1NT OPENING?

Responder's hand	HCP	LP	TP	Responder's initial bid	What does it mean?
♠A75 ♥9754 ♦K5 ♣9532 You are too weak to bid.	7	0	7	Pass	Balanced & weak
♠AKJ84 ♥QT542 ♦Q6 ♣4 This bid promises enough points for game and 5 cards in each major	12	2	14	3S	5-5 Majors
♠KJ74 ♥AT65 ♦A5 ♣985 This bid asks the opener if she has a 4-card major	12	0	12	2C	Stay-man
♠K75 ♥A96 ♦952 ♣Q974 You have just enough to invite partner to bid 3NT	9	0	9	2NT	Invite NT Game
♠K5 ♥Q6 ♦J93 ♣AJ9873 Even though you have a long minor just bid the NT game	11	2	13	3NT	I've enough for game
♠A76 ♥KJ3 ♦QJ4 ♣AQ95 You have the right count to invite slam in NT	17	0	17	4NT	Quanti-tative
♠K765 ♥AQJ62 ♦9 ♣J73 You have a 4-card major so start with Stayman	11	1	12	2C	Stay-man
♠K9865 ♥6 ♦J93 ♣9873 It is right to transfer to your 5-card spade suit.	4	1	5	2H	Jacoby transfer

♠K9 ♥KQ9642 ♦3 ♣AJ94 Transfer at the 4-level with game values and 6 hearts	13	2	15	4D	Texas transfer
♠J542 ♥Q632 ♦J9743 ♣− Bid Stayman on this weak hand planning to pass any response	4	1	5	2C	Garbage Stayman
♠95 ♥Q6 ♦QJ9873 ♣732 Get out of NT with this weak hand. After partner bids 3C, correct to 3D	5	2	7	2S	2S Relay
♠K5 ♥AQ6 ♦KJ9 ♣AJ873 You have the values for 6NT so just bid it	18	1	19	6NT	Slam!
♠852 ♥KJ9652 ♦K3 ♣92 Transfer at the 2-level and then raise hearts to invite a heart game	7	2	9	2D	Jacoby transfer

ANSWERS TO EXERCISE 2
AFTER OPENING 1NT, WHAT DO YOU REBID WHEN THE RESPONDER BIDS AS INDICATED?

Opener's hand	TP	Responder's bid	Meaning?	Your rebid?
♠KQ75 ♥AJ79 ♦K87 ♣K5 2C asks for a 4-card major, with both, bid hearts first	16	2C	Stay- man	2H
♠AK4 ♥QT5 ♦KQ6 ♣K974 The 2D response says "no 4-card major"	17	2C	Stay- man	2D
♠KQ7 ♥AJ9 ♦KQ75 ♣Q94 With maximum points, bid 3NT	17	2NT	Invites 3NT	3NT
♠KQ5 ♥AJ9 ♦KQ75 ♣Q76 Just complete the transfer for now – see what partner does next	17	2H	Tranfer to 2S	2S
♠KQ5 ♥AJ9 ♦KQ75 ♣Q76 You're on the top so go for it, bid 6NT	17	4NT	Invites 6NT	6NT
♠KQ7 ♥AJ8 ♦Q75 ♣KQ76 Good partners do what partner asked - just bid 3C	17	2S	Relay to 3C	3C
♠KQ5 ♥AJ ♦K75 ♣Q7632 Just complete the transfer by bidding 4H	15	4D	Texas transfer	4H
♠KQ65 ♥A9 ♦KQJ5 ♣Q76 With 17 points and 4 great spades, super accept the transfer by jumping in spades	17	2H	Transfer to 2S	3S

♠KQ5 ♥AJ9 ♦K975 ♣Q76 With a minimum, decline the invitation by passing	15	2NT	Invites 3NT	Pass
♠Q53 ♥AJ9 ♦KQ97 ♣KQ6 Partner's bid required you to bid at least 6NT and to bid 7NT with a maximum – you have it – what fun - 7NT	17	5NT	Invites 7NT	7NT

ANSWERS TO EXERCISE 3
WHAT WILL BE YOUR REBID ON THE AUCTIONS BELOW?

Responder's hand	Your total points	Your initial bid	Opener's response	Your rebid?	The bid shows?
♠K765 ♥AQJ62 ♦9 ♣J73 5-4 majors start with 2C and jump in your 5-card major after a 2D response	12	2C	2D	3H	4 spades and 5 hearts
♠AKJ84 ♥QT542 ♦Q6 ♣4 With 5-5 majors strong bid 3S and pass opener's choice unless you have enough for slam	14	3S	4S	Pass	A fit and game
♠KJ74 ♥AT65 ♦A5 ♣985 Stayman finds a fit so bid game with 10-15 points.	12	2C	2H	4H	A match and game values
♠K9865 ♥6 ♦J93 ♣9873 Transfer to your 5-card major & pass with < 9 TP	5	2H	2S	Pass	Too weak to bid again

Hand					Bid 1	Bid 2	Bid 3	Bid 4	Meaning
♠95 ♥Q6 ♦QJ9873 ♣732 Relay to 3C and then correct to your long weak diamond suit					7	2S	3C	3D	Weak diamond suit
♠852 ♥KJ9652 ♦Q3 ♣J9 With 6 hearts & 9 TP, transfer and then invite game in the major suit					9	2D	2H	3H	Invite to 4H
♠K5 ♥AQ642 ♦KJ9 ♣973 With only 5 hearts, transfer and then return to 3NT with game points (10-15)					14	2D	2H	3NT	5 hearts & game values
♠K542 ♥6 ♦K9743 ♣KQ5 After failing to find a 4-4 major-suit fit, bid your second suit on this strong unbalanced hand					12	2C	2H	3D	4 spades, < 4 hearts & 2nd Suit
♠A964 ♥KQ2 ♦63 ♣A984 Having no 4-4 fit in spades bid 3NT with these values					13	2C	2D	3NT	Game, no 4-4 major fit
♠K52 ♥AQ62 ♦A743 ♣K4 With no 4-4 fit in hearts & holding slam invitational values bid a **quantitative** 4NT. Partner will pass with 15 HCP and will bid 6NT with 16 or 17 HCP					16	2C	2S	4NT	Invites slam in NT no 4-4 major fit

ANSWERS TO A SHORT QUIZ

1. 25

2. 10-15

3. Zero

4. 16-17

5. 17

ANSWERS TO ANOTHER SHORT QUIZ

1. False – you must complete the transfer

2. True – she may pass with 15 HCP but will bid 6NT with 17

3. True – if you bid 2S you will deny holding four hearts

4. False – he will only bid 3NT if he is at the top of his 1NT opening

5. True – this bid is invitational to slam in the minor suit or NT

HAND #1	
VULNERABLE:	N-S
DECLARER:	South
CONTRACT:	3NT
OPENING LEAD:	T♥

North
♠ A J 8 3
♥ 8 5
♦ K 6 2
♣ A J 5 4

NORTH
13HCP+ 0LP=13TP

West
♠ T 4
♥ K J T 6 4
♦ Q 8 4
♣ 8 7 3

East
♠ 7 6 5 2
♥ Q 3 2
♦ T 5 3
♣ K 9 6

THE BIDDING			
SOUTH	WEST	NORTH	EAST
1NT	P	2C *	P
2D	P	3NT	P
P	P		
* Stayman			

South
♠ K Q 9
♥ A 9 7
♦ A J 9 7
♣ Q T 2

SOUTH
16HCP+ 0LP=16TP
SOUTH OPENS 1NT

The BIDDING: North has enough points for game after the 1NT opening bid but is unsure of the strain. She bids 2C (Stayman) to see if South has four spades which would give the partnership an 8-card fit in spades. South answers by bidding 2D which denies holding a 4-card major and so North settles for the notrump game (3NT).

The LEAD: The TEN OF HEARTS. West has an interior sequence so leads the 10 which promises two higher or none higher. If two higher, one will be the jack and one other higher card (the king or ace – not the queen which would be a solid sequence and the queen would have been led). East can afford to play the queen on this trick to help her partner understand the location of the outstanding high cards.

The PLAY: Declarer can count only eight tricks: Four spades, one heart, two diamonds, and one club. She will need one more trick and the heart suit is very dangerous. South can get her extra trick by finessing in the club suit even if the finesse loses to the king. There is one danger however. If the finesse loses and East has a heart remaining he will be able to return his heart and West will cash four heart tricks and defeat the contract. To prevent this unfortunate happening South holds-up winning her ace of hearts until the third round of the suit. Now when she finesses in clubs East is out of hearts and the contract is made with an overtrick – the defense winning only the first two heart tricks and the king of clubs.

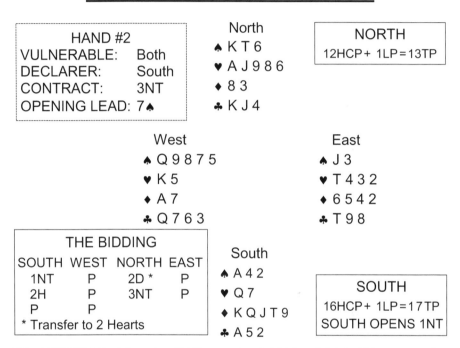

HAND #2	
VULNERABLE:	Both
DECLARER:	South
CONTRACT:	3NT
OPENING LEAD:	7♠

North
♠ K T 6
♥ A J 9 8 6
♦ 8 3
♣ K J 4

NORTH
12HCP + 1LP = 13TP

West
♠ Q 9 8 7 5
♥ K 5
♦ A 7
♣ Q 7 6 3

East
♠ J 3
♥ T 4 3 2
♦ 6 5 4 2
♣ T 9 8

THE BIDDING

SOUTH	WEST	NORTH	EAST
1NT	P	2D *	P
2H	P	3NT	P
P	P		

* Transfer to 2 Hearts

South
♠ A 4 2
♥ Q 7
♦ K Q J T 9
♣ A 5 2

SOUTH
16HCP + 1LP = 17TP
SOUTH OPENS 1NT

The BIDDING: After the 1NT opening bid North bids 2D to transfer to 2H. South dutifully completes the transfer. North now bids 3NT which gives South a choice of games. This sequence of bids shows the values for game and that North holds only five hearts. South passes 3NT since he holds only two hearts. If he had held three or more hearts he would have bid game in hearts instead of passing.

The LEAD: The SEVEN OF SPADES (fourth best from a broken suit)

The PLAY: The declarer has only five top tricks but can establish tricks in hearts and diamonds. But first what does the lead tell us about the spade suit? If you apply the "rule of eleven" by subtracting seven from 11 there are only four cards higher than the seven in the other three hands. Since you can see three higher cards between the dummy and your hand you know that East has only one higher card. When you play a low spade from the dummy and East inserts the jack you know that the queen is with West and so you can also make an extra trick by finessing the 10 of spades at some point in the play.

You will win the ace of spades and play the king of diamonds to drive out the ace of diamonds thereby establishing four diamond tricks bringing your total to nine and enough to make your game. Now it's time to try for overtricks. After winning the ace of diamonds West leads another spade hoping you will play the king but you skillfully finesse the 10 which wins the trick. Now you come to your hand and cash the rest of the diamond winners and then you can try the heart finesse by playing the queen. West covers the queen with the king and you win the ace. The jack of hearts, king of clubs and the spade king bring your total to 11 tricks and a nicely played hand.

CHAPTER 8
COMPETITIVE BIDDING

In this chapter you will learn:

- About the names of the two new players in the auction
- How to enter the bidding after an opponent has opened
- How to describe your hand when both sides are bidding

INTRODUCTION TO COMPETITIVE CONCEPTS

Once the bidding has been opened, the other partnership quite often enters the auction. There are several reasons to compete: You may be able to buy the contract thereby making a score for your side, you will clearly make it difficult for your opponents to complete their bidding, and finally your bid may suggest a good lead against the opponent's final contract.

When both sides are competing for the final contract there are some major differences between the two sides. First are the player's names. You are familiar with the name for the player who opens the bidding, the **opener,** and his partner, the **responder.** The players for the other side also have names. The first person to bid for the other side is called the **overcaller** and her partner is called the **advancer.** Throughout the rest of this book we will refer to the players by name and it is important to remember your name as it will definitely have an effect on your role as the auction continues to a final contract.

The second major difference is in the overcaller's first bid. No longer do you ever start the bidding for your side with a 3-card minor suit. Suit bids will always show length – at least a 5-card suit. Sometimes the overcaller will have two 5-card suits and would like to play in the one that fits with his partner. And finally, with no 5-

card suit to bid, the overcaller will sometimes have a way to tell partner that he has a good hand with some length in all the other suits and ask his partner to select a suit.

There are five ways for the overcaller to enter the auction:

1. You may **OVERCALL** with a suit bid to show a **single-suited** hand.
2. You may **OVERCALL 1NT** to show a **balanced** hand.
3. You may bid the **MICHAELS CUEBID** to show a specific **2-suited** hand.
4. You may bid the **UNUSUAL NOTRUMP** to show a specific **2-suited** hand.
5. Finally you may make a **TAKEOUT DOUBLE** to show a **3-suited** hand.

The two most common options for the overcalling side are the **overcall** and the **takeout double**.

Each of these bids has different requirements which will be defined in the following sections. We will also discuss how the opening side can effectively cope when you interfere in their nice comfortable auction. With everyone bidding the bridge game has now become even more challenging and exciting. Let's learn about these new bids!

THE OVERCALL

After the auction is opened, the other side may enter the auction by overcalling. If the opening bid is 1NT it is wise to be a bit cautious in entering the auction. For now, consider it safe to overcall when you have a 6-card suit and around 9-14 points. More advanced methods for competing after a 1NT opening are available but are beyond the scope of this book. The rest of this will apply to those hands where the opening bid is one of a suit.

You may overcall by bidding a new suit if your hand meets these two requirements:

- Your suit is at least five cards long
- You have 9-17 TP

If your suit can be bid at the 1-level you will need a really good suit and at least 9 TP or a good 11 points if your suit is not so good. To overcall at the 2-level you will need a really good suit and close to an opening hand. A good "rule" for a 2-level overcall is the "**rule of 8**": A 5-card suit with three honors (5+3 = 8) or a 6-card suit with two honors (6+2 = 8) plus around 11 TP.

You may also overcall 1NT which would show the same values and distribution (15-17 balanced points) as an opening bid of 1NT. To overcall 1NT you must meet one other requirement. A 1NT overcall promises a stopper in the suit bid by your RHO.

LET'S LOOK AT SOME EXAMPLES.
The opener has bid 1D

♠ A Q J 8 7 ♥ K 6 4 ♦ 9 6 ♣ 9 5 4

When your RHO opens 1D this hand is a near minimum for an overcall at the 1-level - bid 1S

♠ A Q J 8 7 ♥ K 6 4 ♦ 9 6 ♣ A Q 4

Again I'd overcall 1S with this hand even though it is much stronger than the previous hand

♠ A 8 7 ♥ 9 6 4 ♦ 9 6 ♣ A Q J 10 9 5

This hand has just enough suit length and points for a 2-level overcall - bid 2C

♠ K J 8 7 ♥ K 6 4 ♦ 9 6 ♣ A 10 9 5 4

This 11 HCP hand with a bad suit is not good enough for a 2-level overcall - pass!

♠ A Q 8 7 ♥ K 6 4 ♦ K Q 9 6 ♣ Q 10

With stoppers in diamonds and 16 HCP, this balanced hand should overcall 1NT

RESPONDER'S ACTIONS AFTER AN OVERCALL

When your RHO makes any overcall you are relieved of the responsibility of keeping the bidding open for your partner since she will have another opportunity to bid. Therefore any bid by you will show some solid values. Here are some of your options.

A simple (nonjump) raise of your partner's major suit shows 3-card or 4-card support and 6 to 10 points. A jump raise is exactly the same as it was without competition - WEAK - showing 4-card support and 4-6 points. The other Bergen raises (3C and 3D) and the 2NT bid to show an opening hand with 4-card support can no longer be used. However, you now have a new way to tell your partner that the hand belongs to your side and that you have a fit and at least a limit raise. You will accomplish this by bidding the same suit as the overcaller, a bid called a **CUEBID RAISE.** It is logical to assume that you would not want to play in a suit bid by the opponent so this "coded" conventional bid is your way of telling partner the good news about your fit.

EXAMPLES

After partner opens 1H and the next player bids 1S, what do you bid?

♠ 8 7   ♥ K 6 4 2   ♦ 9 6 4   ♣ Q 5 4 3

With this weak hand and 4-card support for hearts - bid 3H

♠ A 8 7   ♥ K 6 4   ♦ A 6   ♣ 9 8 7 5 4

You have 11 points and great support for your partner so tell him that by cuebidding 2S

♠ Q 8 7   ♥ K 8 6 4   ♦ A 9 6   ♣ 9 5 4

Even though you have 4 cards in support you do not have enough points to cuebid so just bid 2H for now. You will bid one more time if the opponents bid to a higher level.

A single or jump raise of partner's minor suit opening is exactly the same as if the overcall had not occurred. The **jump raise** is still a **limit raise** (11-12 points). The only change in your raise structure is that the **cuebid** of the opponent's suit replaces the **criss-cross raise** to show an **opening hand**.

EXAMPLES

Partner opened 1D and your RHO bid 1H. What do you bid?

♠ J 8 7   ♥ K 6 4   ♦ A J 9 6 4   ♣ 9 5

With a minimum hand and 5 cards in support of partner's diamonds you should raise to 2D

♠ A 7   ♥ A 6 4   ♦ Q J 8 7 6   ♣ 9 5 4

A clear limit raise of partner's diamonds - bid 3D

♠ A J 5   ♥ K 6   ♦ A Q 10 9 6   ♣ 9 5 4

Tell your partner that you have 5-card support and an opening hand by cuebidding - bid 2H

POINTS OF EMPHASIS	TAKE NOTE
The **cuebid** raise is used after an overcall to alert your partner about your fit and strength. After a major suit opening, the cuebid shows a limit raise or better. After a minor suit opening, the cuebid shows an opening hand with 5-card support.	After a minor suit opening some players like the cuebid of the overcaller's suit to show a limit raise rather than an opening hand. We believe the jump to show the limit raise is more effective in obstructing the opponents. When the cuebid shows an opening hand it is more helpful in our side finding the best contract.

Without support for your partner's opening bid suit your only choices are to pass, bid a new suit, or bid notrump. If you bid a new suit it promises five cards and if you must bid your suit at the 2-level the bid also tells your partner that you hold at least 10 points. This bid, a new suit at the 2-level after an overcall, is what we call "five and a dime" - five cards in the suit and 10+ points. Any new suit bid is 100% forcing meaning your partner must bid again and will try to further describe his hand pattern and strength. If you have eight or more points but do not hold a 5-card suit, **double** (see TAKE NOTE below) to ask your partner to name a new suit. Hopefully the new suit will be one which matches your 4-card suit.

POINTS OF EMPHASIS	TAKE NOTE
Bidding a new suit at the 2-level promises 5 cards in your suit and at least 10 points. With only 4-card suits a **double** by the responder asks the opener to name an unbid suit hopefully any unbid major.	When responder's double asks partner to bid a new suit it is called a **negative double**. Most players use this double through at least any overcall up to and including 3D.

If you do not have support or a new suit to bid you may bid notrump if you have a stopper in the opponent's suit.

With:	Bid:
• 6-10 points	1NT
• 11-12 points	2NT
• 13-15 points	3NT

After any notrump bid your partner will know a lot about your hand and should be able to bid to the correct contract. Slam is very unlikely on these auctions so finding a playable contract is your goal.

EXAMPLES
Partner opened 1D and RHO overcalled 1H.
What do you bid?

♠ A 8 7　　♥ K 6 4　　♦ J 9 6 4　　♣ Q 9 5
Bid 1NT with your 10 points and a stopper in hearts

♠ A Q J 7 4　　♥ 6 4　　♦ Q J 8 7　　♣ 5 4
Bid your 5-card spade suit at the 1-level - 1S

♠ A J 5　　♥ K 10 6 4　　♦ A 9 6　　♣ J 9 4
Bid 3NT - you have 13 points and heart stoppers

♠ K 8 7　　♥ 6 4　　♦ J 9 6　　♣ A 10 9 5 4 2
You'd like to bid 2C but do not have enough points to introduce a new suit at the 2-level - pass

♠ A J 5 3　　♥ K 6 3　　♦ 10 9　　♣ K 9 5 4
Double to tell your partner you have good points but no 5-card suits - this double (negative) asks partner to bid a new suit

If your RHO overcalls 1NT and you have 10 or more points just say double. This double is quite the opposite of the double discussed above. That double asked partner to bid a new suit, this double is for penalty meaning you are pretty sure your RHO can't make his contract. Add up the points: Partner's 13, overcaller's 16, plus your 10 = 39 leaving just 1 (or maybe 2 or 3) for the advancer. With good defense the overcaller will not make 1NT and you will score bonus points for doubling. Any other bid by you, including a simple raise, shows less than 10 points. If you bid a new suit it shows five cards and is not forcing, not even encouraging, it just says you want to play at the level and strain which you have just bid.

The bonus points for doubled contracts are quite profitable, especially if the opponents are vulnerable. The chart below shows the points for setting the opponents.

PENALTIES FOR BEING SET

Number Defeated	Not Vulnerable		Vulnerable	
	Not Doubled	Doubled	Not Doubled	Doubled
Down 1	50	100	100	200
Down 2	100	300	200	500
Down 3	150	500	300	800
Down 4	200	800	400	1100

BY THE WAY

A double (the red X in your bidding box) has two meanings.

Sometimes it is for takeout meaning the double asks your partner to bid something and other times it is for penalty meaning you think you can defeat your opponents' contract.

Generally doubles of notrump bids or game bids are penalty doubles – other doubles are for takeout unless both of you have previously bid, then doubles are for penalty as well.

ADVANCER'S ACTIONS AFTER AN OVERCALL

Finally it's your turn to bid! The opener has opened, your partner (the overcaller) has bid and the responder has also made a bid. You may pass when partner overcalls but with some points you may want to bid. Sometimes it's a little hard to believe that everyone had something to say and you have a pretty good hand of your own. It is the nature of competitive auctions that once momentum is started no one wants to give up and let the other side play the hand. So do not be intimidated and try to do your part to compete for the contract. So what are your options after partner overcalls by bidding a suit?

You can show support. Since your partner promises at least five cards in her suit you only need three to raise her suit. Partner may be a bit light but don't worry about that, just raise her suit one level with 6-10 points. With a better hand and support you can **cuebid** the opponent's suit to ask your partner "how good is your overcall"? If your partner repeats her suit it says "I'm a little light" and you would most likely pass. Anything else promises solid opening bid values and you will then raise her suit with 11 or 12 points and bid game with more.

With some points and no support for partner you can bid a new suit or notrump. A new suit by you when everyone is bidding shows around 10 points, a good 5-card suit of your own and tolerance (usually two cards) for partner's suit. This bid is not forcing but since you promise reasonable values the overcaller may bid again. If she returns to her suit it is to play and you will almost always pass. If she bids anything else, including raising your suit, she is showing a good hand and is trying to reach game. You may also compete by bidding notrump but your values will be a bit stronger since partner may be a bit lighter. Bid 1NT with 8-11 points and stoppers in the suits bid by your opponents. Bid 2NT with 12-13 and stoppers in their suits. If you are ever so lucky to have 14 or more points just bid 3NT.

Since everyone may be bidding on these auctions it is often hard to tell whose hand it really is or how high to bid. There is one very useful guide and one bit of advice. Larry Cohen, a well-known world-class bridge professional, has written extensively about the **"Law of Total Tricks"**. This "law" in its simplest form says that you should bid to the level equal to the number of total trumps held by your side. If you know that your side has nine trump cards it is generally safe to compete to the level where you must take nine tricks which would be a bid of three of your suit. With only eight trump cards don't bid past the 2-level (eight tricks). Now for the advice, pay close attention to your partner's bidding and always trust her to have what her bidding says she has. The opponents often are less than truthful about their strength either to try to fool you or because of poor basic bidding skills.

EXAMPLES

Bids displayed in parentheses are bids made by the opponents.
The auction has been:
(1H) - 1S by partner - (2H) - Your turn!

♠ Q 8 7　　♥ 5 4　　♦ K 9 6 4　　♣ Q 9 5 3

Show your support and limited values by bidding 2S

♠ 9 4　　♥ 6 4　　♦ A Q J 8 7　　♣ K 9 3 2

Bid 2D to show your suit and 10 points with tolerance for your partner's suit

♠ A J 5　　♥ 9 7 4　　♦ A K 9 6 3　　♣ J 9

With 13 points and support for your partner's suit, cuebid (3H) to ask partner "how good is your overcall"?

♠ Q 7　　♥ K J 8　　♦ J 10 9 6　　♣ K Q 8 4

Bid 2NT which should be a safe place to play

♠ K 9 7 5　　♥ 6 4　　♦ K 9 6 4　　♣ Q 9 5

With your limited values bid only 2S but since your side has a total of 9 trump cards be prepared to compete to the 3-level if the opponents bid 3H

If your partner has overcalled 1NT, he has shown the same 15-17 balanced points as an opening bid of 1NT. If the responder passes all your bids are the same as when 1NT is opened. Pass, raise notrump, or use Stayman and Jacoby transfers just as you learned in the previous chapter. If your RHO bids 2C just bid double to say "that's what I was going to bid if he had passed" so the double becomes the Stayman bid and all other bids remain the same. If your RHO makes any higher bid all your conventional bids are no longer in play. So how do you compete? With no 4-card major suit just raise notrump to the appropriate level. With only 4-card suits, just bid the appropriate number of notrump or double to ask partner to bid a suit hoping to find a match. With a 5-card major bid it at the 2-level with 5-8 HCP and jump to the 3-level with 9+ HCP. When you hold a 6-card major suit and less than 8 TP bid the suit at the 2-level and jump to the 4-level with more points.

POINTS OF EMPHASIS	TAKE NOTE
The "Law of Total Tricks" (LTT) is an effective way to determine how high to compete (# of trump cards = highest level). If an opponent bids 2C after a 1NT opening or 1NT overcall and the next player doubles it is what is called a "stolen bid" meaning it is Stayman.	After a 1NT overcall, some play that a new minor suit bid at the 3-level is invitational only and may be passed. Some also play that a cuebid of any 2-level bid other than 2C is Stayman. For now using the double to ask partner to bid a new 4-card major suit works just fine.

BY THE WAY

If you opened 1NT and the overcaller bids a suit then your partner, the responder, may compete in exactly the same way as the advancer does, as outlined above. A double of 2C is Stayman and responder is asking the opener if she has a 4 card major. If the overcall is higher than 2C and responder has only a 4-card major then a double is like Stayman and asks the opener to bid a 4-card major if she has one. With a 5-card suit of her own the responder can bid it at the 2-level or 3-level depending on her points. With a 6-card major suit and 7 or more points the responder bids it at the 4-level on her own.

THE TAKEOUT DOUBLE

The takeout double is one of the most frequently used bids in bridge and is a very effective way to enter the auction after it has been opened. There are again two requirements for making a takeout double:

- At least 3-card support for all the unbid suits
- An opening hand - 13 SP

You may occasionally have only two cards in support of an unbid minor suit but will always have at least three cards in any and all unbid major suits. In essence you are telling partner that you do not have a suit of your own but will be able to support any suit he may have. Also since you are asking partner to name the trump suit you will be the dummy so can add points for being short in the suit that was opened – and you will almost always have two or less cards in the opponent's suit.

EXAMPLES

Your RHO opens the bidding with 1S, what would be your bid in the overcaller's seat?

♠ 7   ♥ K Q 5 4   ♦ Q 10 6 4   ♣ A 10 7 3

Even with only 11 HCP (but 14 SP) this hand is perfect for a takeout double because of your singleton spade and 4-card support for all unbid suits

♠ 9 4   ♥ A J 9 6   ♦ K 9 8 7   ♣ K Q 2

This hand is less perfect but has at least 3-card support for all unbid suits and 14 SP. Double for takeout.

♠ 8 5   ♥ K Q 10   ♦ A J 9 6   ♣ K Q 8 7

With 16 SP this hand is OK for a takeout double even though you have only 3 hearts and would like to have 4 cards in the unbid major

♠ Q 7   ♥ K J 8   ♦ K 10 9 6   ♣ K 9 8 4

This hand with a wasted value in spades and only 12 HCP and only 3 hearts is just too weak for a takeout double - pass is best

♠ 9   ♥ A Q J 6 4   ♦ K 9 5 4   ♣ Q 9 5

With 5 hearts this hand is better suited for an overcall of 2H than a takeout double even though it meets the requirements for either bid.

RESPONDER'S ACTIONS AFTER A TAKEOUT DOUBLE

When the overcaller makes a takeout double it changes some of your normal responses while many remain unchanged. There are, however, two very significant changes: A new suit bid at the 2-level is no longer game forcing, in fact, it is not even forcing. Secondly, 1NT is no longer forcing after a major suit opening. One notrump after a takeout double now shows a bit better hand (8-9 points) than without competition and a real desire to play notrump.

The takeout double has added a new bidding tool to your bidding arsenal. You may **redouble!** The redouble card is the blue XX in your bidding box. This new bid is used to tell your partner you have at least 10 points and no convenient bid on this round. This redouble tells your partner your side has at least 23 points. With this much strength you will probably win the auction or be able to double the opponents and extract a big penalty if they are too frisky in the auction. Let's see what bids remain the same, what bids change, and when to use this new bidding tool - the redouble.

When the opening bid is a major and your RHO makes a takeout double and you have four cards in support of the opener's major suit show it with the appropriate Bergen raise or by bidding 2NT with 13+ support points. With only 3-card support, bid two of the major with 6-10 points and **redouble** with a stronger hand.

When the opening bid is a minor suit and you have support bid exactly the same as you would have bid without the takeout double: Simple raises, limit raises and criss-cross raises are all in play.

Without support for the opener's suit you can bid a new suit or notrump. A new suit at the 1-level is forcing as always. A new suit at the 2-level is not forcing and shows a long suit (six cards) and a desire to play it right there. One notrump after a takeout double is never forcing and shows about 7-9 HCP. With more HCP and a balanced hand redouble first planning to either double the opponents or bid two or three notrump later. If you have a strong hand with a long minor or are unsure about what to bid and have 10 or more points just redouble to tell partner the good news. Since your side has the majority of points and you both have bid you may get an opportunity to double the opponents for penalty.

EXAMPLES

The bidding has been 1S – (double) – what is your bid on the following hands?

♠ Q 8 7   ♥ A 5 4   ♦ K 9 6 4   ♣ Q 9 5 3

With only 3-card support for partner's suit and 11 HCP you should redouble

♠ K J 8 4   ♥ 6 4   ♦ Q J 9 7   ♣ K 9 2

With 4 cards in support of spades and 11 SP bid the Bergen raise of 3C

♠ 9 5   ♥ 9 7 4   ♦ A K J 9 6 3   ♣ J 9

With only 9 HCP but a great diamond suit bid 2D which is not game-forcing or even invitational. The bid tells partner that is the contract you would like to play.

♠ J 7   ♥ K J 8   ♦ J 10 9 6   ♣ K 9 8 4

Bid 1NT which is not forcing after a takeout double; the bid shows 7-9 points and a desire to play it right there unless partner has extras

♠ K 10 7 5   ♥ A 6 4   ♦ K Q J 4   ♣ 10 9

Bid 2NT to show your opening hand and 4-card support for your partner's spade suit

---

ADVANCER'S ACTIONS AFTER A TAKEOUT DOUBLE

After a takeout double your bids are quite simple since partner has announced adequate support (three cards) for any 4-card suit you may hold. So you are assured of an adequate fit if you have any suit which is at least four cards long. Now all you need to do is tell your partner about the fit and your strength. If you have more than one 4-card suit you should prefer a major suit over a minor suit. If your RHO passes you must bid even with zero points. If RHO bids you may pass but should consider bidding with a 5-card suit and four or more points or a 4-card suit and six or more points. If you bid your suit at the cheapest level it shows eight or less points. With 9-11 points, jump in your longest suit but prefer a 4-card major to a 5-card minor. With 12 or more points, jump to game in your major suit when you have a 4-card or longer suit.

If you hold four cards in both major suits and at least nine points it is generally best to ask your partner which of his major suits is four cards long thus making sure of finding your best fit. You can accomplish this by **cuebidding** a suit bid by an opponent. Remember we do not want to play in a suit bid by the opponents so this cuebid passes the buck back to your partner asking her to name your trump suit. If partner names a major suit at the cheapest level you will raise with 9-11 points and bid game in the major with 12 or more points.

Occasionally you will not have a 4-card suit to bid. In this case consider bidding notrump if you have a stopper in the suit bid by your opponents. One notrump will show 7-10 points and 2NT will show 11-12 points. Note that 1NT is a bit stronger than on other auctions. This is because your partner is usually very short in the opponent's suit so making notrump will be a bit more difficult. With a really bad hand (0-6) and only 3-card suits just bid your cheapest 3-card suit and hope and pray that partner passes.

EXAMPLES

The bidding has been (1D) – Double – (Pass) – your bid?

♠ Q 8 7 6   ♥ 5 4 3   ♦ 9 6 4   ♣ Q 9 5 3

You must bid so show your partner that you have less than 9 points by bidding 1S

♠ K Q 8 4 3   ♥ 6   ♦ J 8   ♣ A K 9 3 2

With a great 5-card suit and 15 TP bid the game you know you should be able to make - 4S

♠ A J 5 3   ♥ K J 9 4   ♦ 6 3 2   ♣ Q 9

With 11 points and two 4-card majors ask your partner which major to play by bidding 2D (a cuebid of the opponent's suit)

♠ Q 7 3   ♥ K J 8 5   ♦ 9 6   ♣ K J 8 4

Jump to 2H to show your 4-card suit and 10 points

♠ 10 9 8   ♥ Q 6 4   ♦ J 9 6 4   ♣ 10 9 5

What a horrible hand! Just bid 1H and hope partner passes; don't bid 1NT with such a bad hand

ADVANCER'S POINTS	ADVANCER'S SUIT LENGTH	ADVANCER'S BID
0-8 Pts	4-card or 5-card major or no major but four or more cards in a minor suit	Bid your suit at the cheapest level; always the major if at least four cards long
9-11 Pts	4-card or 5-card major or no major but four or more cards in a minor suit	Jump a level in your suit: majors first
9+ Pts	Four cards in both majors	**Cuebid** to let partner name her 4-card major
12+ Pts	4-card or 5-card major	Jump to game in your major suit
0-7 Pts	No 4-card suit	Your cheapest 3-card suit
8+ Pts	No 4-card suit	1, 2, or 3 notrump based on your points

THE TAKEOUT DOUBLER'S REBIDS

With a minimum hand (12-15 SP) for the takeout double you should pass any minimum bid by the advancer. With an invitational hand (16-18 SP), raise gently (one level) remembering that partner had to bid and may have zero points. Finally, caution is once again called for when you hold what would normally be seen as a game-going hand (19-21 SP). It is prudent to use a jump raise rather than a game bid to describe your hand and allow the advancer to get out of the auction short of a game when she is very weak (< 6 points).

When the advancer jumps a level to show 9-11 points, you should bid game with 15 or more support points and pass with less. If the advancer cuebids any suit bid by an opponent, show your only or best 4-card major at the cheapest level with 13 or 14 points and jump a level with 15 or more points. The jump bid promises enough values for game.

If the advancer bids some number of notrump, assume the minimum. Add your points to the values she has shown, and bid the notrump game if the total values add up to 25 or more points.

EXAMPLES

The bidding has been:

(1C) - X - (P) - 1H

(P) - ?

What is your rebid?

♠ Q J 8 7   ♥ A K 5 4   ♦ K 9 4   ♣ 9 4

You have a minimum takeout double so you should pass as partner has less than 9 points

♠ K Q 9 4   ♥ A J 6 4   ♦ A Q J 8   ♣ 9

You have 20 SP so you should jump to 3H to show your great hand. Partner needs very little to make game and should bid 4H with 5 or more points.

♠ A J 5   ♥ K 9 7 4   ♦ A K 9 3   ♣ J 9

A simple raise to 2H shows 16-18 SP so that would be your best bid on this hand

---

THE 2-SUITED OVERCALLS: THE MICHAELS CUEBID AND THE UNUSUAL 2NT

When the overcaller has two 5-card suits it is best to make a bid which shows both suits at once rather than overcalling one suit and hoping to get a chance to show the other suit later. There are two conventions which the overcaller may use to show her 2-suited hand: The **Michaels Cuebid** and the **Unusual 2NT**. The overcaller chooses the convention which specifically shows her two suits. Most players bid on 2-suited hands with seven or more HCP since partner is likely to match one of the suits shown by the overcall.

The Michaels cuebid shows both majors if a minor suit is opened. If a major suit is opened, the Michaels cuebid shows the other major and an unspecified minor. To summarize:

THE MICHAELS CUEBID

OPENING BID	OVERCALLER'S CUEBID	THE CUEBID SHOWS
1C	2C	Hearts and Spades
1D	2D	Hearts and Spades
1H	2H	Spades and a Minor
1S	2S	Hearts and a Minor

The Unusual 2NT bid also shows two specific suits: The two lowest unbid suits. Note that this bid is a jump to 2NT immediately after an opening bid by your RHO. To summarize:

THE UNUSUAL 2NT

OPENING BID	OVERCALLER'S JUMP TO 2NT	THE BID SHOWS
1C	2NT	Hearts & Diamonds
1D	2NT	Hearts & Clubs
1H	2NT	Clubs & Diamonds
1S	2NT	Clubs & Diamonds

EXAMPLES

On the following auctions the bidding has been opened with a bid of 1S, what would you bid to show your 2-suited hand?

♠ 5   ♥ Q 8 6 43   ♦ A 5   ♣ Q J 9 5 3

With 9 points and two 5-card suits, you have just enough to bid 2S (Michaels). This bid describes this minimum 2-suited hand with hearts and an unspecified minor.

♠ 3   ♥ K Q J 6 5   ♦ A 8   ♣ A K 9 3 2

With this great 2-suited hand, begin by bidding 2S (Michaels) to let partner know about your distribution. Later you will bid more to define the strength of your hand.

♠ 5   ♥ 9 3   ♦ A Q J 6 3   ♣ K Q 9 8 6

With 12 HCP and two 5-card minor suits, the unusual 2NT would describe this hand to a tee

♠ 7   ♥ K 5   ♦ K Q J 9 6   ♣ A K J 8 4

Jump to 2NT to show this 2-suited hand even though it is much stronger than the last hand

♠ 10 8   ♥ Q 6 4 3 2   ♦ K J 9 6 4   ♣ 5

While you have the required 2 suits for a Michaels cuebid your hand is just too weak - pass!

RESPONDER'S ACTION AFTER A 2-SUITED OVERCALL

When your RHO makes one of these 2-suited overcalls the auction is much more difficult than if the darn opponent would just be quiet but that's the whole idea! They have taken away many of your normal bids meaning it will often be impossible to accurately describe your hand. But let's try!

If you have support for your partner's suit be aggressive especially with four cards in support. Raising to the 3-level shows about 8-10 points. You will gamble a bit and bid game with 11 or more points.

With no support and holding five or more cards in a suit not specifically shown by the overcaller, consider bidding your suit. To bid you will need about 11 points or more because bidding a new suit at the 3-level is forcing. Another possibility is to consider doubling the opponents for penalty. If you have length in one of their known suits and about 10 points, double to alert your partner that a penalty double might be the best contract for your side. This double encourages your partner to double if his RHO bids a suit he likes. Otherwise he should pass the bid back to you for a possible penalty double.

These methods will work fairly well for now. You will not always get it right but that's the nature of the beast when it comes to competitive auctions. Remember also you can always pass and let the opponents try to find a safe and profitable place to play the contract.

EXAMPLES

The bidding has been 1H – (2NT Unusual) - Your bid?

♠ Q J 7 6   ♥ Q 4 3   ♦ 9 6 4   ♣ Q 9 5 3

Even though you have 3 hearts you are just a bit too weak to support hearts at the 3-level – pass

♠ K Q J 8 4 3   ♥ K 6   ♦ J 8   ♣ A 9 3

With a decent 6-card suit and 14 HCP you are good enough to force the bidding - bid 3S

♠ A J 5 3   ♥ K J 9 4   ♦ 6 3   ♣ Q 9

With 11 points and 4-card support for hearts go ahead and bid the game - it may not make but you are under the gun with no way to show some good values other than just bidding 4H

♠ K 7   ♥ 8 5   ♦ A J 9 4 2   ♣ K J 8 4

With nice values and great cards in both of the opponent's suits, bid double to let your partner know that a penalty double is probably the best contract for your side on this hand

---

ADVANCER'S ACTION AFTER A MICHAELS CUEBID OR AN UNUSUAL 2NT OVERCALL

The most important thing for the advancer to remember is that partner has promised two 5-card suits and really, really wants you to pick one of them. If you have less than a 3-card fit for both of partner's suits you will not like it but you must pick one of them provided your RHO passes. Assume your partner has the weakest hand possible (about 7-8 HCP) and bid accordingly. Partner will bid again if she has a really good hand. If you know what suit you want to play but are very weak or lack sufficient support just bid the suit at the lowest level. If you have a hand that wants to invite game in a known suit, jump a level (if possible) when you advance the bid. If after a

---

Michaels bid where the minor suit your partner holds is unknown and you want to play in the minor, you can ask partner to name the minor by bidding 2NT.

The most important thing for the overcaller to remember is that her partner was under duress and may have picked a suit he really was not happy to bid. Therefore, it is paramount that the overcaller does not bid again unless she has better than an opening hand, like 15 or more points. These bids are very powerful competitive tools but are often abused which in many cases have resulted in disastrous results. Have fun with the bids but don't keep bidding the same distribution and values when partner makes minimum bids. Also pay attention to the vulnerability and be less frisky when you are vulnerable and they are not.

EXAMPLES

Your LHO opened 1H and partner bid 2H (showing spades and a minor), your RHO passed and it is now your turn.

What is your bid?

(1H) - 2H - (P) - ?

♠ J 9 2   ♥ J 9 3   ♦ 8 2   ♣ K 7 5 4 2

Partner promised 5 spades so you have an 8-card fit but your hand is very weak so 2S it is

♠ K 10 8   ♥ 9 4   ♦ Q 9 5 3   ♣ A J 9 5

With your 10 HCP and fits with partner in spades and also in whichever minor suit he holds, invite partner to bid a game by jumping to 3S

♠ 8   ♥ K 8 5 3   ♦ J 9 6 4   ♣ K 8 3 2

With a weak hand and no fit for spades, bid 2NT to ask partner which minor suit he holds and pass his rebid

♠ K 9 6 4 2   ♥ 8 6   ♦ 7   ♣ A Q 9 6 4

Bid 4S, with lots of spades and likely shortness in partner's second suit it is very possible that you will make the game. If you can't make game, it will be quite difficult for the opponents to compete further.

♠ 7 2   ♥ K 9 7 6 5   ♦ 9 5 2   ♣ 8 6 4

Your worst nightmare - no fit and no points. Bid 2S and hope the opponents bid some more and that your partner does not bid again!

POINTS OF EMPHASIS	TAKE NOTE
If the responder passes after a 2-suited overcall by your partner, you must bid even with no fit and poor points. Bid 2NT after a Michaels overcall to ask partner which minor suit she holds.	Advanced players use the cuebid when advancing a 2-suited overcall. The cuebid shows a fit in partner's suit and at least invitational values.

Bridge Etiquette
Avoid "post-mortem" discussions at the table following the play of a hand or round of bridge at a duplicate game. Other players are in hearing range of your discussion about the contract and the result. It also delays progression of the game. Discuss hands with your partner after the game is over.

PLAY TIP: TAKING TRICKS IN THE RIGHT ORDER

Many factors affect your ability to make your contract. You must save enough trump cards in the dummy to ruff your losers. You will need to play the high card from the short side when cashing your tricks. You may need to set up a long suit to pitch a loser. Finally you will need an entry to your established suit. You also have to be careful about when you let the opponent's gain the lead. All this means you must make a good plan before you start playing the hand and you must attempt to take your tricks in the right order. Let's look at a hand with a few of these factors involved and see how to proceed.

The contract is 4H and the lead is the queen of diamonds.

As declarer you have a spade loser, a diamond loser, and the potential for two

DUMMY'S HAND
♠ K Q J
♥ 6 5 4 3 2
♦ K 7 4
♣ 6 3

DECLARER'S HAND
♠ 9 6
♥ A K J 9 8
♦ A 8 5
♣ K Q 8

club losers. The spade loser is unavoidable and you see that an extra winner will be available after the ace is driven out. If your timing is right you can pitch the diamond loser on that extra winner. Finally, you can use the king of clubs to drive out the ace, then cash the queen and ruff the last club. So what should be your order of play? It is important to win the first diamond in your hand so you have a quick entry to the dummy to use the long spade after the ace is played. You did notice that while dummy has lots of trump they are smaller than the trumps in your hand so there is no trump entry to the dummy. So you will win the opening lead in your hand and draw the outstanding trumps – no need to wait on that! Now it is critical that you work on spades next – not the clubs or the opponents can gain the lead and remove your diamond entry before you set up the spades. After they win the ace of spades they should lead another diamond (their best play). You win the second diamond trick in dummy and use the spades to pitch your losing diamond. Now it's time for the club play – a small card to the queen to force out the ace, win any return, cash the other high club and ruff your small club in the dummy. With this carefully timed play you made an overtrick just like the pros!

DEFENSIVE TIP: LEADING PARTNER'S SUIT

When you are the opening leader and partner has bid, lead his suit unless you have a very good reason not to or you want a new partner ☺. There are two good reasons why you may elect not to lead partner's suit. One is that you hold the ace and suspect that the declarer has the king. In this case you want to wait for partner to lead the suit in order to capture the king with your ace. The other reason is that you strongly believe you have a better lead such as a singleton or a strong honor card sequence. By leading your singleton you may be able to get a ruff when partner gets on lead.

If you decide to lead partner's suit which card do you lead? Lead top of any two touching honor cards and also top of any doubleton. With a singleton, you have no choice - lead it! With three or more cards headed by an honor lead small, except when your honor card is the ace, lead the ace. When you hold three small cards in partner's suit you should lead small if you have not supported (raised) the suit and the top card if you have supported his suit. The reasoning is that a raise always promises 3-card support so after a raise you want to let partner know if you hold an honor card or not. Without the raise leading a small card alerts your partner that you have some length in his suit with or without an honor card.

When on opening lead and partner has bid a suit then lead the underlined card with any of the following (or similar) holdings in partner's suit:

K 8 <u>4</u>   <u>Q</u> J 7   <u>J</u> 8   <u>A</u> 9 5   J 8 <u>5</u>   <u>9</u> 5

If you have the following (or similar) holding in partner's suit

9 5 3

then lead as follows:

You supported partner	You did NOT show support
Lead the <u>9</u>	Lead the <u>3</u>
You promised 3-card support so partner will not interpret this as high from a doubleton NOR is partner likely to think you hold an honor in the suit	Leading the 9 looks too much like you are leading from a doubleton and partner needs to get an idea of the suit's overall distribution

SUMMARY

➤ After an opening bid the other partnership may and often does enter the auction. The first person bidding for the competing side is called the **overcaller** and his partner is the **advancer**.

➤ The overcaller may enter the auction by:
- Overcalling = a single-suited hand
- Making a takeout double = a 3-suited hand
- Bidding Michaels or the Unusual 2NT = a 2-suited hand

➤ A suit overcall shows:
- At least a 5-card suit and
- 9-17 TP

➤ A notrump overcall shows:
- 15-17 HCP
- A stopper in the opener's suit

➤ After an overcall: 1NT forcing, 2/1, most Bergen raises, and criss-cross raises no longer apply. The responder may:
- Raise the opener's major suit by bidding at the 2-level with 6-9 SP, jump to the 3-level with 4 trump and 4-6 points, and cuebid the overcaller's suit with 10+ points and 3-card or 4-card support
- Jump in opener's minor suit to show a limit raise and cuebid to show an opening hand
- Bid a new suit with "5 and a dime" - 5 cards and 10 points
- Bid 1NT = 6-10 TP, 2NT = 11-12 TP, or 3NT = 13-15 TP

➤ After an overcall, the advancer may:
- Raise the overcaller's suit with 3-card support
- Bid a new 5-card or longer suit with 10+ TP
- Cuebid with a strong hand to ask the overcaller "How good is your overcall?"

➤ A takeout double promises 3-card support for all unbid suits and 13 SP

➤ After a takeout double responder's 2/1 and 1NT forcing bids no longer apply. However, all major and minor suit conventional raises still apply. The responder may also **redouble** to show 10+ points and await developments in the auction.

➤ If the responder does not bid over a takeout double, the advancer is obligated to bid even with zero points Advancer's bids are:
  • Bid your longest suit (prefer majors over minors) at the 2-level with 0-8 TP
  • Jump in your suit with 9-11 TP
  • Bid game in your suit with 12+ TP
  • May also cuebid with both majors and 9+ points

➤ When the advancer makes a minimum bid after a takeout double, the overcaller's rebids are:
  • Pass with 12-15 SP
  • Raise one level with 16-18 SP
  • Jump raise with 19 -21 SP

➤ The Michaels cuebid and unusual 2NT bids show two 5-card suits
  • The cuebid after a minor suit opening = both majors
  • The cuebid after a major suit opening = the other major + a minor
  • The unusual 2NT shows the two lowest unbid suits

➤ After a 2-suited overcall, the responder bids aggressively with support and may double to suggest playing for a penalty double

➤ When partner makes a 2-suited overcall, the advancer:
  • Picks one of the suits at the cheapest level even with poor support if the RHO passes
  • Jumps in a known suit to invite game
  • Bids 2NT after a Michaels cuebid if she wants to know what minor the overcaller holds

➤ It is important to make a plan so you play suits in the right order

➤ Lead partner's suit unless you have a compelling reason not to

A SHORT QUIZ

1. What is the bridge name for the partner of the overcaller?

2. How many points are needed for an overcall at the 1-level?

3. What does it mean when the overcaller bids "double"?

4. What does it mean when the responder bids the same suit as the overcaller after the bidding is opened with 1H?

5. What does it mean when the advancer bids the same suit as the opener?

EXERCISE 1
WHAT DO YOU BID ON THE FOLLOWING HANDS WHEN YOUR RHO OPENS AS INDICATED?

Your hand	Your points?	Opening bid	Your bid?
♠AQJ97　♥98　♦K85　♣J96		1H	
♠A97　♥98　♦K85　♣QJ965		1H	
♠AQJ7　♥9　♦J853　♣AJ96		1H	
♠AQJ97　♥98　♦K9532　♣J		1H	
♠97　♥9　♦KQ853　♣AJ965		1H	
♠AJ97　♥K98　♦K852　♣A6		1C	
♠A97　♥KJ98　♦K8　♣AJ96		1C	
♠QJ752　♥QJ985　♦K8　♣6		1C	
♠97　♥K6532　♦AK852　♣J		1C	
♠AQ7　♥J98　♦KQJ85　♣96		1S	

EXERCISE 2
WHAT IS YOUR BID ON THE FOLLOWING HANDS?

Your hand	Opener's bid	Partner's bid	RHO's bid	Your bid?
♠K96 ♥98 ♦QJ965 ♣965	1H	1S	P	
♠K96 ♥A8 ♦KQ965 ♣965	1H	1S	P	
♠K6 ♥9 ♦QJ965 ♣KJ965	1H	2H	P	
♠62 ♥K98 ♦QJ965 ♣965	1H	2NT	P	
♠K96 ♥QJ8 ♦QJ965 ♣96	1C	2C	P	
♠K9652 ♥K98 ♦97 ♣965	1C	1NT	P	
♠KQ96 ♥JT98 ♦KQ53 ♣5	1C	Double	P	
♠A4 ♥KJ9852 ♦QJ65 ♣9	1C	2NT	P	
♠96 ♥KJ983 ♦Q3 ♣K965	1S	Double	2S	
♠A4 ♥98 ♦QJ965 ♣K965	1S	2C	P	

ANSWERS TO A SHORT QUIZ

1. Advancer

2. 9-17 TP

3. It is for takeout showing at least three cards in all the unbid suits and 13+ SP

4. It is a cuebid showing support for the opener's major suit and at least 10 points

5. It is a cuebid asking partner (the overcaller) "how good is your overcall?"

ANSWERS TO EXERCISE 1
WHAT DO YOU BID ON THE FOLLOWING HANDS
WHEN YOUR RHO OPENS AS INDICATED?

Your hand	Your points?	Opening bid	Your bid?
♠AQJ97 ♥98 ♦K85 ♣J96 A nice overcall	12 TP	1H	1S
♠A97 ♥98 ♦K85 ♣QJ965 Too weak for an overcall at the 2-level	11 TP	1H	Pass
♠AQJ7 ♥9 ♦J853 ♣AJ96 Takeout double asking partner to bid any other suit	16 SP	1H	Double
♠AQJ97 ♥98 ♦K9532 ♣J Michaels cuebid showing spades and a minor suit	13 TP	1H	2H
♠97 ♥9 ♦KQ853 ♣AJ965 Unusual 2NT showing the two lowest unbid suits	12 TP	1H	2NT
♠AJ97 ♥K98 ♦K852 ♣A6 Takeout – 3-card support for any other suit	16 SP	1C	Double
♠A97 ♥KJ98 ♦K8 ♣AJ96 A normal 1NT overcall (15-17 HCP - balanced)	16 TP	1C	1NT
♠QJ752 ♥QJ985 ♦K8 ♣6 Michaels showing both majors - 7+ points	11 TP	1C	2C
♠97 ♥K6532 ♦AK852 ♣J Unusual 2NT to show two lowest unbid suits	13 TP	1C	2NT
♠AQ7 ♥J98 ♦KQJ85 ♣96 Enough on this hand for the 2-level overcall	14 TP	1S	2D

ANSWERS TO EXERCISE 2
WHAT IS YOUR BID ON THE FOLLOWING HANDS?

Your hand	Opener's bid	Partner's bid	RHO's bid	Your bid?
♠K96 ♥98 ♦QJ965 ♣965 You have a simple raise	1H	1S	P	2S
♠K96 ♥A8 ♦KQ965 ♣965 Cuebid to ask how good partner's overcall was	1H	1S	P	2H
♠K6 ♥9 ♦QJ965 ♣KJ965 2NT to ask which minor partner has	1H	2H	P	2NT
♠62 ♥K98 ♦QJ965 ♣965 Partner has diamonds and clubs - bid the fit	1H	2NT	P	3D
♠K96 ♥QJ8 ♦QJ965 ♣96 Partner has both majors so pick one - either OK	1C	2C	P	2H
♠K9652 ♥K98 ♦97 ♣965 Bid 2H to transfer to 2S	1C	1NT	P	2H
♠KQ96 ♥JT98 ♦KQ53 ♣5 Cuebid to ask partner to name his 4-card major	1C	Double	P	2C
♠A4 ♥KJ9852 ♦QJ65 ♣9 Partner has hearts and diamonds – you fit both so bid game	1C	2NT	P	4H
♠96 ♥KJ983 ♦Q3 ♣K965 Partner asked you to bid so compete in hearts	1S	Double	2S	3H
♠A4 ♥98 ♦QJ965 ♣K965 Just a simple raise	1S	2C	P	3C

HAND #1	
VULNERABLE:	None
DECLARER:	South
CONTRACT:	2S
OPENING LEAD:Q♥	

North
♠ K 6 5
♥ J T 8 3
♦ A T 7
♣ A J 2

NORTH
13HCP+0DP=13TP

EAST
12HCP+1LP=13TP
Opens 1H

West
♠ Q 8 4
♥ Q 4
♦ J 8 6 2
♣ 9 8 6 3

East
♠ 9 2
♥ A K 7 5 2
♦ K Q 4
♣ T 7 5

THE BIDDING			
EAST	SOUTH	WEST	NORTH
1H	1S	P	2H
P	2S	P	P
P			

South
♠ A J T 7 3
♥ 9 6
♦ 9 5 3
♣ K Q 4

SOUTH
10HCP+ 1LP=11TP
Overcalls 1S

The BIDDING: After East opens 1H, South, with a nice spade suit and 10 HCP, overcalls 1S. North holding 13 points cuebids 2H to ask South "how good is your overcall"? South answers by rebidding his suit to show less than the 13 points. Armed with this information North passes the 2S bid which is a very good decision since 4S does not make. Three notrump can be made on this hand but with only 23 points between the two hands it is a bit hard to get to that contract.

The LEAD: The QUEEN OF HEARTS (top of a doubleton in partner's bid suit)

The PLAY: South has two heart losers and two diamond losers plus the potential for a spade loser. With the jack and 10 in his hand the declarer could finesse either player for the queen of spades. It is certainly reasonable to play the opening bidder for the queen by playing low to the king of spades and then lead a small spade and if East plays low put in the 10. This play loses to the queen but you still make your contract. If you had elected to finesse by playing the jack and letting it ride thereby finessing West for the queen you would have made an overtrick.

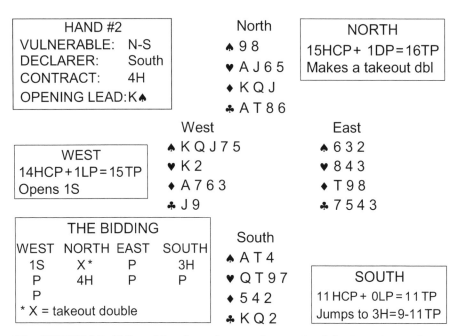

HAND #2	
VULNERABLE:	N-S
DECLARER:	South
CONTRACT:	4H
OPENING LEAD:	K♠

North
♠ 9 8
♥ A J 6 5
♦ K Q J
♣ A T 8 6

NORTH
15HCP+ 1DP=16TP
Makes a takeout dbl

WEST	
14HCP+1LP=15TP	
Opens 1S	

West
♠ K Q J 7 5
♥ K 2
♦ A 7 6 3
♣ J 9

East
♠ 6 3 2
♥ 8 4 3
♦ T 9 8
♣ 7 5 4 3

THE BIDDING			
WEST	NORTH	EAST	SOUTH
1S	X*	P	3H
P	4H	P	P
P			
* X = takeout double			

South
♠ A T 4
♥ Q T 9 7
♦ 5 4 2
♣ K Q 2

SOUTH
11 HCP + 0LP = 11 TP
Jumps to 3H=9-11TP

The BIDDING: When North makes a takeout double showing at least 3-card support for all unbid suits, South jumps in his best suit to show 9-11 points. North understanding what the jump bid promises knows that his 16 points are more than enough to bid the heart game.

The LEAD: The KING OF SPADES (top of a solid sequence)

The PLAY: South wins the opening lead in his hand with the spade ace. Next South takes a successful finesse for the heart king. After drawing all the remaining trumps, South drives out the ace of diamonds. The defense can now cash a spade but that is the last trick for the defense as the declarer can ruff the next spade and play the good clubs. The declarer cashes the clubs by playing the high cards (the king and queen) from the short side first, noting the fall of the jack, and then a small club to the ace and then cashes the good 10 of clubs. Making five hearts which is exactly what the top players in the world would make.

CHAPTER 9
STRONG OPENING BIDS

In this chapter you will learn:

- About the requirements for strength-showing opening bids of 2C, 2NT and 3NT
- How to respond to strong opening bids
- How opener rebids to describe her strong hand after an opening bid of 2C
- About the keycard-asking bid called 1430

MORE ABOUT BIG HAND BIDDING

All unbalanced hands with 22+ TP (or 9 playing tricks) will be opened with a bid of 2C. Some hands that are balanced with lots of HCP will also be opened with a bid of 2C and then rebid with some number of notrump. Other balanced big hands are opened with either 2NT or 3NT.

Big hands immediately grab your partner's attention because you announce one with an opening bid of 2C, 2NT or 3NT. These are the hands bridge players describe as beautiful, gorgeous or as rock crushers. The opener has or almost has enough strength in her hand alone for game. Not only are they pretty with lots of colorful face cards (honors) but with potential to reach slam and a big score for you and your partner. After a 2C opening bid the responder will most of the time bid 2D (called a waiting bid) to allow the opener to describe what kind of hand she holds. If her hand is unbalanced she will next show what long strong suit she holds. If she is balanced she will rebid some number of notrump to show how many HCP she holds.

THE BIG NOTRUMP BIDS

As we learned in Chapter 2 a balanced hand with 20-21 HCP should be opened with a bid of 2NT. Bigger balanced hands are opened with either 2C or 3NT. With a balanced hand and 25-26 HCP, your opening bid will be 3NT. All other big balanced hands are started with an opening bid of 2C. Open 2C and rebid 2NT with 22-24 HCP and to further delineate your point count when you have a really huge hand with 27+ HCP (fairy tales sometimes do come true) open 2C and rebid 3NT.

EXAMPLES

What do you open with the following hands?

♠ K Q 4   ♥ A J 8   ♦ K Q 8   ♣ A Q 10 7   21 HCP

Open this pretty hand 2NT - with just a little help from partner game is likely

♠ A K 7   ♥ A J 8   ♦ A Q 5   ♣ A K 6 2   25 HCP

Open this prettier one 3 NT - with a favorable lead, a bit of luck regarding card placement, and a few points from partner everything's rosy

♠ A Q 7   ♥ K Q 4 2   ♦ A J 10 4   ♣ A K   23 HCP

Open this lovely hand 2C planning to rebid 2NT to show your balanced hand with 23 HCP

♠ A K 7   ♥ A Q 4 2   ♦ A Q J 10   ♣ A K   27 HCP

With 4 more points open 2C and jump to 3NT on your rebid to show this whopper

POINTS OF EMPHASIS	TAKE NOTE
With a balanced hand and: 20-21 HCP - open 2NT 22-24 HCP - open 2C & rebid 2NT 25-26 HCP - open 3NT 27-28 HCP - open 2C & rebid 3NT	Some more experienced players use the 3NT opening bid for some other purpose like "gambling" with a long solid minor suit.

RESPONDING WITH A BALANCED HAND: NO 4-CARD OR 5-CARD MAJOR

When your hand is balanced with sufficient points and no 4-card or 5-card major you should respond in notrump. Your HCP will determine the level of your bid. Since the opener needs more points to open notrump higher than the 1-level, it follows that responder needs fewer points to respond. If the opener's initial bid is 2NT or a rebid of 2NT after a 2C opening you may pass. You should, however, bid when your points added to the opener's are sufficient for at least game (five after 2NT and three after a 2NT rebid). Since a 3NT opening is game you should pass unless you have seven or more points and visions of slam. The following chart shows appropriate responses to big notrump opening bids.

RESPONDER'S BIDS IF BALANCED
Notes: 4NT invites 6NT - 5NT requires 6NT and invites 7NT

Opening Bid → Responder's Points ↓	2NT 20-21 HCP	2C then 2NT 22-24 HCP	3NT 25-26 HCP	2C then 3NT 27-28 HCP
0-3	Pass	3NT	Pass	Pass
4-6	3NT	3NT	Pass	Pass
7-8	3NT	3NT	4NT	6NT
9-10	3NT	4NT	6NT	7NT
11-12	4NT	6NT	7NT	7NT
13-14	6NT	5NT	7NT	7NT
15	5NT	7NT	7NT	Can't have
16	7NT	7NT	Can't have	Can't have

EXAMPLES
Partner has opened 2NT, what do you bid?

♠ Q 4 3   ♥ A J 8   ♦ K 9 8   ♣ 10 7 6 3   10 HCP

Partner has promised 20-21 points so your partnership has enough values for game but not slam - bid 3NT

♠ 9 7 3   ♥ K J 8   ♦ 10 9 6 5   ♣ T 6 2   5 HCP

You have just barely enough for game - bid 3NT

♠ Q 7 4   ♥ K Q 4   ♦ Q J 10 4   ♣ K 7 4   13 HCP

Your points + what partner has shown = slam - bid 6NT

♠ Q 9 7   ♥ 9 4 2   ♦ 10 8 6 3   ♣ 9 6 3   2 HCP

With this hopeless hand, just pass 2NT and hope partner can make it

---

LOOKING FOR A 4-4 MAJOR-SUIT FIT: THE STAYMAN CONVENTION

As with a 1NT opening bid, if the responder has a 4-card major, she will use the Stayman convention (3C after a 2NT bid or rebid and 4C after a 3NT opening or rebid) to try for a 4-4 major suit fit with partner. When partner has opened 2NT, as few as 4 TP will be enough for game. If partner bids the major suit you hold bid the major suit game and if partner bids the wrong major return to notrump at the appropriate level. If partner has opened 3NT she has game in her own hand. While you would need zero points to play in four of a major if a fit is found remember that you will need to return to notrump at the 4-level if there is no fit. For this reason, it is often prudent to just pass 3NT even with a 4-card major and use Stayman only if you have three or more points.

If your Stayman inquiry uncovers a major-suit fit and your points added to what partner has shown with her notrump bid equal the values needed for slam, just bid six of the major. You could also invite slam by bidding five of the agreed major suit if you need partner to have the top of her bid. If the opener answers your Stayman request by bidding the wrong major or by bidding diamonds to deny a 4-card major, you will return to notrump at the appropriate level as defined in the chart on page 201.

EXAMPLES

Partner opened 2C, you responded 2D, and the opener rebids 2NT
What do you bid now?

♠ K Q 4 2   ♥ A 8 7 5   ♦ Q J 8 7   ♣ 2   12 HCP
With two 4-card majors and enough points for slam, bid 3C (Stayman) and if partner names a major, bid 6 of that suit and if partner bids 3D, bid 6NT in spite of your singleton

♠ A 9 7 6   ♥ J 8 7   ♦ Q 7 6 5   ♣ 9 2   7 HCP
Bid Stayman and raise a spade response to game - bid 3NT if partner bids 3D

♠ 10 7 5 2   ♥ 9 4 2   ♦ 10 9 6 4   ♣ J 9   1 HCP
Even though you have a 4-card major you are not strong enough for a Stayman bid - pass 2NT

♠ 10 8 7 4   ♥ Q 8 4   ♦ A 4 3 2   ♣ 9 7   6 HCP
Start with Stayman by bidding 3C - If the opener's answer is 3D or 3H you will bid 3NT. Your hand is not strong enough to think beyond game because your combined total points are no more than 30 and both hands are balanced. If partner responds to your major suit query by bidding spades, bid the spade game.

FINDING 5-3 AND 6-2 MAJOR-SUIT FITS: THE JACOBY AND TEXAS TRANSFER CONVENTIONS

The **Jacoby** and **Texas** transfer conventions are used following a big notrump opening or rebid. If you (the responder) have a 5-card or 6-card major, you use one of these conventions. After a 2NT opening or a 2NT rebid by the opener, you will bid 3D to transfer to hearts and 3H to transfer to 3S. After you partner completes the transfer you should pass with too few points for game. With more points and just a 5-card major, transfer and then bid the appropriate level of NT. Remember 5NT is "pick a slam" either 6NT or six of the major. With a 6-card major and sufficient values for game (5 TP after 2NT and 3

TP after 2C followed by a 2NT rebid), use the Texas transfer where 4D transfers to 4H and 4H transfer to 4S and then pass. After using the Texas transfer at the 4-level, bid five of your suit if you have the values to invite slam. With slam values bid six of your suit or bid 4NT to ask for keycards (see the next section).

If the opening bid is 3NT or 2C followed by 3NT, all transfers will be at the 4-level (4D → 4H and 4H → 4S). Remember you already know that your partnership has the values for at least game. With a 6-card major suit and zero points it is OK to transfer at the 4-level and pass because you know you have an 8-card fit. Be a bit careful about transferring to a major suit with only five cards and no points because if you pass you may be playing in a 5-2 fit and if you bid 4NT next you may get the partnership too high.

POINTS OF EMPHASIS	TAKE NOTE

Stayman and transfers can and should be used after 2NT and may be used after 3NT bids by the opener.
 	
    When the opener has more points, the responder needs fewer points for game and slam bids.
    2NT and 3NT bids may be passed.
	Some players use an ace asking bid called **Gerber** before bidding slams. After a 1NT or 2NT bid, a direct **jump** to 4C is Gerber.
	
	    The opener shows her ACES by bidding:
	    4D = 0 or 4 4H = 1
	    4S = 2 4NT = 3

EXAMPLES
Partner has opened 2NT, what is your bid?

♠ 10 8 7 4 2   ♥ 8 6   ♦ 4 3 2   ♣ 9 7 2   0 HCP

A very disappointing hand opposite your partner's 2NT opener! It happens so try to make the glass half full by using the transfer bid of 3H to get to spades. Now you will pass and hope that 3S plays better than 2NT.

♠ K Q 4 3 2   ♥ J 8   ♦ Q 9 8   ♣ 10 9 7   8 HCP
With a 5-card major transfer to spades by bidding 3H and then bid 3NT to show game values and less than enough points for a slam - partner will choose to pass 3NT with only two spades and will bid 4S with three or more cards in spades

♠ 7 6   ♥ A J 8 7 5 2   ♦ Q 7   ♣ J 6 2   8 HCP
Transfer to hearts by using the Texas transfer and then pass as your hand is just a bit light for slam

♠ 9 7 6 5 3 2   ♥ 4 2   ♦ 10 4 2   ♣ 8 4 2   0 HCP
A 6-card suit but no points - transfer at the 3-level by bidding 3H and pass partner's 3S bid

THE STRONG 2C OPENING BID
WITH UNBALANCED HANDS

All unbalanced, strong hands are opened 2C. This is the strongest opening bid in bridge. To open 2C you should have 22+ TP or nine playing tricks; a strong 5-card or longer suit, or two 5-card or 6-card suits; at least four **quick tricks**; and no more than four total **losers**. Your 2C bid is conventional saying nothing about clubs but saying you have a big hand and that you will describe your hand further on your next bid. A 2C bid is absolutely forcing and partner may not pass. In fact, a 2C opening bid is forcing to at least game unless responder makes a "second negative" bid which is described below.

EXAMPLES
What do you open with the following hands?

♠ A 7   ♥ A K Q 5 4 2   ♦ A Q 10   ♣ A 9
Your hand has 23 HCP and two LP for the 6 hearts. You have 5 ½ QT, 3 losers (missing the K of spades, K of diamonds, and the K of clubs), and a strong 6-card heart suit. Open 2C planning to rebid 2H.

♠ –   ♥ A K Q J 8   ♦ A K Q 10 4 2   ♣ K 3

With 22 HCP, 3 LP, 4 ½ QT, and 1 loser open 2C. Your first rebid will be in diamonds because it is longer than your heart suit. This hand is obviously a powerful playing hand with 11 ½ playing tricks.

♠ A 6   ♥ A K Q 10 8 7 6   ♦ Q 3   ♣ A 5

Despite having only 19 HCP and 3 LP, you do have 4 QT and only 4 losers - open this hand 2C

RESPONDING TO A 2C OPENING BID

When your partner opens 2C, you may not pass. It is a forcing bid. If you have at least a 5-card suit that contains two of the top three honors (A, K, or Q) and at least 8 HCP, bid it. Bid your suit at the 2-level if it is a major and at the 3-level if it is a minor suit. This bid is called a positive bid because it shows the values just described. Lacking any one of these three requirements, your bid will be 2D. Your two diamond bid is called a **waiting bid** because you are waiting to hear what type of big hand your partner has: a big balanced hand or a hand with a long strong suit. This 2D bid may be made with a totally broke hand or one which has some very nice values but does not have the right kind of suit for a positive response.

EXAMPLES

On the following hands, what is your response to partner's 2C opening bid?

♠ 8 6 7   ♥ A K 8 4 2   ♦ Q 4   ♣ 7 5 3

Bid 2H - you have the values for a positive first response - 9 HCP and 2 of the top 3 honors in your 5-card heart suit

♠ 8 6 7   ♥ A 9 8 4 2   ♦ Q 4   ♣ K 7 2

Bid 2D waiting - your HCP are adequate but your suit is not strong enough for a 2H bid. Do not attempt to show your points by bidding 2NT. Your partner's next bid might be in notrump and you want the strong hand concealed should the final contract be in notrump.

♠ 8 6 7   ♥ A 9 8 4 2   ♦ 7 4   ♣ Q 7 2

Neither your HCP nor your strength is adequate for a 2H bid - your correct bid is 2D

♠ 8 6 7   ♥ 10 9 8 4 2   ♦ 7 4   ♣ 8 7 2

As much as you might like to, you cannot pass - the 2C opening bid is forcing - bid 2D!

You owe partner at least 2 bids after a 2C opening

OPENER'S SUIT REBIDS FOLLOWING A 2C OPENER

If the responder's bid is 2D you will bid to describe your hand. We have already addressed the rebids of 2NT and 3NT so this section will be all about suit rebids. Bid your longest (5+) suit. If you have two suits of equal length, bid the higher-ranking one first.

EXAMPLES
2C – 2D
?

♠ A Q J 8 5   ♥ A K Q J 10   ♦ 6 4   ♣ A

After a 2C opening bid and a 2D waiting bid, you will bid 2S at your next turn to show your higher-ranking long suit

♠ A 8   ♥ A K Q J 10 9   ♦ K Q 6 4   ♣ A

Open 2C and rebid 2H at your next turn to show your fantastic suit

RESPONDER'S REBID FOLLOWING
A BIG SUIT REBID BY THE OPENER

If the opener bids a suit for which you have three or more cards in support, jump to game in the opener's suit when you hold no ace or king, and no singleton or void. This is another example of the **principle of fast arrival**. It shows no values to proceed toward a slam. Raise opener's suit one level with support (three or more cards) to show a hand which is better than an immediate jump to game. This single level raise shows at least an ace or a king or shortness in a side suit; all features which might be useful in reaching a slam.

If partner bids a suit for which you have no support but you have a 5-card suit which did not meet the requirement for a positive response, bid the suit now. Partner will know its relative strength because of your initial 2D waiting bid.

If your hand is worthless, no support and no points, bid the cheaper minor suit (usually 3C) which describes your hand as hopeless and indicates to partner that this is likely your last bid. You are warning partner not to count on anything of value from you and that even game is in doubt if his hand is minimal for the 2C opening. This bid commonly is called a "**second negative**". Once you make this negative bid you are not required to bid again unless your partner next bids a new suit.

Strong opening bids almost always reach game contracts and often are the gateway to a slam.

BY THE WAY
There is only one rebid after a 2C opening that responder may pass before making the obligatory second bid. That bid is 2NT. All other rebids by the opener after a 2C opening require the responder to bid at least twice.

EXAMPLES

Partner opens 2C, you responded 2D waiting, and partner rebid 2H. What is your rebid?

$$2C - 2D$$
$$2H - \ ?$$

♠ A Q   ♥ 8 7 3   ♦ 10 8 4 2   ♣ J 8 4 3

Your correct bid is 3H which tells partner you have support for hearts and at least an A or a K or shortness in a suit if she wishes to explore for slam

♠ Q 8   ♥ 8 7 4 3   ♦ 10 8 3   ♣ 8 7 4 3

Jump raise to 4H to tell partner you have heart support and not much else

♠ Q 8 4   ♥ 8 7   ♦ 10 8 4 3   ♣ 8 7 4 3

Bid 3C which is now a second negative bid (cheaper minor) which tells partner you are broke

♠ A Q 8 5 4   ♥ 8   ♦ 8 4 3   ♣ 8 7 4 3

Bid 2S which denies heart support, promises at least 5 spades and indicates either your strength in spades or HCP were inadequate for a positive response on your first bid

---

SLAM BIDDING

This is part of the fun stuff that keeps us coming back to the bridge table and going to the experts' books to learn how to bid slams we missed and how to play those successfully that we messed up.

How do we know when our hands fall in the slam-producing realm? In previous chapters we have talked about bids that are slam-invitational, e.g., a 4NT response to a 1NT opening bid which tells partner that you have enough points for slam if she is at the top of her bid. Recall that 33 points is the number usually cited for a small slam and 37 points are needed for a grand slam. When both hands are balanced and the HCP for the two hands total these numbers or are close, such as when both hands have game-forcing values with a little extra, you should definitely be thinking slam. Slams can be made with fewer points when the partnership has a good fit or fits in more than one suit. With highly distributional hands, e.g., 6-5-0-2, slams can be made with many fewer points. Since you will need to take 12 tricks in a slam contract, you have to avoid bidding a slam when you have two quick losers. There are conventional bids to use that can help you avoid bidding all the way to six when you have two quick losers. Two quick losers may occur if we are missing two aces or one ace and the king of trump. For this reason the four aces and the king of the trump suit are called "**keycards**" and we avoid slams when we are missing two of these five cards. We will soon learn how to ask partner how many of these keycards he holds.

NOTRUMP SLAM BIDDING

Notrump slams are usually bid and made when the two hands are powerful and balanced. A strong 5-card suit (or longer) contributes

---

to the success of a notrump slam when both hands are relatively balanced. Notrump slams as we have seen are bid quite successfully by simply adding your HCP to the HCP shown by your partner's notrump bid. Even when a major-suit fit is found after a Stayman inquiry slams may be bid by simply totaling up the points. Remember bidding one above game either in notrump or a major suit (after a fit is found) is an invitation to slam. Partner is asked to bid the slam if she has the top values for her notrump bid. So in notrump bidding we will not use any fancy conventions to check for keycards except when we have a distributional hand with a long major suit and have first bid the Texas transfer. We never need an ace or keycard asking bid if we use the Jacoby transfer bid to show a 5-card suit because our next bid will be in notrump and will describe our points. Just remember that directly asking for aces (keycards) is history if you transfer at the 3-level.

POINTS OF EMPHASIS	ANOTHER POINT OF EMPHASIS
There is no ace-asking bid after a 3-level transfer! Bidding one above game in NT or a suit where a fit exists is an invitation to slam.	The **Texas transfer** always shows at least a 6-card suit and is used when you just want to play game or when you want to ask for **keycards** which are the four aces and the king of trump.

Inviting slam after strong notrump bids

#1

Opener's hand ♠ A J 7 6 ♥ K Q 2 ♦ A K 2 ♣ K J 7	Responder's hand ♠ K 8 5 4 ♥ A 9 6 3 ♦ 7 4 2 ♣ A 8
2NT	3C
3S	5S
6S	Pass
2NT = strong & balanced 3S = my 4-card major 6S = I am at the top so I accept the invite	3C = Stayman 5S = invites slam in spades Pass – great

#2

Opener's hand ♠ A K 7 3 ♥ A Q 2 ♦ A Q 4 ♣ K Q 9	Responder's hand ♠ Q 5 4 ♥ K 7 6 3 ♦ 7 4 ♣ A J 6 2
2C	2D
2NT	3C
3S	4NT
6NT	Pass
2C = big opening 2NT = I'm balanced 3S = my 4-card major 6NT = I'm at the top!	2D = waiting 3C = Stayman 4NT = no major-suit match – inviting slam in notrump Pass – I'm happy!

SUIT SLAM BIDDING: THE ROMAN KEY CARD BLACKWOOD-ASKING BID "1430"

The **1430** keycard-asking bid is a spinoff of the earliest asking bid called **Blackwood** which asked partner how many aces she held. This was followed by an improved asking bid called Keycard Blackwood which included the king of the trump suit in the answer. Later Keycard Blackwood became Roman Keycard Blackwood because of variation in the way the asking bid was answered. Finally, along came the variation we will learn which is called **1430**. The 1430 inquiry asks partner how many of the five keycards (the four aces and the king of trump) he holds. After the partnership determines that they have the combined values to be in the slam range a successful slam in a suit contract will require a strong combined trump holding and at least four of the five keycards. Hands that often produce slams include those with a fit after a 2C opening, those with suit agreement after a 2/1 response, and those where the responder bids 2NT to show 4-card support and an opening hand in support of a major suit opening. Occasionally a suit slam is possible without a fit when the responder has a hand with a long strong suit opposite an opening bid.

With an agreed upon suit, the person with the stronger hand usually should be the originator of the query about keycards. She should have first or second round control of all the suits. An ace or a void is a first round control, a supported King (K x) or a singleton is a second round control. She should have no suit with two or more small cards (no control), and should not have a void. The query begins with a 4NT bid which actually asks, "How many of the five keycards do you have?" The responses are:

5C	1 or 4 Keycards
5D	0 or 3 Keycards
5H	2 Keycards without the Queen of trump
5S	2 Keycards with the Queen of trump

Notice that when you hold two keycards you also get to talk about the queen of the trump suit. Wow! Is that some kind of information gained from a simple query? Often the final contact is placed from this response. If all keycards are held, however, a grand slam try can be made by asking about kings. A 5NT bid asks about kings. The trump king is excluded from the answer because it was included in the original keycard request. A return to the trump suit denies holding any side suit king. Identify your lowest-ranking king by bidding six of that suit. If the bid which would identify your king would take you past your trump suit, just bid six of the agreed upon suit lest you get too high.

BY THE WAY
This keycard asking bid is referred to as "1430" because the first two response steps show 1 or 4 and 3 or 0. Bridge players are only too familiar with the score (1430) of a vulnerable major suit small slam bid and made. This mnemonic association helps to correctly reply to and interpret the response.

TWO SAMPLE AUCTIONS
USING THE 1430 KEYCARD ASKING BID:

#1

Opener's hand	Responder's hand
♠ A K J 9 7 6	♠ 8 4
♥ K Q 10 8 2	♥ J 9 6 3
♦ A K	♦ Q J 7 4 2
♣ 7	♣ A 8
2C	2D
2S	3D
3H	4H
4NT	5C
6H	PASS

2C = strong opening	2D = waiting
2S = my long suit	3D = my suit
3H = my second long suit	4H = I have 4 hearts
4NT = keycard ask	5C = one keycard
6H = we're missing a keycard	

#2

Opener's hand	Responder's hand
♠ A K 7 3	♠ Q 5
♥ A J 10 9 8 2	♥ K 7 6 3
♦ A Q	♦ K 7 4
♣ 9	♣ A J 6 2
1H	2NT
4NT	5H
5NT	6D
7H	PASS

1H = Opening hand with 5 + hearts	2NT = opening hand + 4 hearts
4NT = keycard ask	5H = 2 keycards – no queen of trump
5NT = show me a king	6D = king of diamonds
7H = I hope I can make it	

Keycard asking using 1430 can also be used after a Texas transfer. Four notrump (4NT) in this case is not quantitative because there is suit agreement in the major: The opener has at least two cards in the major suit and the responder has at least six. Here are the sequences:

1NT- 4H   = transfer to four spades
4S - 4NT = how many keycards do you have in spades?

2NT - 4D = transfer to hearts
4H - 4NT = 1430 keycard asking for hearts.

Ace-asking conventions are designed to keep you out of bad slams. Don't initiate standard ace-asking conventions with a void or worthless doubleton. In these instances, once you have suit agreement, you can show slam interest by bidding a control in a new suit. **A bid of a side suit above the 3-level of an agreed upon major suit shows either a first or second round control in the suit bid.** A first round control is an ace or a void and a second round control is a king or a singleton. Once either partner initiates control bidding the other is expected to cooperate by bidding a control if she holds one. Controls are bid at the cheapest level up the bidding ladder. A control bid at the 5-level guarantees that it is first round control, i.e., an ace or void. You do not bid controls in the trump suit as these are shown via the keycard-asking bid. These bidding methods are designed to assist you in reaching good slams which make and staying out of slams which do not make.

To bid a slam you must have first or second control in all side suits. You must also have at least four of the five keycards. You will also try to stay out of slams if you are missing one keycard and the queen of your trump suit unless you have at least 10 trump cards between the two hands.

EXAMPLE OF CONTROL-BIDDING TO SHOW SLAM INTEREST AFTER MAJOR SUIT AGREEMENT:

Opener's hand	Responder's hand
♠ A K 7 3	♠ 4 2
♥ A K J 5 3	♥ Q 7 4 2
♦ K 2	♦ A 7 4
♣ 9 2	♣ A J 8 3
1H	3C
3S	4C
4NT	5S
6H	Pass

1H	= 5-card suit - 18 HCP	3C	= Bergen 10-11 SP
3S	= interest in slam - bidding a control in spades	4C	= I have a control in clubs
4NT	= that's what I needed - keycard ask	5S	= two keycards with the queen of hearts
6H	= we'll try the slam since we have all the keycards and the queen of trump	Pass	= you're in charge

---

PLAY TIP: GETTING HELP FROM THE OPPONENTS

There are some fancy ways to play suits in order to gain extra tricks. The experts are good at using these techniques among which are squeezes and dummy reversals. Other times it is advantageous to force the opponents to lead a suit thereby helping you find a critical card. One of these maneuvers is called an **endplay**.

EXAMPLE OF AN ENDPLAY AT A SLAM CONTRACT

You have arrived at a 6S slam with the following hands.

Dummy's Hand
♠ A J 8 3 2
♥ A Q
♦ K J 8
♣ 10 8 7
Declarer's Hand
♠ K Q 10 9 4
♥ 7 5
♦ A 10 7
♣ A K Q

The opening lead is the jack of hearts. If you finesse the queen of hearts and it loses you will have to find the queen of diamonds to make your contract. And it looks like your finesse isn't going to work - so what can you do? Win the ace of hearts and draw your trumps where you have no losers. Even if you have to play trump three times to get them all in you will still have trumps left in each hand. Next cash all three of your club winners. Now it is time to lose the heart trick so lead your little heart eliminating hearts from both hands. As you can see whichever opponent wins the heart trick will be forced to help you in the diamond suit. He may elect to lead diamonds which you will let ride to the high honor last to play to the trick. In this way you can capture the queen if it is played or win the trick with the lower honor card. If he doesn't lead diamonds, he will have to lead either a heart or club (he's out of spades) which will give you a **"ruff and sluff"**. You will pitch (sluff) the losing diamond from one hand and ruff in the other hand. Pretty neat play and just the way the experts would play. Exciting isn't it? This technique (the endplay) is often possible when you have equal length in all four suits in the two hands, a situation called **"mirror distribution"**.

A side suit singleton lead against a suit contract can be a great way to defeat a slam when partner has the right ace (either the ace of the suit led or the ace of trump). Partner will immediately win the trick with the ace of the suit led or later with the ace of trump and will return the suit you led to give you a ruff with a low trump.

A short suit lead is not best when you have natural trump tricks such as a QJ10 holding in the trump suit - look for a different lead. Also leading a short suit is not recommended when you have length in trump. When this situation occurs it is generally best to lead your long suit hoping to force the declarer to ruff thereby reducing his trump holding to the same length as yours. With luck you may be able to gain control of the hand by making declarer ruff a second time.

A singleton may also be a great lead at a lower-level contract when you have a second way to get to your partner's hand for a second ruff. Partner can help you by telling you where he has an outside **entry** (a way to get back to his hand). The card he leads back tells you how to reach his hand for another ruff. A high card asks for the higher-ranking suit of the remaining two (disregard the trump suit) and a low card asks for the lower-ranking suit. This signaling method is called giving **suit preference** and is an extremely powerful tool in enabling the defenders to defeat a seemingly unbeatable contract.

EXAMPLES

Partner has led the nine of clubs against a four heart contract. You are really sure partner's lead is a singleton and that you can give him a ruff or two. You will win the trick with the ace of clubs and return the underlined card to indicate which suit partner should lead back to find your entry.

Hand #1	Hand #2	Hand #3
♠ A 9 6 4	♠ 7 6 5	♠ 9 6 4
♥ 4	♥ T 4	♥ T 4 3
♦ 7 6 5	♦ A 9 6 4	♦ 7 6 5
♣ A <u>T</u> 6 2	♣ A T 6 <u>2</u>	♣ A T <u>6</u> 2
The 10 asks for a spade return	The deuce asks for a diamond return	The six shows no preference

---

MORE ABOUT SIGNALING

You give critical information to your partner when trying to defeat a contract through defensive signals. To be effective, the signals must be correct, and your partner must watch for them and interpret them correctly.

Two other signals were discussed in previous tips. **Attitude**, the most common, is given when partner leads an honor and you encourage with a high spot card and discourage with a low one. Attitude can be conveyed also when discarding where the size of the card you play shows whether you like the suit or not.

Count signals are used when declarer is leading and it is important for your partner to know how many cards declarer has in a particular suit. When you tell partner how many you have by playing a **low** card with an **odd** number and a **high** card with an **even** number, partner will know how many are in the unexposed declarer's hand.

Our final signal is the **suit preference signal** which is used to ask partner to lead a specific suit. In addition to the situation discussed above the suit preference signal can be used in another common situation. When the dummy has a singleton in the suit led the defense is not going to get any more tricks in that suit. So, when playing third to the trick you can signal what suit you'd like partner to switch to. Again the size of your card suggests which suit you'd like led. Disregarding the suit led and the trump suit, a **low card** asks for the **lower** of the remaining two suits and a **high card** asks for the **higher** suit.

BRIDGE ETIQUETTE

Even though you and your partner have agreed to play some "coded" or conventional bids, you may not keep the meaning of these bids a secret from your opponents. They are entitled to know that they are artificial and what the meaning is. When your partner makes one of these bids you are required to say "**alert**" and to display the alert card from your bidding box. If either opponent wants to know what the bid means he may ask at his turn to bid. If neither asks, say nothing more.

Likewise, you are entitled to the same information from your opponents. However, it is best not to ask about their bids during the auction if you do not intend to bid. Asking may allow your opponents to exchange information about their bids that actually may have been misunderstood. You can always request disclosure once the auction is over.

➤ All big hands (22+ TP) are opened with a bid of 2C which is artificial and forcing

➤ After a 2C opening the responder should bid 2D (waiting) unless she can make a positive suit response. To bid a suit she should have a 5-card or longer suit with two of the top three or three of the top five honors and 8 or more HCP.

➤ Big balanced hands are opened:
  • 2NT with 20 -21 HCP
  • 2C and then rebid 2NT with 22-24 HCP
  • 3NT with 25 -26 HCP
  • 2C and then rebid 3NT with 27-28 HCP

➤ After a big NT opening (whether preceded by 2C or not) the responder should::
  • With a balanced hand, and no 4-card or longer major suit, pass or raise notrump to the appropriate level based on her points
  • Use Stayman to look for a 4-4 major suit fit
  • Use the Jacoby transfer to try for a 5-3 major suit fit
  • Use the Texas transfer to play in a 6-2 or longer major suit fit

➤ Big unbalanced hands (22+ TP, at least one 5-card or longer suit, 4QT, and no more than 4 losers) are opened 2C (artificial and forcing) and rebid by naming the long suit. After a suit rebid the responder should:
  • Raise opener's suit with at least 3 cards in support. She jumps to game with no ace or king and no side suit singleton or void (fast arrival). With support and any of the above features, the responder makes a stronger bid by raising partner's suit one level.
  • With 3+ points and no support for opener's suit, bid a 5-card or longer suit which was not good enough for an initial bid.

- With a worthless hand, show a "**second negative**" by bidding the cheaper minor (there is no "second negative" if opener's suit is diamonds).

➢ If the opener rebids 2NT or any game bid after opening 2C, the responder may pass. If the opener rebids a suit, the responder is required to make 2 bids and must make a third bid if the opener bids a new suit on her third bid.

➢ Notrump slams require a combined total of 33 HCP for a small slam and 37 HCP for a grand slam and are usually bid by adding responder's points to the points shown by the opener's notrump bid

➢ Slams in suits where a fit exists may be bid with less points but require a strong trump holding, 4 of the 5 keycards and controls in all 4 suits

➢ With suit agreement a bid of 4NT is the **1430** keycard-asking convention. There are 5 keycards - the 4 aces and the king of the trump suit. The answers are as follows:
  - 5C = 1 or 4 of the 5 keycards
  - 5D = 3 or 0 of the 5 keycards
  - 5H = 2 of the 5 keycards without the queen of trump
  - 5S = 2 of the 5 keycards with the queen of trump

➢ If the partner who asks for keycards continues by bidding 5NT, she is looking for a grand slam and wants you to bid your lowest-ranking king (but not the trump king - you have already told her about that one). If your answer would go past the trump suit, just bid the small slam.

➢ When looking for slam, control bids are used when you have 2 or more little cards in a suit or a void suit:
  - First round controls are an ace or a void and second round controls are a protected king or a singleton
  - Control bids show slam interest and are side suits, bid up the ladder, to indicate a first or second round control
  - Controls bid at the 5-level promise first round control

- Do not bid a control in the trump suit - use the keycard asking bid for that.
- Good slams are when you have controls in all suits and at least 4 of the 5 keycards.

➢ Get help from the opponents by forcing an endplay

➢ Lead a singleton against a suit contract to try to get a ruff

➢ The suit preference signal tells partner where you have an entry

A SHORT TRUE (T) OR FALSE (F) QUIZ

_____ 1. A 2C opening bid is forcing for one round only

_____ 2. A 2NT opening bid is not forcing at all

_____ 3. Stayman can be used with 1NT, 2NT, and 3NT opening bids

_____ 4. A 2D waiting bid shows a bust hand

_____ 5. A jump raise to game of partner's suit following her 2C opener shows slam interest

_____ 6. A 4NT response to a 2NT opening bid is quantitative showing the number of HCP held

_____ 7. There is no ace-asking bid after a Jacoby transfer at the 2-level or 3-level

ANSWERS TO A SHORT TRUE (T) OR FALSE (F) QUIZ

1. False - Responder is required to bid twice after a suit rebid and again if opener introduces a new suit at her third bid

2. True

3. True

4. False - It is a waiting bid, not necessarily a negative one. You should make a positive response when you have at least eight HCP and a suit which is at least five cards long with two of the top three honors.

5. False - It tells partner you have support for her suit but not much more

6. True - And it is definitely not ace-asking

7. True

EXERCISE 1

What is your opening bid on the following hands?

1. ♠ A J 8   ♥ K Q 9 2   ♦ A K   ♣ K Q J 3

2. ♠ A Q 9   ♥ A K J 2   ♦ A J 5 4   ♣ A K

3. ♠ K Q J 10 5 4 2   ♥ A 3   ♦ 5   ♣ A K J

4. ♠ A J 10 3   ♥ K Q J 4   ♦ A K   ♣ J 10 9

ANSWERS TO EXERCISE 1

1. Open 2C. You are balanced with 23 HCP. Next bid 2NT to show your strength and shape.

2. Open 3NT. This bid shows 25-26 points and that's what you have.

3. Bid 2C. You have 18 HCP + 3LP, 4 QT, and no more than four losers.

4. You are one point short for a 2NT opening. Open 1C planning to jump to 2NT on your next bid.

EXERCISE 2

Partner opened 2C. What is your response?

1. ♠ 9 5 2   ♥ 10 8 6   ♦ K Q J 6 3   ♣ A 10

2. ♠ Q 9 3   ♥ A 10 9   ♦ 6 5 2   ♣ K 8 7 6

3. ♠ K Q J 10 8 7   ♥ K 10 9   ♦ 4   ♣ 6 3 2

4. ♠ 9 5 4 2   ♥ 9 4 2   ♦ 6   ♣ J 6 5 3 2

ANSWERS TO EXERCISE 2

1. Bid 3D to show your good 5-card suit with two of the top three honors and your 10 HCP. Do not bid 2D, which is a waiting bid and denies the values you have.

2. Bid 2D waiting, not 2NT. If partner wants to rebid NT at her second turn, you want her to be declarer at NT, not you. You can show your values by continuing to bid.

3. Bid 2S. This bid shows your spade suit and values.

4. Bid 2D and await developments. If partner's bid is other than damonds or NT, your singleton may be helpful.

EXERCISE 3

Partner opened 2C, you responded 2D, and partner rebid 2NT.

2C – 2D
2NT – ?

What do you rebid with the following hands?

1. ♠ K J 8 4 3 2   ♥ 9 4 2   ♦ 8 6   ♣ 4 8

2. ♠ 10 7 6   ♥ 9 4 3   ♦ 8 5 4 2   ♣ 7 6 5

3. ♠ K Q J 8   ♥ 8 7   ♦ A 8 3   ♣ Q 7 4 2

ANSWERS TO EXERCISE 3

1. Bid four hearts. Use the Texas transfer to get to a spade game and then pass. You have a combined, maximum 28 HCP, enough for game but no more.

2. Pass. One of those sad moments in bridge but there is no other choice.

3. Begin with 3C (Stayman) looking for a 4-4 fit in spades. Your combined points (34 minimum) are enough for a small slam. If partner answers Stayman by bidding 3D or 3H, bid 6NT. If partner bids 3S, bid 6S.

EXERCISE 4: QUESTIONS AND ANSWERS

Partner opened 2C, you responded 2D, and partner rebid 2H.

2C - 2D

2H - ?

Q. What did your 2D bid say?

A. You do not have a 5-card or longer suit with two of the three top honors and eight HCP. You may have quite a few points and a long suit but your hand does not meet the three requirements for an immediate positive response.

Q. What does partner's 2H bid say about her hand?

A. The 2H bid shows at least five hearts, about 22+ HCP, at least 4 QT, no more than four losers and that her hand is unbalanced.

Q. Holding the following hands, what would you rebid?

#1　　♠ K 8 7 6　　♥ 8 5 4　　♦ Q 8　　♣ 10 9 8 7

A. 3H. Your hand qualifies for an encouraging raise because you have 3-card support for hearts and a king.

#2　　♠ 10 8 7 6　　♥ 8 5 4　　♦ Q 8　　♣ 10 9 8 7

A. 4H. This jump raise shows heart support and absolutely no slam interest.

#3　　♠ 10 8 7 6　　♥ 8 5　　♦ Q 8 4　　♣ 10 9 8 7

A. 3C. This bid is called a second negative and it shows a hopeless hand without support for partner's suit.

Q. After your raise to 3H on hand #1 above, partner bids 4NT. What does her bid mean?

A. She is asking for keycards for the agreed trump suit of hearts.

Q. What is your response?

A. 5D. This bid shows 0 or 3 keycards (surely 0).

Q. Partner now bids 5H. What does that mean?

A. It is a signoff bid. She wants to play 5H because the partnership is missing two keycards.

EXERCISE 5: QUESTIONS AND ANSWERS

You open 2C, your partner responds 2D, you rebid 2NT and she next bids 3C and you bid 3S. Finally partner bids 5S.

2C   – 2D

2NT – 3C

3S   – 5S

Q. What does your 2NT rebid show?

A. 22-24 HCP.

Q. What was the meaning of her 3C bid?

A. Do you have a 4-card major?

Q. What did your 3S response show?

A. I have four spades and I definitely do not have four hearts.

Q. What was the meaning of responder's 5S rebid?

A. It is a slam invitational bid showing a fit and asking me to bid 6S if I'm at the top (23-24 HCP) of my 2NT bid and to pass if I only have 22 HCP.

EXERCISE 6: QUESTIONS AND ANSWERS

You open the bidding 1H, your partner bids 3C, you next bid 4D, and she next bids 4S.

1H - 3C

4D - 4S

Q. What does 3C say?

A. It is a limit raise showing 4-card heart support and 10-12 SP.

Q. What is the meaning of the 4D bid?

A. Since we have heart agreement, I am showing slam interest by bidding diamonds to show a first or second round control in that suit.

Q. What does the 4S mean?

A. Partner is cooperating in the slam investigation by bidding a first round control in spades (first round because it is above game in our agreed trump suit).

Q. If I next bid 4NT, what does that bid mean?

A. I am asking for keycards in hearts.

Q. If you hold 2 keycards and the Q of hearts, what is your bid?

A. 5S.

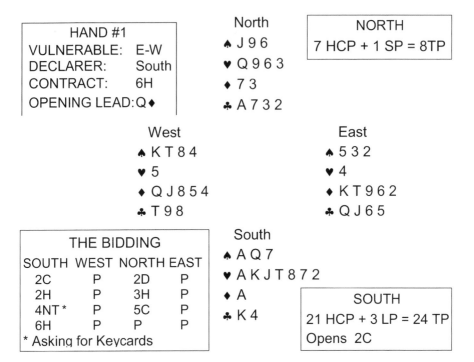

HAND #1	
VULNERABLE:	E-W
DECLARER:	South
CONTRACT:	6H
OPENING LEAD:	Q♦

North
♠ J 9 6
♥ Q 9 6 3
♦ 7 3
♣ A 7 3 2

NORTH
7 HCP + 1 SP = 8TP

West
♠ K T 8 4
♥ 5
♦ Q J 8 5 4
♣ T 9 8

East
♠ 5 3 2
♥ 4
♦ K T 9 6 2
♣ Q J 6 5

THE BIDDING			
SOUTH	WEST	NORTH	EAST
2C	P	2D	P
2H	P	3H	P
4NT*	P	5C	P
6H	P	P	P
* Asking for Keycards			

South
♠ A Q 7
♥ A K J T 8 7 2
♦ A
♣ K 4

SOUTH
21 HCP + 3 LP = 24 TP
Opens 2C

The BIDDING: South has a great heart suit and sufficient values (21 HCP) for the artificial 2C bid promising a big hand. North bids 2D, a waiting bid which keeps the auction low to allow South to describe her hand. When South bids 2H showing a long strong heart suit, North raises to the 3-level to show a hand with heart support and some interest in slam. South next asks for keycards by bidding 4NT. North's response of 5C shows one or four keycards (must be one) and South bids the small slam.

The LEAD: The QUEEN OF DIAMONDS (top of two touching cards against a suit contract)

The PLAY: South wins the ace of diamonds and draws the outstanding trumps, an easy task on this hand. Next she leads a club to the dummy and takes a losing finesse in spades. Making six hearts is surely fun as everyone loves bidding and making slams.

HAND #2	
VULNERABLE:	None
DECLARER:	South
CONTRACT:	4H
OPENING LEAD:9♦	

NORTH
♠ J T 8 3
♥ K Q 6 3
♦ J T 3
♣ T 3

7 HCP+ 0 LP = 7 TP

West
♠ 9 5 2
♥ 9 8 5
♦ 9
♣ Q J 8 7 6 2

East
♠ 7 6 4
♥ T 2
♦ A 8 6 5 2
♣ A 5 4

THE BIDDING

SOUTH	WEST	NORTH	EAST
2C	P	2D	P
2NT	P	3C *	P
3H	P	4H	P
P	P		
* Stayman			

South
♠ A K Q
♥ A J 7 4
♦ K Q 7 4
♣ K 9

SOUTH
22 HCP + 0 LP = 22 TP
Opens 2C

The BIDDING: South opens with the strong artificial bid of 2C. North's 2D bid is a waiting bid. South rebids 2NT to show a balanced hand with 22-24 HCP. North bids Stayman and South shows her 4-card major suit and North bids the heart game.

The LEAD: The NINE OF DIAMONDS – leading a singleton may work on this hand as you have some hope that partner can win an early trick and return a diamond for you to ruff.

The PLAY: East wins the opening lead with the ace of diamonds and returns the deuce of diamonds. This low diamond is a suit preference signal suggesting that West return a club (the lower of the other two suits) when he gains the lead. West ruffs the diamond return and sends back a club which East wins with the ace and gives West another ruff. Poor South, with good defense the opponents have defeated the contract before she even gains the lead. A good hand with what looked like two or maybe three losers has all of a sudden been defeated because the defense found a way to get four tricks – it happens and we go on to the next hand. Another hand where 3NT will make but most players will be in hearts. With less than perfect defense, South will make her 4H contract for a better score than 3NT.

CHAPTER 10
WEAK OPENING BIDS

In this chapter you will learn:

- About weak opening bids called preempts
- The guidelines for opening 2-level, 3-level, and 4-level preemptive bids
- How responder and opener proceed after weak opening bids
- About weak jump overcalls

MORE ABOUT WEAK OPENING BIDS

Opening bids at the 2-level, 3-level, and 4-level, even the 5-level, are weak and are called preemptive bids. Preemptive opening bids do not have opening hand values. They are defensive bids designed primarily to make it difficult for the opponents to find their optimal contract because the higher-level opening has used up their bidding space. They have a secondary purpose in that they describe your hand to your partner in fairly graphic terms when you adhere to common guidelines for these higher-level bids. And a third purpose is to suggest an opening lead should you defend the hand. The best preemptive hands are those with their strength concentrated in the long suit giving you playing strength (ability to take tricks) and with little defensive strength such as outside aces or kings.

THE OPENING WEAK TWO-BID

Since we have used the 2C bid as the opening for all strong hands, we cannot make a preemptive bid in clubs. Not to worry. All other suit opening bids at the 2-level will be weak (preemptive) bids called "**weak twos**". The lower the level of our preemptive bid the less effective it is in interfering with the opponent's auction so 2D is only minimally effective as a deterrent. When we preempt we are telling our partner (and the opponents) that we have a 1-suited hand that is going to be useful only if our suit is trumps. The requirements, or guidelines, to open with a weak two-bid of 2D, 2H or 2S are:

WEAK TWO-BIDS

- 5-10 HCP, no more
- A 6-card suit headed by two of the top three honors or three of the top five honors in the suit
- No good side 4-card major suit
- Usually no voids
- Usually no outside ace(s)

In 3rd seat the guidelines are less restrictive because your partner has already passed; it is unlikely we will preempt our side out of a game contract. So feel free to act with a bit of recklessness. There is no preempt in 4th seat; a preemptive-type bid in 4th chair shows opening hand values and a long suit.

EXAMPLES

Let's look at some hands with 6-card suits for their preemptive appropriateness:

♠ K 4 2   ♥ K 8 7 4 3 2   ♦ 7   ♣ 8 5 2

Your point count and shape are right but your suit is too weak for a weak 2H opening bid – pass.

♠ K J 10 8 4 2   ♥ A 4   ♦ 6   ♣ Q 8 6 3

With 12 TP (and "rule of 20" hand) your hand is too strong for a weak two-bid - open 1S

♠ A J 10 9 6 3   ♥ Q J 7 4   ♦ 10 4   ♣ 5

Pass because you have a good outside 4-card major suit. Your preemptive bid may prevent finding a 4-4 heart fit with partner. But in 3rd seat open 2S with your nice spade suit. You have robbed the opponents of 2 levels of bidding.

♠ J 7 2   ♥ A Q 8 6 3 2   ♦ 7 6   ♣ 8 4

This is an acceptable weak two opening preempt. You have 2 of the top 3 honors in hearts and a 6-card suit - bid 2H.

♠ A K J 10 7 2   ♥ 9 7 5   ♦ 9 8 7   ♣ 4

This hand has all its strength in spades – perfect; make a preemptive weak two-bid of 2S

BY THE WAY

Since a 2D preemptive bid may not be much of a deterrent to the opponents when they have strong hands, many players use the 2D as an artificial bid to show one of a number of hand patterns which are difficult to bid. These bids have interesting names such as Flannery, Mexican 2D, and Multi among others.

For now, we will stick to the basic meaning of a 2D bid, i.e. a "weak two" preempt with a 6-card diamond suit.

CONTINUING THE BIDDING AFTER A WEAK TWO-BID

It is important to be disciplined when making a preemptive opening bid so that partner can make an informed decision about how to proceed. With support for the opener's suit and a weak hand the responder should up the ante (called "furthering the preempt") by raising the opening bid. With a good hand she will look for the best contract for your side. With no support and minimal points, she'll have to pass.

With 3-card support and a weak hand (<13HCP), she will further the preempt by raising the opener's suit to three. The opener must pass.

With 4-card support and a weak hand, she will raise to four. Again the opener must pass.

With two or more cards in opener's major suit and at least 16 HCP she will raise to game, expecting to make it. Once again the opener must pass.

A jump to 3NT or game in a new suit is to play. Opener is expected to pass.

With interest in game (at least 14 HCP) the responder may bid 2NT, an artificial forcing bid, which asks the opener to further describe her hand. This bid shows interest in two aspects of the opener's hand: Is her hand minimum (5-7) or maximum (8-10) for her opening bid and, if maximum does she have an outside **feature** which would be an ace or a protected king or queen.

The 2NT **feature asking** bid may also be used when the responder has a big hand with slam interest. If she finds that the opener has a maximum, she can next check for keycards by bidding 4NT and bid the slam when four of the five keycards are held by the partnership.

The opener answers the 2NT inquiry by bidding:

Opener's hand	Opener's rebid
• Minimum hand 5-7 points	Three of the original suit
• 8-10 points with an outside **feature** (an A, Kx, or Qxx)	Bid the suit of the feature at the cheapest level
• 8-10 points with all the points in the opening bid suit (AKQxxx)	Bid 3NT to show a solid suit with no outside feature

Finally, if the responder has game interest and holds a strong suit of her own which is five or more cards long, she may bid the suit to force the opener to bid again. The opener continues by raising the new suit with 3-card support or a doubleton honor. Without support for the responder's suit, the opener should rebid her original suit with a minimum (5-7 HCP) opening and bid a new suit or notrump with a maximum (8-10 HCP).

EXAMPLES

Your partner has opened 2H and RHO has passed. What is your response?

♠ A J 8   ♥ 9   ♦ K Q J 7 5   ♣ A K 8

Bid 2NT asking for a feature. You want to know if there is a way to get to partner's hand to use hearts for a 3NT contract.

♠ K Q J 8 6 5   ♥ 7   ♦ A 5   ♣ A Q 7 4

You have a good hand and a good suit. Make a 2S forcing bid hoping to get to a game contract.

♠ A 6   ♥ 8 6 4 2   ♦ 7 4 3 2   ♣ 7 5 3

Further the preemptive bid by bidding 4H since you have 4 of them. Your LHO likely has a big hand and your bid will cause him all kinds of grief since he will have to come into the bidding at the 4-level or 5-level.

♠ A 8 5 3   ♥ 9 7 6 5   ♦ K Q J   ♣ A J

Again bid 4H, this time with expectations of making the contract

♠ A Q J 8 6 4 3   ♥ 5   ♦ 6 3   ♣ 8 6 4

Pass - don't preempt over a preempt --- whether it is your partner or your opponent

♠ A 8   ♥ 6 3   ♦ A K Q J 8 7 5   ♣ K 6

Jump to 3NT - you have 8 sure tricks in your own hand and 9 with a club lead

POINTS OF EMPHASIS	TAKE NOTE
A raise of a preemptive bid is not an invitation – the opener must pass.	Some partnerships play that a new suit is not forcing. To force the responder must first bid 2NT then introduce the new suit to force.
2NT or a new suit are **forcing bids** asking the preemptive bidder for more information.	
A **feature** is an ace, a protected king (Kx), or a protected queen (Qxx).	Other partnerships play that a new major suit is forcing but a new minor is not.
	Let's play forcing for now!

HIGHER-LEVEL PREEMPTIVE OPENINGS AND RESPONSES

Preemptive opening bids of 3C, 3D, 3H, and 3S are comparable to those made at the 2-level but usually have seven cards rather than six. A quality suit is needed but honor card requirements are less stringent than for a weak two opener because you have more of them. Preemptive opening bids of 4H and 4S are made holding eight of the bid suit. Eight-card minor suit preempts at the 4-level are not recommended (especially in 1st and 2nd seats) because you have gone past 3NT and may have preempted your side past a 3NT game contract. Five-level minor suit preempts are made with eight or nine cards in the suit. One common aspect of all preempts is that the opener does not have the values for an opening suit or notrump bid at the 1- level or any of our big hand bids.

Unlike after a weak two-bid where the responder can use the 2NT inquiry on game invitational hands, responding to higher-level preempts is more a matter of just bidding the game or passing. Often you will pass. Less often you will have enough quick tricks and a fit that a game is possible and you will just bid it. Finally, it is already more difficult for the opponents to find their fit and level after the higher-level preempt but you certainly want to further the preempt when you have a fit for the opener and a weak hand.

EXAMPLES

Your partner has opened three diamonds, RHO passes. You hold:

♠ 8 5   ♥ 5   ♦ A 8 7 5   ♣ 7 6 5 4 3 2

Put maximum pressure on LHO with your first bid - bid 5D. Maybe even 6D is correct. He is going to have to guess his best bid.

♠ 7   ♥ Q 9 6 3   ♦ 8 6 4 2   ♣ K J 8 4

Make the defensive bid of 5D. What will your LHO do?

♠ A Q J   ♥ 5   ♦ 8 7 5 3   ♣ A 9 7 5 3

Bid 5D. The contract just might make with your shape and support. If not, you have no defense against a heart contract.

♠ K 6   ♥ A 9 7   ♦ A J 8   ♣ A 9 8 6 2

Bid 3NT - if partner has the king of diamonds (very likely) you will have 7 diamonds and 2 aces for 9 tricks

Remember that preemptive bids, by definition, are defensive bids. You may not to make your contract unless partner has an unexpected surprise for you like a really good hand. Remember, too, the opponents can double you for penalty. You need to be aware of vulnerability which will affect the size of the penalty should you be set. When you are vulnerable and the opponents are not (unfavorable vulnerability), you can afford to be set only one trick, doubled, before the likely positive score moves in favor of the opponents. Example: If your contract is 4S doubled, going down only one (-200) and the opponents likely could have made 4H for a positive 420, your net loss is only 200 rather than 420. However, if you are set two tricks for -500, the opponents have scored more than if you let them play the four heart game for a score of 420. When there is equal vulnerability, you can afford a two trick set. When the vulnerability favors your side (you NV, opponents V), you can afford a three trick set. Sometimes you get lucky and get to play a sacrifice bid without a double. Dreamer!

BY THE WAY

When you bid game because you are weak with a good fit you are **sacrificing**. A **sacrifice bid** is one made with the knowledge that you probably will go down but with the intent that the penalty will be less than the opponents will make in a successful contract of their own. When it works that way, it is a successful sacrifice. When it doesn't work out that way, you may go down a bunch (sorry, partner). If you originated the preemptive bid, your partner should be the one to make a sacrifice, not you. She knows your hand; you don't know hers.

PREEMPTIVE BIDS BY THE OVERCALLER

So far we have talked only about the opening bidder making a preemptive call. The overcaller may also make a preemptive bid by jumping on his initial bid. A jump to the 3-level is virtually identical to an opening preempt and is meant to disturb the opponent's auction and to suggest an opening lead. A jump overcall to the 2-level looks exactly like a weak two-bid but is called a "weak jump overcall". Therefore, a 2D, 2H, or 2S overcall after a 1C opening would show a strong 6-card suit and a weak hand. The advancer would answer the overcaller's preempt in much the same way as the responder answered an opening preemptive bid.

It is important to learn that only one side gets to preempt. If the opening is a strong bid, the overcaller may make a preemptive bid. If the opening bid is a preemptive bid, then the overcaller's bid will be strong. How strong and how to compete will be discussed in the following section.

COMPETING AFTER A PREEMPTIVE OPENING BID

When the opponents open with a preemptive bid they are trying to make your entry into the auction more difficult. You will be able to enter the auction in much the same ways as you did after an opening bid at the 1-level. However, since the level is higher you will need a stronger hand to enter the auction. Any bid you make will show at least a solid opening bid (about 14 HCP).

An overcall promises a good 5-card or longer suit and sound opening values (14-17 TP).

A jump overcall by you will be strong since they are weak so it would show 18-20 HCP and a really good 6-card or 7-card suit.

A notrump bid following a weak two-bid shows the strength for a notrump opening bid (15-18 HCP) and the opponent's suit well-stopped. A notrump bid after a preemptive bid at the 3-level shows a balanced hand with stoppers in the opponent's suit and anywhere from 15 to 22 points.

A takeout double still shows solid opening values and at least 3-card support for all unbid suits. The shorter you are in the opener's preemptive suit the more you should try to bid. It is desirable to have 4-card support for the other major if the preempt was in a major suit. The double of preemptive bids all the way through 4H is for takeout while a double of 5C or 5D is generally for penalty. A double of a preemptive bid of 4S is optional for the advancer (pass for penalty or bid a long suit).

If the opponent opens with a 2H or 2S preempt, a cuebid of that suit asks your partner to bid 3NT with a stopper in the suit. You will have a hand with a long running minor suit. After a 2H opening, bid 3H with something like:

♠ K 8   ♥ 6 3   ♦ A K Q J 8 6 3   ♣ A 8

Partner will bid 3NT with a stopper in hearts; otherwise she will bid 4C to ask you to play in your long minor suit (pass or correct to 4D).

If the opponent opens with a bid of 2D, a 3D cuebid would still be Michaels showing both majors with at least five cards in each suit. There is no unusual 2NT bid after a preemptive bid; remember 2NT is now a natural balanced hand with 15-17 HCP.

All of these bids are available to the overcaller whether she is bidding right after the opening bid (**the direct seat**) or after two passes (**the balancing seat**).

POINTS OF EMPHASIS	TAKE NOTE
Bids over a preempt show solid values - 14+. There is no unusual 2NT after a preempt. A cuebid of a 2H or 2S opening is not Michaels; it asks for a stopper for NT.	**Direct seat** means the overcaller bids right after the opening bid. **Balancing seat** means the overcaller is the last person to bid - there have been two passes. These bids may be a tad lighter than direct bids.

PLAY TIP: ENTRIES ARE EVERYTHING

As we learned in Chapter 4, entries are a means to get from one hand to another in order to lead from the entered hand. Entries enable you to take established tricks or to be in the correct hand in order to finesse in some suit. Sometimes you have easy access to either hand but don't count on it. Entries should be part of your initial plan so don't be careless and play to the first trick without consideration of the transportation between the two hands.

Watch the spots on a suit you plan to run to be sure you're not blocked from reaching those in the opposite hand. You need to carefully plan for the number of entries required to establish a long suit on which to pitch losers. Be especially wary when playing a notrump contract that you have an entry into the hand with established tricks. Consider this hand where your contract is 3NT:

```
DUMMY'S HAND
♠ 7 5 2
♥ A K 9 5 2
♦ A
♣ K 8 4 2

DECLARER'S HAND
♠ K 8 3
♥ 7 3
♦ K Q J 10 6
♣ A 4 2
```

The lead is the queen of clubs

You need to take nine tricks to make your contract. You have two sure heart winners, five diamond winners, and two club winners...nine winners right off the top so you're home free. However, if you quickly play to the first trick and carelessly win the trick by playing the ace in your hand you have no quick entry back to your hand to take the good diamond tricks after playing the ace in the dummy. You must preserve the only entry to your hand by taking the first trick with the king of clubs in the dummy.

DEFENSIVE TIP: COUNTING

Become an astute defender and a formidable opponent. Count!! Make a plan to beat the contract you are defending. Start by counting the HCP displayed in dummy's hand, add them to yours, add presumed points held by declarer based on his bidding, then subtract the total from 40 to arrive at the approximate number of points held by your partner. If you can figure out where those points might be it will be extremely helpful in defending the hand. On the following hand the opening bid has been 1NT (15-17 points) and the responder has bid 3NT.

Dummy's hand:

♠ Q 7 6
♥ A Q 2
♦ K 9 7 5 3
♣ 7 4

Lead

J♠

Your hand:

♠ K 8 5 2
♥ K 6 3
♦ 6 4
♣ Q J 10 4

The opening lead has been the jack of spades (denying any higher spades - J denies) on which the declarer plays the six of spades from the dummy. You play low and the declarer wins the trick with the ace and takes a heart finesse which you win with your king. If you haven't counted yet it's time to stop and count.

Declarer has 15-17 points, let's give him 16, and dummy has 11 we can see. We have nine so partner has four give or take a point. Where could that be to allow us to set the contract? He has shown one point (the jack of spades) but will need to have four more (the ace of clubs) to have any hope of setting the contract. You should immediately fire off the queen of clubs hoping to trap declarer's king. If partner has the ace of clubs, hopefully he will be able to win the first or second trick and have a club left to return to your remaining good clubs and down goes the contract.

This is just one aspect of counting. As you gain experience you will start to count other things like distribution. It always helps the defense to determine the pattern of declarer's hand. You will learn to use clues from the bidding, the lead, and the count signals your partner provides to establish exactly how many cards declarer holds in each suit. Armed with this information you will be able to defeat more and more contracts.

BRIDGE ETIQUETTE
DIRECTOR CALLS

We end with the hope that we will soon see you at the bridge table in our over 3200 duplicate bridge clubs across the United States, Canada, Mexico, and Bermuda. At each club you will find a **director** who organizes and runs games and tournaments sanctioned* by the American Contract Bridge League † (ACBL). The director keeps things operating smoothly, knows and enforces the rules of the game, and generally is a bridge player's good friend. When an irregularity occurs at the bridge table, any player, except the dummy, may raise her hand and call the director to the table by saying "director, please". The director will listen to the player's discussion of the problem and then make a ruling about how to proceed and may in some instances assign a penalty to the offending side. The most common irregularities during the bidding are insufficient bids and bids which are out of turn. Common irregularities during play are leads out of turn and revokes. A revoke is failure to follow suit when holding cards in the suit led.

* Sanctioned games award masterpoints to the players who win and place in the overall results. Masterpoint rankings are considered achievement levels: the number of points awarded increase with the difficulty of the competition.

†The ACBL, the largest bridge organization in the world, manages all duplicate activities on the North American continent, Puerto Rico and Bermuda. Their website (www.acbl.org) is a valuable resource for learning bridge and getting information about bridge activities.

> A 2D, 2H, or 2S opening bid is called a "weak two" and in 1ˢᵗ or 2ⁿᵈ seat shows:
>   • A 6-card suit with 2 of the top 3 or 3 of the top 5 honors
>   • 5-10 HCP
>   • No good side 4-card major suit
>   • Usually no voids and no outside aces

> A weak two in 3ʳᵈ seat is less restrictive so be a bit frisky

> Respond to an opening weak two-bid by:
>   • Raising preemptively to the 3-level with 3 trump and to the 4-level with 4 trump
>   • Raising to game with support and at least 16 HCP planning to make it
>   • Bidding 2NT with game or slam interest (at least 15 HCP), to ask how good the preempt was and if the opener has a feature like an A, Kx, or Qxx
>   • Bidding a new suit with game interest and at least 5 cards in the suit
>   • Bidding a game in a new suit or 3NT to play with game values
>   • Inviting slam by jumping to 5 in the opener's major

> The opener's continuations after an opening weak two-bid:
>   • Passes all nonforcing and game bids
>   • Answers 2NT by showing a feature with 8-10 HCP, bidding 3NT with AKQ in the weak two suit, or returning to the weak two suit with 5-7 HCP
>   • Answers a new suit bid by raising with 3 or a doubleton honor, otherwise shows a feature or returns to her suit

> 3-level opening bids show 7 cards and less than an opening hand; responder generally passes but may raise preemptively or to make

➤ 4-level opening bids in the majors show 8 cards and less than opening bid values

➤ A sacrifice bid is made to lessen the opponents' score when they are likely to succeed in a game or slam contract; be aware of vulnerability when considering a sacrifice

➤ Weak jump overcalls attempt to thwart the opponents in the same way as a preemptive opening bid

➤ After a preemptive opening bid, the overcaller may bid but will have solid values as only one side gets to be weak. He may:
  • Overcall with about 14 TP
  • Bid notrump at the cheapest level with 15-17 HCP
  • Make a takeout double over all preempts through 4H
  • Cuebid at the 3-level in a major suit to ask for a stopper for notrump
  • Cuebid 3D after a 2D opening to show both majors
  • Not bid the unusual 2NT over a weak two-bid; a 2NT bid here would be natural showing 15-18 balanced points

➤ Plan for movement between hands using available entries

➤ Counting is critical to accurate defense – try to count points

A SHORT TRUE (T) OR FALSE (F) QUIZ

After an opening weak two-bid:

_____ 1. Responder's 2NT bid is game-forcing

_____ 2. Responder's 2NT bid is asking opener to further describe her hand

_____ 3. With a weak hand and four cards in opener's suit, responder should pass

_____ 4. Responder's 2-level bid in a new major suit is game-forcing

_____ 5. Following responder's 2NT bid, opener should pass with no feature and a minimum (5-7) hand

EXERCISE 1

YOU ARE THE OPENER - WHAT DO YOU BID?

Your hand is	Your HCP?	Your TP?	Your bid?
♠84 ♥AKJ864 ♦75 ♣842			
♠KJ74 ♥84 ♦KQ9743 ♣8			
♠T96 ♥A8 ♦AKJ984 ♣84			
♠984 ♥84 ♦AJ8432 ♣A6			
♠84 ♥AQJ86432 ♦97 ♣5			
♠84 ♥AQ98643 ♦75 ♣54			
♠8 ♥AQJ9642 ♦JT98 ♣4			

ANSWERS TO A SHORT
TRUE (T) OR FALSE (F) QUIZ

1. False - it is forcing for only one round

2. True - she is asking about the strength of the preempt and for a feature

3. Definitely not - she should further the preempt and probably to game if vulnerability is favorable

4. False - it is only a one-round force

5. False - she should return to her original suit

EXERCISE 2
RESPONDING TO AN OPENING WEAK TWO-BID
PARTNER HAS OPENED 2H; WHAT DO YOU RESPOND?

Your hand is	Your HCP?	Your TP?	Your bid?
♠98 ♥J86 ♦Q975 ♣8742			
♠T98 ♥84 ♦Q975 ♣8764			
♠QJ6 ♥A8 ♦AKQ984 ♣A4			
♠K83 ♥Q7 ♦AQ752 ♣KQ4			
♠KQJ874 ♥4 ♦A4 ♣AQ93			
♠AQJ ♥64 ♦AK2 ♣AKQJ2			
♠84 ♥AJ96 ♦JT987 ♣A4			

ANSWERS TO EXERCISE 1
YOU ARE THE OPENER - WHAT DO YOU BID?

Your hand is	Your HCP?	Your TP?	Your Bid?
♠84　♥AKJ864　♦75　♣842 A classic weak two-bid	8	10	2H
♠KJ74　♥84　♦KQ9743　♣8 Pass with a strong side 4-card major suit	9	11	Pass
♠T96　♥A8　♦AKJ984　♣84 Too strong for a weak two-bid; open 1D	12	14	1D
♠984　♥84　♦AJ8432　♣A6 The suit is a bit ratty for a weak two in 1st or 2nd seat – OK in 3rd seat!	9	11	Pass or 2D
♠84　♥AQJ86432　♦97　♣5 8-card suit and < an opening hand - bid 4H	7	11	4H
♠84　♥AQ98643　♦75　♣54 7-card suit and < an opening hand - bid 3H	6	9	3H
♠8　♥AQJ9642　♦JT98　♣4 With a weak hand and lots of distribution - take a gamble on 4H	8	11	4H

ANSWERS TO EXERCISE 2
RESPONDING TO AN OPENING WEAK TWO-BID
PARTNER HAS OPENED 2H; WHAT DO YOU RESPOND?

Your hand is	Your HCP?	Your TP?	Your Bid?
♠98　♥J86　♦Q975　♣8742 Raise preemptively with 3-card support	3	4 SP	3H
♠T98　♥84　♦Q975　♣8764 Pass - no support - no points	2	2	Pass
♠QJ6　♥A8　♦AKQ984　♣A4 Bid what you can make! You have 8 tricks and the lead or partner will give you one more	20	22	3NT
♠K83　♥Q7　♦AQ752　♣KQ4 Bid 2NT to ask partner for information to try for game in hearts or notrump	16	17	2NT
♠KQJ874　♥4　♦A4　♣AQ93 2S is forcing and asks partner for support - game is likely	16	18	2S
♠AQJ　♥64　♦AK2　♣AKQJ2 Bid 2NT to see how big partner is - you are definitely looking for slam	24	25	2NT
♠84　♥AJ96　♦JT987　♣A4 Bid 4H - it will not make but you have no defense so they may even make a slam - increasing the preempt is a good move!	10	12	4H

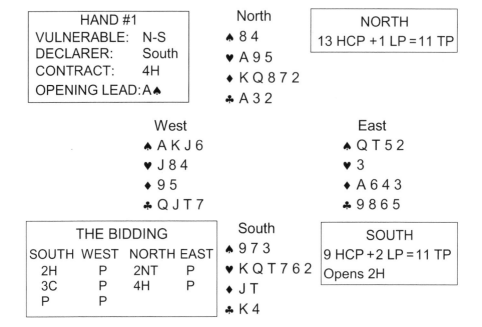

HAND #1		North	NORTH
VULNERABLE:	N-S	♠ 8 4	13 HCP +1 LP = 11 TP
DECLARER:	South	♥ A 9 5	
CONTRACT:	4H	♦ K Q 8 7 2	
OPENING LEAD:A♠		♣ A 3 2	

West	East
♠ A K J 6	♠ Q T 5 2
♥ J 8 4	♥ 3
♦ 9 5	♦ A 6 4 3
♣ Q J T 7	♣ 9 8 6 5

THE BIDDING

SOUTH	WEST	NORTH	EAST
2H	P	2NT	P
3C	P	4H	P
P	P		

South
♠ 9 7 3
♥ K Q T 7 6 2
♦ J T
♣ K 4

SOUTH
9 HCP +2 LP = 11 TP
Opens 2H

The BIDDING: South bids 2H - a weak two-bid. North has just enough to bid 2NT which asks South to bid a feature if she is at the top of her bid. South has 9 HCP so shows her feature, the king of clubs, and North bids the heart game.

The LEAD: The ACE OF SPADES (ace from AK against a suit contract)

The PLAY: With three spade losers and a diamond loser, the declarer must be careful to ruff a spade in the dummy before drawing all the outstanding trumps. A nice game bid and made.

HAND #2			
VULNERABLE:	E-W		
DECLARER:	South		
CONTRACT:	4S		
OPENING LEAD:K♦			

North
♠ A K 4 3
♥ K J 9 7
♦ 7
♣ K 9 7 6

NORTH
14 HCP + 3 SP = 17 TP
Doubles

West
♠ 9 7 5
♥ 4
♦ K Q T 9 8 5 2
♣ Q 5

WEST
7 HCP + 3 LP = 10 TP
Opens 3D

East
♠ 6
♥ Q 8 6 5 3
♦ J 6 4
♣ A 8 3 2

South
♠ Q J T 8 2
♥ A T 2
♦ A 3
♣ J T 4

THE BIDDING			
WEST	NORTH	EAST	SOUTH
3D	X	P	4S
P	P	P	

South
12 HCP + 1 LP = 13 TP

The BIDDING: West opens with a preemptive bid of 3D showing a hand with seven diamonds that was too weak for an opening bid at the 1-level. North being short in diamonds makes a takeout double asking South to bid any of the other suits. South with 13 TP and a 5-card spade suit bids the spade game.

The LEAD: The KING OF DIAMONDS (top of a 2-card sequence against a suit contract)

The PLAY: South wins the opening lead with the ace of diamonds and draws all the trumps held by the defenders. She sees that West had three spades and West's bid showed seven diamonds so West has only three other cards. In your hand with the queen of spades you play the jack of clubs which West covers with the queen, you play the king and East wins with the ace. A diamond is returned which you ruff in the dummy. Next you play a club to your 10 and a club to the nine in the dummy. When the clubs don't break 3-3 you will need to play the heart suit hoping to avoid a loser in the suit. You can finesse either way. Which way should you play the suit? It's time to finish counting West's hand – he had three spades, seven diamonds, and two clubs for 12 of his 13 cards so he can have only one heart. You should play the king of hearts and if West's solo heart isn't the queen you will play the jack intending to finesse East for the queen of hearts. Counting is sometimes real hard but after a preemptive bid it is a lot easier as you can see on this hand. Counting is also fun and exciting when we get it right like you did on this hand.

GLOSSARY

Advancer

The partner of the player who makes an overcall or takeout double

Alert

The word used by the partner of the player who has made an artificial bid to ensure the opponents know the bid is not natural

Artificial bid

A call that is not natural in that its meaning is belied by the strain and perhaps the level e.g., a 2C response to a 1NT opening bid asks the opener for a 4-card major suit, having nothing to do with clubs

Auction

The determination of the contract through the players' bids

Balanced hand

One with no voids, no singletons, and no more than one doubleton

Balancing seat

The player in the seat to make the final call when the opponents are winning the auction and should she pass, the auction is over

Bid

A declaration to win a specific number of tricks in a specified strain

Bidding boxes

A container holding cards which are used to make a call during the auction

Boards

Holders for the hands used in duplicate games to keep the hands as they were originally dealt

Bonus points

Score above trick value for partscores, games and slams bid and made for the offense and points made by the defense when a contract is defeated

Book

The first six tricks taken by the declarer

Broken sequence

A sequence of honor cards in a suit where the third card from the top is missing but not the next one(s) e.g. A K J x, K Q 10 9, Q J 9

Call

A pass, bid, double, or redouble

Chicago-style scoring

A system in which the vulnerability rotates: first hand no one is vulnerable, second and third hands dealer is vulnerable and fourth hand both are vulnerable

Clubs

The lowest ranking suit, one of the minors, with a black symbol sometimes described as puppy paws. Clubs are also considered one of the "rounded" suits because of the shape of its symbol.

Coded bid

An artificial or conventional bid

Coded lead

A lead convention, where "jack denies, 10 or nine implies" which helps partner discern the meaning of your lead when you are leading from an interior sequence (honor cards where the two lower cards are in sequence: K J 10 7). Your lead of the jack denies having a higher honor such as J 10 9 7 but the lead of the 10 or nine says you have two or none higher such as K J 10 7 or 10 9 8 7.

Competitive auction

Both sides are involved in the bidding process

Constructive raise

An encouraging raise of partner's suit that is about 7-9 points and shows less than a limit raise which is 10-11 points

Contract

The final bid in the auction expressed in both level and strain such as 4H

Control bid

Showing a first (ace or void) or second (king or singleton) round control of a suit by bidding it when the partnership is exploring for slam

Convention

A call or bid with a defined meaning which often is artificial

Convention card

Information on a form which duplicate players are required to have available for opponents to review to understand what systems and conventions the partnership plays

Criss-cross raise

A jump bid in the other minor suit (2D after 1C and 3C after 1D) used to show an opening hand and support (five cards) for opener's minor suit. This conventional bid is still used if the opponent makes a takeout double but is off after an overcall.

Cuebid (opponent's suit)

An artificial, forcing bid used in several situations: Responder can show support for partner's suit by cuebidding the overcaller's suit; advancer can show support or a good hand by cuebidding the opener's suit; overcaller can show a 2-suited hand using the Michaels cuebid convention. A cuebid may also be used as a general forcing bid.

Danger hand

The opponent declarer does not want in the lead because of her position to make a damaging lead or because she has enough established tricks to set the contract.

Dealer

The player who distributes the cards and has the first opportunity to bid or pass

Declarer

The offensive player of the contract by virtue of first naming the strain of the winning auction

Defeat

Set the contract

Defenders

The pair that did not win the auction

Denomination (strain)

The suit or notrump specified in a bid

Diamonds

The third-highest ranking suit and one of the minors; a "pointed suit" because of the shape of the symbol

Direct seat

A player in a position to make a call immediately following an opponent's bid

Discard

Play a card to a suit that is different from the suit led but is not a trump; synonymous with "sluff" or "pitch"

Distribution

The number of cards held in each suit by a particular player, also referred to as hand pattern

Dog

Slang for a bad hand

Double

A call that increases the bonus for making or defeating a contract called a penalty double; double is also used to ask partner to bid, a takeout double

Doubleton

A holding of two cards in a suit

Dummy

The player who is declarer's partner and also the hand of declarer's partner that is placed face up on the table after the opening lead is made

Dummy points

Points used in place of length points when you have support for partner's suit and your hand will be the dummy

Void = 5 points, singleton = 3 points, doubleton = 1 point

Duplicate

A form of bridge in which the partnerships play the same deals

Endplay

The technique of forcing an opponent to make a favorable lead, usually toward the end of the hand when other options are exhausted

Entry

A means of getting from one hand to the opposite one

Favorable vulnerability

When your side is non-vulnerable and the opponents are vulnerable

Finesse

A play technique to establish extra tricks by trapping an opponent's high card

First seat

The dealer who has the first chance to bid or pass

Fit

A combined partnership holding of eight or more cards

Follow suit
Play a card in the suit that was led

Forcing bid
One that partner is expected not to pass

Forcing 1NT
Conventional agreement that when opener bids 1H or 1S and the next player passes, a 1NT bid by responder is 100% forcing; it is a critical element of the 2/1 system

Fourth highest
A lead of the fourth card from the top

Fourth seat
Player to the dealer's right
The fourth player to have a chance to make a call

Fourth-suit forcing
A conventional bid that forces the partnership to at least game

Game
A contract that results in trick values of at least 100 points

Game-forcing bid
A bid that forces the partnership to at least game

Game-forcing hand
The opener has a game-forcing hand with 19-21 points and the responder has a game-forcing hand with 13+ points

Game-forcing raise
A bid by the responder which forces the partnership to game, i.e., 2NT after a 1-level major suit opening, criss-cross after a 1-level minor suit opening and all splinter bids

Gerber convention
An artificial jump bid of 4C which asks partner to show the number of aces held. It is most often used after a natural notrump bid or rebid. A subsequent bid of 5C asks for kings in a grand slam try.

Grand slam
A contract to take all 13 tricks

Hand
The cards held by one player

Hand evaluation
Assessment of a particular hand using high card points and suit length

Hand pattern
A synonym for distribution

Hearts
The second-highest ranking suit, one of the majors also called "rounded suit" because of the form of its symbol

High card points (HCP)
The values assigned to honor cards A = 4, K = 3, Q = 2, J = 1

Hold-up
Allowing the opponents to take a trick that you could win

Honors
The aces, kings, queens, jacks and 10s

Interior sequence
A holding of honor cards in which the two lower cards are in sequence and the higher card is not such as A J 10 9

Invitational hand
An opener's hand is invitational to game with 16-18 points and the responder's hand is invitational with 11-12 points

Jacoby transfer
A convention used in response to a notrump opening bid when holding five or more cards in a major suit. A 2D bids asks opener to bid 2H and a 2H bid asks opener to bid 2S. The transfer allows the stronger hand to remain concealed.

Jacoby 2NT
A conventional raise of partner's major suit which is forcing to game

Jump rebid
A rebid of the same suit at a higher level than is necessary

Jump shift
A jump bid one level higher than necessary in a new suit, this bid shows a strong hand and is game-forcing

Key cards
The four aces and the trump king

Law of total tricks
A competitive bidding concept which in its simplest form says to bid to the level which is equal to the total number of trump cards held by the partnership

Lead
The first card played to a trick

Length points (LP)
Value assigned to long suits in a hand for evaluation; every card over four in a suit gets one point: a five card suit = 1 point, a six card suit = 2 points, a seven card suit = 3 points, etc

Level
The number of tricks over book a partnership contracts to take when it makes a bid

LHO
Left-hand opponent

Limit raise
A raise of partner's minor suit from the 1-level to the 3-level which is game invitational

Loser
A trick that is potentially lost to the opponents

Loser on a loser play
Discarding a card that must be lost on a losing trick in another suit

Major suit (majors)
Spades or hearts

Michaels cuebid
A bid by the overcaller of the same suit as the opener to show a 2-suited hand

Minimum hand
The opener has a minimum hand with 12-15 points and the responder has a minimum hand with 5-10 points

Minor suits (minors)
Diamonds or clubs

Mirror distribution
Identical suit distribution as partner

MUD
An acronym for the opening lead where the middle card from a worthless tripleton is led followed by the higher card and finally the lowest card

Negative double
Conventional use of responder's double of an overcall as takeout rather than for penalty

New suit
A suit that has not been previously bid

Nonforcing bid
A bid partner may pass

Non-vulnerable
Status of partnership when bonuses and penalties are less than when vulnerable

Notrump

A contract without a trump suit where the highest card in each suit wins the trick

Old suit

A suit previously bid by the partnership

One level

The lowest level of bidding representing seven tricks

Opener

The player who first makes a bid

Opening bid

The first bid in the auction

Opening lead

The card led to the first trick
The player to the left of the declarer makes this lead

Overcall

A bid made after the opponents have opened the bidding

Overcaller

The player who first bids for the competing partnership after the bidding is opened

Overruff

To ruff with a higher trump after a prior ruff on the same trick

Overtake

Play a higher card in the suit led when the partnership already is taking the trick

Overtrick

A trick in excess of the number required to make the contract

Partnership

The two players facing each other at the table

Partscore
A contract that does not receive a game bonus if made but receives 50 bonus points above trick value

Pass
A call specifying no bid at this turn

Passed hand
A player who passed when given the chance to open and therefore is assumed to have less than 13 points

Penalty
Bonus awarded the defenders for defeating a contract

Penalty double
Double made with the expectation of defeating the opponents' contract

Point count
A method of hand evaluation which includes points for high cards and distribution

Preemptive bid
A bid made with a weak hand and a long suit at a higher level than is necessary meant to interfere with the opponents' auction by taking away bidding space

Preemptive raise
A weak raise of partner's suit with length in the suit and few points

Preference bid
Choosing one of partner's suit without necessarily showing support

Principle of fast arrival
In a game-forcing auction when one of the partners jumps to game it shows a hand that it is suitable for game but has no slam potential

Quantitative raise

A jump to 4NT after partner has bid a natural one or two notrump. The bid asks partner to bid slam with maximum values for his bid. A raise of 1NT to 4NT invites slam if opener has 16-17 points.

Quick loser

An immediate loser if the opponents gain the lead

Quick trick

A supplementary hand evaluation system of high-card holdings which assesses the ability to take early tricks; A = 1QT; AK in same suit = 2QT; AQ in same suit =1½QT; Kx = ½ QT

Rank

The priority of suits in bidding; from lowest to highest: clubs, diamonds, hearts, spades. Notrump outranks all suits.

Rebid

Second bid by opener or responder

Redouble

A call that increases the bonuses for making or defeating a contract that has already been doubled. Used by the responder to show 10+ points after a takeout double by the overcaller.

Relay

An artificial bid that requires a specific bid from partner; e.g., 2S after a 1NT opening bid requires partner to bid 3C

Responder

The partner of the opening bidder

Reverse

A rebid of a higher-ranking suit which shows more cards in the first suit than the second suit. Opener's reverse shows 16-21 HCP and is forcing for one round. Responder's reverse shows 13+ points and is game-forcing. In both cases the reverse requires partner to bid one level higher in returning to the original suit.

Reverse Bergen raises
Artificial bids used to show 4-card support and hand strength for the major suit partner has opened; 3D = 7-9 points, 3C = 10-11 points

Revoke
Failure to follow suit when holding a card(s) in that suit; often incurs a penalty

RHO
Right-hand opponent

Roman Key Card Blackwood (RKC)
A bid which asks how many of the five keycards (four aces and the king of trump) are held. A variant called 1430 uses these responses: 5C =1 or 4 keycards, 5D = 0 or 3 keycards, 5H = 2 keycards without the trump queen and 5S = 2 keycards with the trump queen

Rubber bridge
A form of contract bridge where vulnerability is earned by making a game

Ruff
Play a trump to a trick when holding no cards in that suit

Ruff and Sluff
To ruff in one hand and sluff (often a loser) in the other hand of the same partnership

Rule of eight
Strength and length guideline in order to overcall a suit at the 2-level: With five cards, three honors; with six cards, two honors

Rule of 11
When partner has led fourth highest in a suit, subtract the value of the card from eleven to determine the number of higher cards in the remaining three hands

Rule of 15

With a marginal opening hand in 4th seat, open the bidding when high card points and the number of cards held in the spade suit equal 15

Rule of 20

With a marginal opening hand (~12 HCP) in 1st or 2nd seat, open the bidding when HCP and the number of cards held in the two longest suits equals 20

Sacrifice bid

An intentional overbid meant to surrender fewer points than opponents would gain in their successful contract; usually done with favorably vulnerability

Second hand play

The card played by the defender who is second to play to a trick: usually this player will play low

Second (2nd) seat

The player to the left of the dealer who has the second opportunity to make a call

Semi-balanced hand

A hand that contains two doubletons

Sequence

A holding of two or more consecutive honor cards; also four honor cards which are separated by only one card

Set

Defeat the contract

Side suit

A suit other than the trump suit

Small slam

A contract to take 12 tricks

Signals
Conventional agreements and plays made by the defenders to give each other information

Signoff
A bid that asks partner to pass

Singleton
A holding of one card in a suit

Slow loser
A trick the opponents can take once the higher cards have been played

Spades
The highest-ranking suit, one of the majors, also called the master suit and a "pointed suit" by virtue of its symbol

Splinter raise
A conventional double jump in a new suit to show 4-card support for partner's suit and a singleton or void in the bid suit. A single jump is a splinter bid after a 2/1 bid by the responder.

Spot cards
The cards two through nine

Stayman convention
An artificial response of 2C to an opening bid of 1NT to ask partner for a 4-card major suit. Used after higher notrump openings as well.

Stopper
A high card holding in a suit which can prevent the opponent from immediately taking all the tricks in the suit

Strain
The suit, or notrump, specified in a bid

Suits

The four groups of cards in the deck distinguished by colors and symbols ranked from top to bottom: Spades, hearts, diamonds, and clubs

Super-accept

To bid one level higher than necessary when partner requests a transfer after a 1NT opening to show at least four cards in the suit and 17 HCP

Takeout double

A double which asks partner to bid an unbid suit

Texas transfer

A conventional bid at the 4-level after a 1NT or 2NT opening asking partner to bid (transfer to) hearts or spades; see Jacoby transfer

Texas two-step

Slang for the process of using two bids to show 3-card trump support

Third hand play

Playing only as high as necessary to try to win the trick when third to play to a trick

Third (3rd) seat

The third player to have the opportunity to opening the bidding

Total points

High card points + length points

Trick

The four cards contributed, one by each player, during each round of play in clockwise procession

Trump

A premium or wild card suit determined during the auction

Trumping

Slang term for ruffing

Two notrump-forcing after a major suit raise
A bid used to ask the opener for more information about a raise.

Two-over-one
A bid at the 2-level after a 1-level opening bid
Also used to describe a popular bidding system

Two spade relay
A response of 2S after a 1NT opening bid asking the opener to bid 3C

Unbalanced hand
A hand with a void, a singleton, or more than one doubleton

Undertrick
Each trick by which declarer fails to make the contract

Unusual 2NT
A jump to 2NT by the overcaller to show the two lowest unbid suits

Void
A holding of no cards in a suit

Vulnerability
The status which affects the size of bonuses for making or defeating a contract; in duplicate bridge vulnerability is predetermined by board number, in rubber bridge you become vulnerable after scoring a game

Weak jump overcall
A preemptive jump bid in a new suit after the opponents have opened the bidding

XYZ
A convention used by the responder after any three bids at the 1-level

Made in the USA
San Bernardino, CA
17 March 2015